JAPANESE WOODWORKING AND JOINERY

A BEGINNER'S GUIDE TO THE TOOLS & TECHNIQUES USED BY MASTER CARPENTERS IN JAPAN

CARPENTERS TOOL STUDY GROUP

Contents

Why We Wrote This Book

In the world of woodworking, planning and conceptualizing the project or piece can be just as enjoyable (and as complicated!) as actually fashioning it, bringing it into being. From initial inspiration to the finished object, planning then realizing the piece is the challenge both experienced and beginning woodworkers seek. There are so many things to consider. What's the goal? What look are you going for? Which approach works best: the mechanized route or hand tools all the way?

Sometimes referred to as sashimono, the Japanese technique for assembling furniture and other wooden items without nails, using both simple and highly complex wood joints, stretches back centuries. Mortises or grooves called hozo are carved into the wood in order to join two boards in a joint that's not visible from the surface.

Of course, many of these processes can be done efficiently by relying on machinery. In some cases, it may not make sense to use hand tools to accomplish tasks for which ultimately it doesn't matter whether it's done by machine or by hand. However, in some cases, detailed work that just can't be performed by machine is required.

Maybe you want to make simple, practical, basic or affordable items using Japanese joinery and joint techniques. Or perhaps you have loftier goals, producing bespoke one-of-a-kind treasures that reflect the peak of your artistry and craftsmanship. DIY woodworking projects are a chance to fuse process and tradition with your own vision and three-dimensional originality. For joinery methods, a range of options present themselves. Once you've mastered the tools, techniques and processes, there's nothing you won't be able to make!

Many of these processes can be performed more efficiently by relying on mechanization. But machines and mechanized tools have limits in terms of the precision and refinement they supply. This is where your hands come in, providing the essential, fine-grained finishing touches that will really set your pieces apart!

The book introduces a number of joinery techniques that are widely used in furniture and hand-hewn works, and explains the processes and procedures required. Are you a weekend hobby carpenter with a passion for creating high-quality pieces, but not quite the equipment or budget to match?

Do you want to apply Japanese ingenuity of design to everyday furniture and give them a special character? Japanese joinery is an ancient carpentry skill developed in a time before mass production, when ingenuity and character of design still mattered. Now, you can revive this ancient art and introduce it to your own carpentry designs. Whether you're a weekend hobbyist or a master carpenter, a whole new world of woodworking and furniture building awaits!

—Carpenters Tool Study Group

When actually using the hand tools described in this manual, please do so with the utmost care and at your own risk. If any injury or other serious accident should occur as a result of following the instructions in this manual, we will assume no responsibility whatsoever. The names and words used in this manual may vary from region to region.

Furniture Making and Hand-Tooled Finishes

Wooden furniture and wood-based components and accessories, to oversimplify, are made by joining pieces together, firmly, snugly, permanently. Boxes need to store objects. Desks and tables need to provide flat, smooth surfaces for working and eating. Chairs need to be sturdy enough to support the human body in all its forms.

Longitudinal connections are called joints, and the method of joining two or more pieces at a certain angle is called joinery. In the field of furniture and fittings, however, joints are referred to as inserts, braces or just joinery. There are several types of attachment methods used to assemble each component, such as joints to accommodate the warping and twisting of the wood.

First, we'll look at the joints of actually assembled furniture and other pieces from the works of professional woodworkers.

Although many parts of a professional woodworker's work are machined (because efficiency is a priority), hand tools are still used for the finer processes and refinement required on a given piece. That's why your here: to learn the traditional techniques and approaches that will set your pieces apart and lift your artistry to the next level.

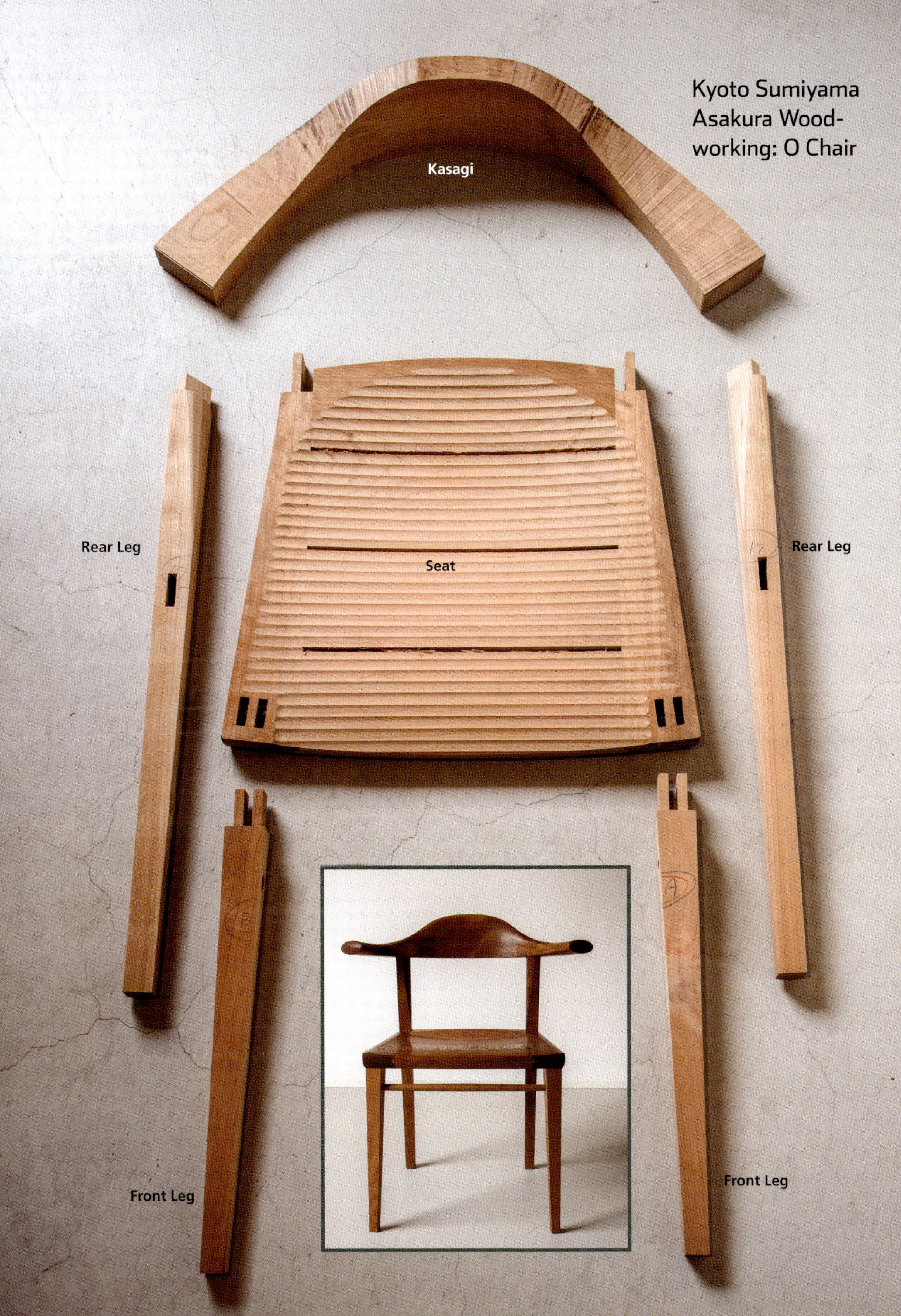
Kyoto Sumiyama Asakura Woodworking: O Chair
Kasagi
Rear Leg
Seat
Rear Leg
Front Leg
Front Leg

O Chair

The rounded arm is made of three components joined in a five-piece assembly. One of the five pieces is shaped like the letter O, which is the origin of the chair's name.

Total Height: 718 mm (28.25 in)
Seat Width: 475 mm (18.7 in)
Seat Height: 430 mm (16.93 in)

The headboards of round-armed chairs are often made of bent wood or laminated veneer. Here a wider piece is used for comfort, but due to its width the five-piece construction is used for added strength.

The seat is composed of four boards and the ends joined to the legs with shiba mortise and tenon. The back and middle two boards are mortise and tenon jointed with a four-way mortise and tenon joint, and the frontmost board is mortise and tenon jointed with a small root.

The seat surface and end-fit finish. The mortise is thicker here for added strength. The mortise at the end-fitting end is joined to the rear leg.

O Chair

The joint between the headstock and the rear legs is a mortise and tenon. Because the headstock is inclined at an angle, that makes it easy to lean back when seated, and because the rear legs are also rolled, the mortise and tenon must be made to match the angle. In addition, the mortise is machined at an angle from the wood edge to allow it to be parallel to the rounded grain of the arm.

The ends of the back legs and the seat are joined by a mortise and tenon joint with a split wedge. The mortises are deliberately made longer and chamfered by hand (right). In addition to the mortise and tenon, the seat surface also shows the gentle texture that can only be achieved by handwork. This one is processed with a four-sided warping canner (bottom).

Butsudan (Buddhist Altar)

This butsudan was made using figured horse chestnut wood. The top and side boards are joined with a balance tenon joint, while the middle board and side boards are joined with a dovetail tenon joint. Spalted wood is used for the base frame.
Dimensions: height 1270 mm (50 in) x width 480 mm (18.9 in) x depth 360 mm (14.17 in)

Round-Legged Wooden Curtain Table

The tabletop is made of cherry wood, and the connection between the crosspiece and the tabletop is made with a dovetail joint. It is important to accommodate warping, twisting, and expansion in wide boards.
Dimensions: height 330 mm (12.99 in) x width 940 mm (37.01 in) x length 1900 mm (74.80 in)

In the showroom near the workshop, you can see representative and signature pieces as well as shelves that can serve as references for custom furniture orders.

KYOTO SUMIYAMA ASAKURA WOODWORKING TORRU ASAKURA AND RENA ASAKURA

A furniture workshop started by a husband and wife in 2009, currently, they have two additional production staff members to fulfill requests for household and commercial furniture. There's also a showroom near the workshop where you can see the actual pieces before placing an order. https://www.asakuramokkou.com/

Here, instead of using the angled joint commonly used in Korean style four-sided shelves, the traditional Japanese three-way miter joint is employed. It's characterized by having all three joints mitered. This technique, which requires strength as it joins only through the use of pillars, is highly challenging. The material being used is yellow poplar.

Mokugei Ichikawa: Yellow Poplar Four-Sided Table

Height: 1200 mm (47.24 in)
Width: 450 mm (17.72 in)
Depth: 420 mm (16.54 in)

The crosspiece supporting the middle board and the pillars is joined with a dovetail tenon joint.

Zataku (Low Table) with Keyaki Lacquer Finish

Height: 320 mm (12.6 in)
Width: 1100 mm (43.3 in)
Depth: 1100 mm (43.3 in)

A low table made from a single plank of keyaki wood. Natural wood needs special care to prevent shrinkage and warping.

The legs and crosspieces are joined with a four-way mortise and tenon joint. As the legs are shaved into the crosspiece, they're recessed by about 5 mm (0.2 in) to prevent gaps in the mortise area.

The tabletop includes dovetail crosspieces to accommodate the warping and shrinkage of the top, ensuring the dovetail grooves don't appear on the edges.

The legs and support crosspieces are joined with a double mortise and tenon joint for added strength.

The legs and crosspieces are lacquered. The tenons of the crosspieces are cut at a 45° angle as they meet within the mortise holes of the legs.

The joint between the armrest plate and the rear legs is a four-sided mortise and tenon joint with dovetail joints on the sides of the rear legs to enhance the joint.

Craftsman Ichikawa Armchair (Tamo Wipe Lacquer)

Total Height: 830 mm (32.67 in)
Seat width: 500 mm (19.7 in)
Seat height: 420 mm (16.54 in)

Joints between the front legs, seat and armrests. The front legs and armrests are joined by a four-way mortise and groove joint, and the joint with the seat is an irregular seven-piece joint.

The finish on the seat side. The rear-legs joint is made by joining the legs together.

Ichikawa Zelkova Sunken Hearth Table

Shachi-jime is a type of mortise and tenon used for hearths and fireplaces. This technique is used when especially strong joints are required. Measurements: 650 mm/25.6 in (length), 1300 mm/51.2 in (width), 950 mm/37.4 in (depth).

MORTISES AND TENONS: ATTACHMENT AND CLOSURE

This method produces a strong joint that can't be removed without removing the orca plug. A mortise and tenon are made and then fastened to the mortise. Both mortise and tenon are made with or without an orifice, and then inserted into the orifice with an orifice stopper to ensure that there's no gap between the mortise and tenon and that the joint is secure.

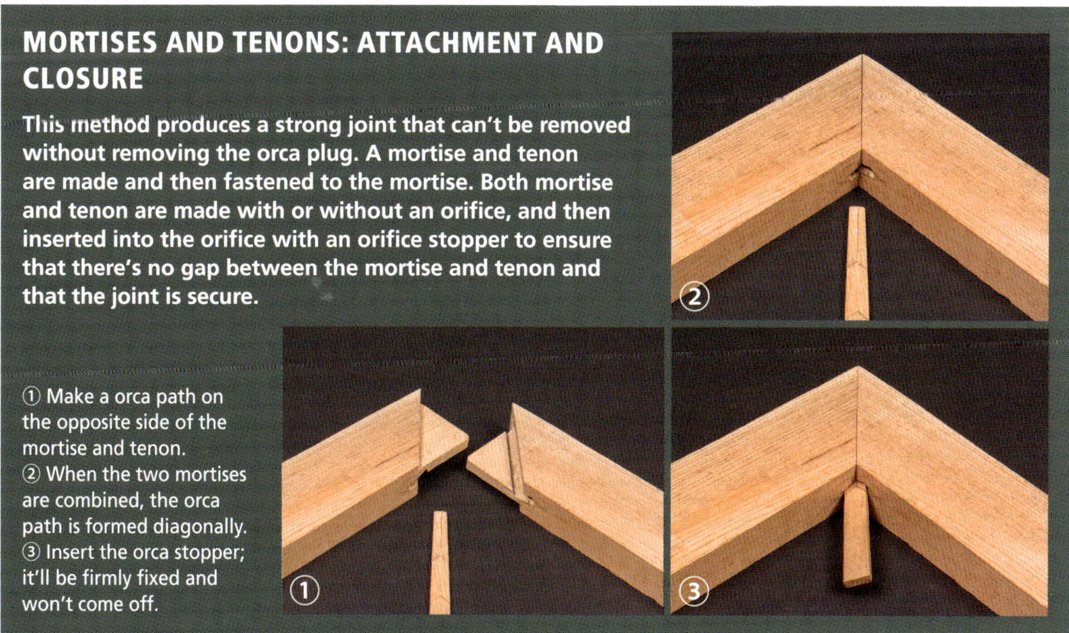

① Make a orca path on the opposite side of the mortise and tenon.
② When the two mortises are combined, the orca path is formed diagonally.
③ Insert the orca stopper; it'll be firmly fixed and won't come off.

Craftsman Wiped Lacquer Box

125 mm/4.92 in (top), 335 mm/13.2 in (width),
175 mm/6.9 in (depth)

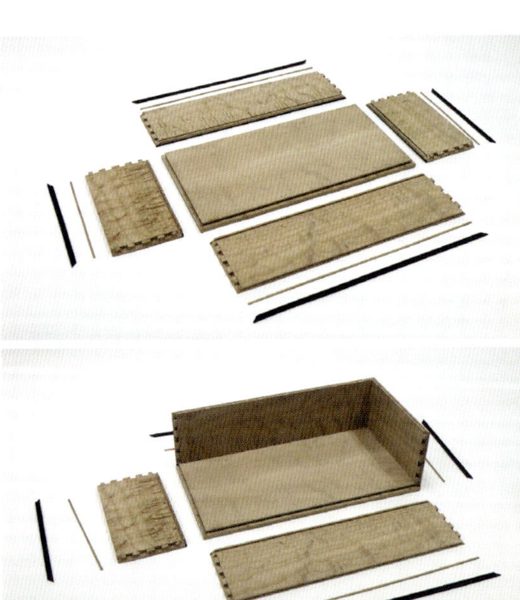

The body of a lacquered box. The tamegatagata (hidden dovetail joint) is a widely used technique for making hand-finished boxes.

The workmanship of tea ceremony utensils is not meant to be shown, so the basic rule is to keep it hidden. The complicated finishing is for the sake of strength and durability. The three photos on the left show the structure of the lid. The joints are made with a hidden dovetail joint in the shape of a clasp, and the cover ring is made with a hired tool or toinukuri-zane. After assembling, the top is scraped off with a planer (above).

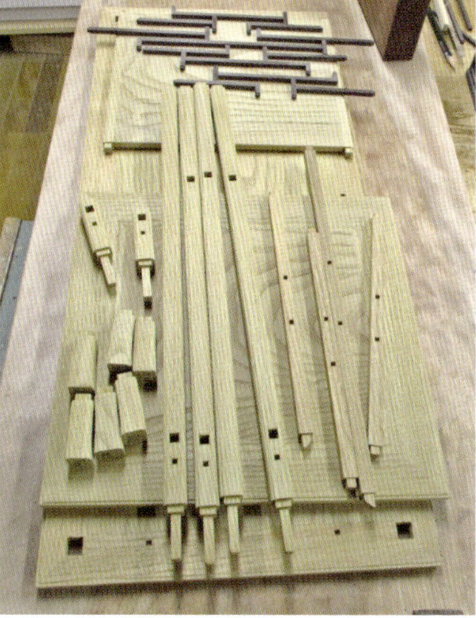

A candle mortise and tenon joint (box mortise and tenon joint) is often used in decorative shelves, penetrating the base plate and joining the post and legs. It's sometimes used for parts that need to be removed, such as a folding screen in front of a fireplace. The top and bottom are 420 mm/16.5 in, the width is 585 mm/23 in, and the depth is 260 mm/10.25 in.

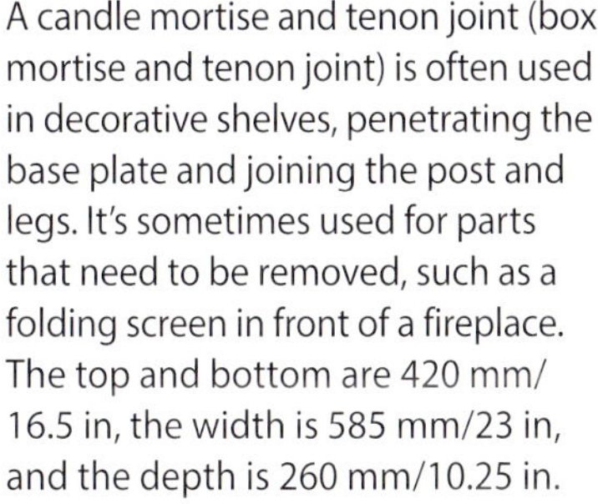

ICHIKAWA MASATO

Self-taught in the art of shimono, which he's practiced for about 40 years, he currently exhibits his work at the Japan Traditional Crafts Exhibition, the Japan Sencha Crafts Exhibition and other venues. In addition to sencha utensils and various types of handwork, he makes chairs, tables and other pieces to order. He's also a member of the Japan Crafts Association.

https://blog.goo.ne.jp/chikuma_2008

Tools Used for Joinery and Furniture Making

Woodworking with Hand Tools

Joining components is of course a key component in the production of furniture and fingerings. While there are quick and easy ways to join parts using screws and nails, other somewhat more difficult approaches can yield even more satisfying results. This approach requires its own sets of tools, but when the joints are successfully and seamlessly assembled, the finished piece is worth it.

With the right woodworking tools and a basic understanding of their function and use, you can make boxes, desks and anything you conceive by machining and assembling the various pieces. It may take some time and investment for the weekend hobbyist to assemble the required components and tools, but once you do, a range of possibilities opens up at your fingertips. Here's an overview of some of the pieces and elements you'll need.

Photography assistance provided by
Carpentry Tools Mandalaya

Rulers

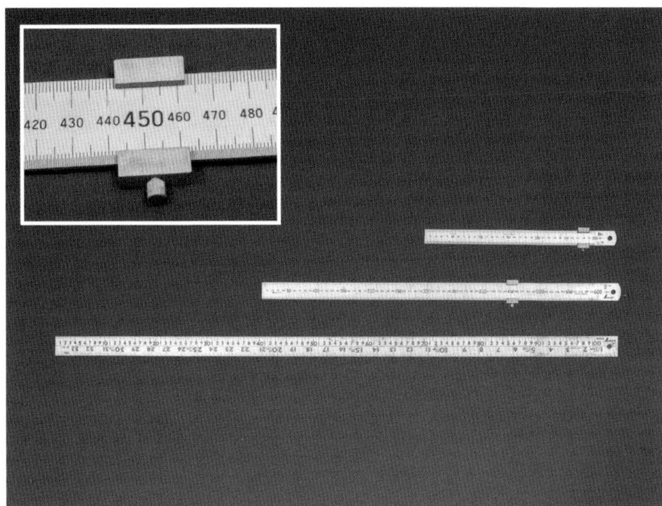

Straight Edge

In woodworking, 30 cm (just less than a standard foot), 60 cm (23.6 in), and 100 cm (39.4 in) lengths are often used. Currently, stainless steel is the most common type of ruler. When a stopper is attached, it's possible to accurately mark multiple pieces of the same size.

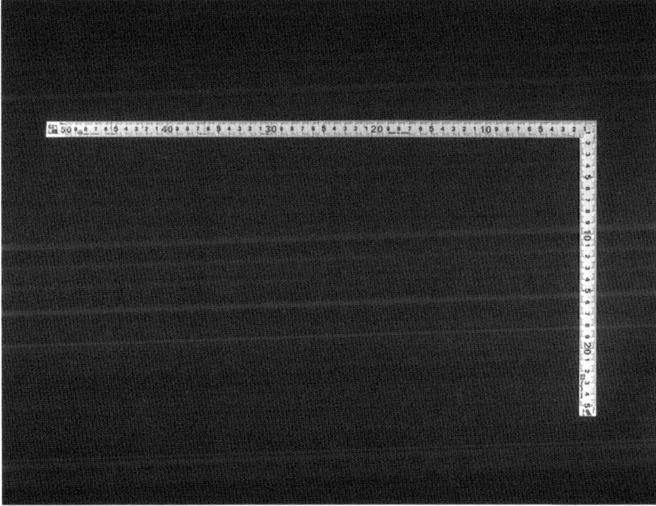

Carpenter's Square

The longer side is often called the "long hand," with the shorter naturally referred to as the "short hand." The reverse or back side is engraved with a scale of √2 times the size of the front. This ruler is used not only for measuring length but also for drawing straight or curved lines, making a gradient and many other purposes. Also called a curved rectangle.

Square

Used for drawing right-angled lines and measuring right angles, the shorter gable end is thicker and sandwiched between the thinner longer end. Both the inside and outside are right angles. These commercially available products are typically made of iron, stainless steel, brass and other metals. They range in length from 5 cm (1.97 in) to 50 cm (19.7 in).

Measuring Tools

Miter Square

While a square is used to check right angles, this tool is used to check or draw 45° angles. It can also be homemade using a wood with minimal warping.

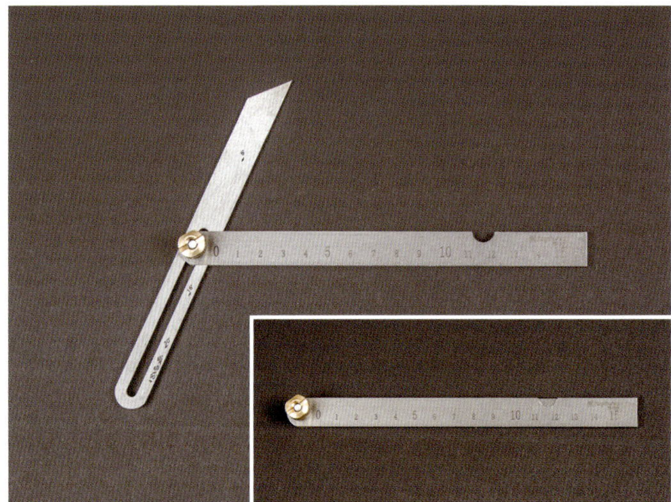

Adjustable Square (Bevel Gauge)

Used to measure or mark arbitrary angles, it's often employed to set and mark the angle of dovetail tenons. You adjust the angle by loosening the screw attached to the long side. It's also known as a free angle square.

Fixing the Adjustable Square to a 2-cm Slope

The adjustable square is useful when marking dovetail tenons. Here is an example of how to use the adjustable square fixed to a 2-cm (0.79-in) slope.

① From the corner of the board where the end grain and edge are at a right angle, mark 10 cm (3.94 in) along the edge and 2 cm (0.79 in) along the end grain.
② Align the square to the two marked points and draw a line with a pencil.
③ Align the long side of the adjustable square to the edge of the board and fix the screw at the point where the grooved side meets the pencil line.

①

②

③

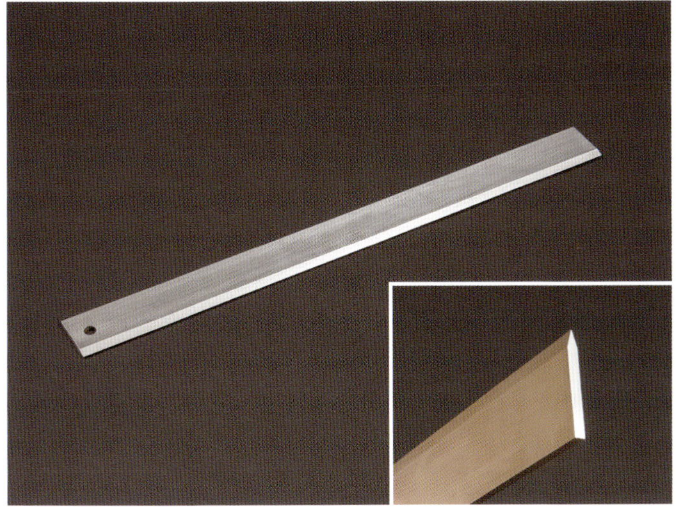

Bottom Plane Gauge

This tool is used to check the flatness of the bottom of a plane's base. It's traditionally made from stable quartersawn wood and crafted in pairs. By fitting the two gauge surfaces together, you can check the straightness of a cut or line. Recently, high-precision stainless steel gauges have become more common.

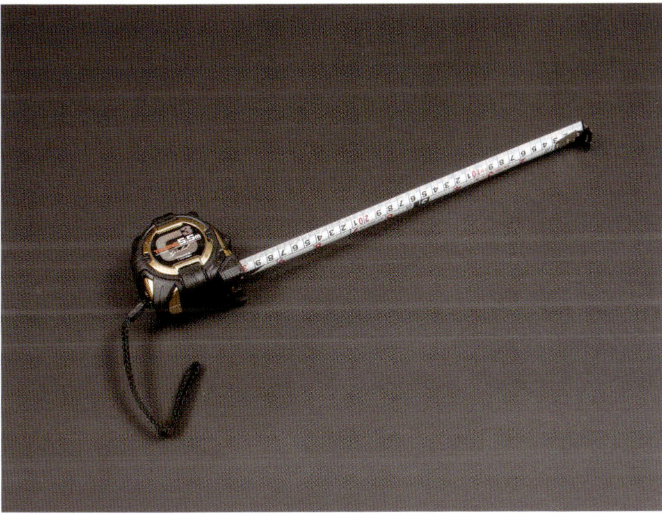

Measuring Tape

Unlike a straight edge, a measuring tape is a compact tool that stores the tape, made of fabric or metal, by rolling it up inside a plastic or metal cartridge. It measures much longer lengths compared to a straight edge. In woodworking, a tape measure with a thin metal tape, known as a convex, is often used.

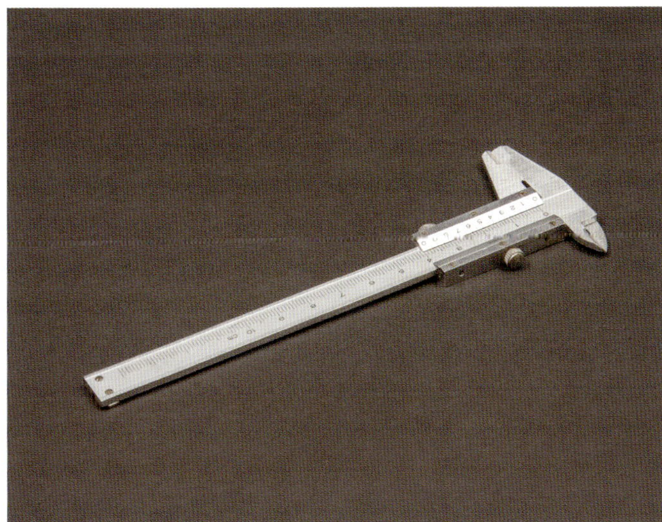

Vernier Caliper

A measuring instrument that can accurately measure thickness, width, external diameter, internal diameter and even the depth of holes. There are also vernier calipers that can digitally display the measured values.

Marking Tools

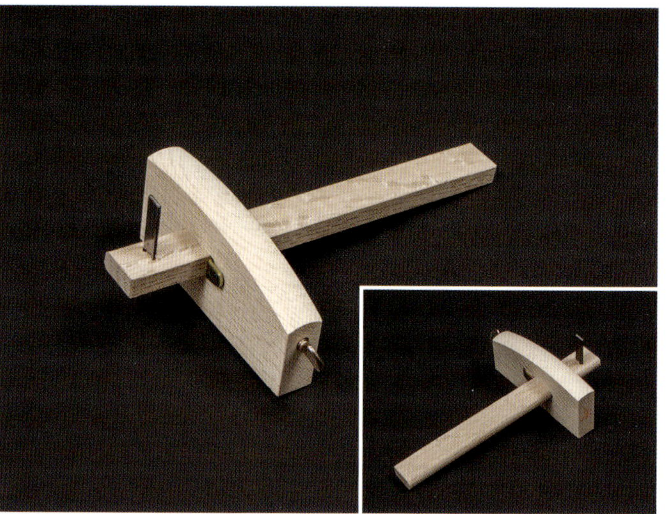

Sujikebiki (Marking Gauge)

Typically consists of a comb-shaped ruler board, a bar and a marking blade. This tool is used to draw parallel lines from a reference surface by placing the ruler board against the material. The bar, inserted at a right angle into the ruler board, is adjusted to the desired width between the ruler board and the marking blade, then fixed with a wedge or screw. The marking blade is set into the bar with the back of the blade facing outward. A similar tool called the "wari-kebiki," used for splitting thin boards, is larger overall with a thicker and larger blade.

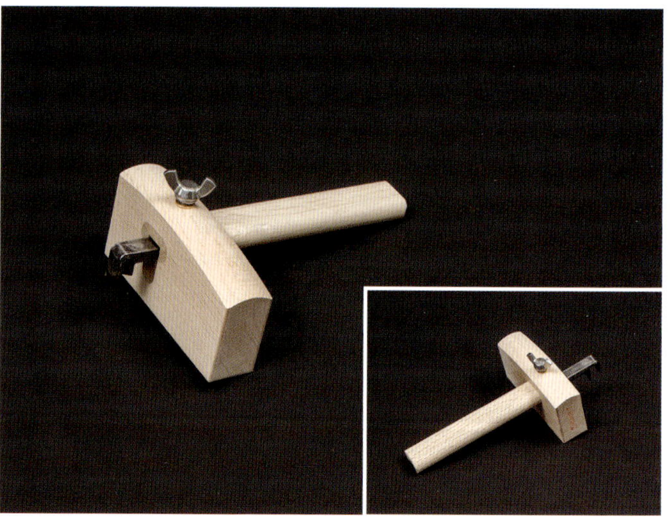

Kamakebiki (Double Blade Marking Gauge)

While the sujikebiki uses a single blade on the bar, the kamakebiki has two L-shaped blades set into the bar, allowing it to draw two lines simultaneously. The longer blade has the back facing outward, while the shorter blade faces the ruler board, ensuring that the width of the lines is consistent on the outside of the two lines.

About the Blades of Marking Gauges

Generally, the blade of a sujikebiki has the front of the blade facing the ruler board, while the two blades of a kamakebiki face each other. When drawing lines on the material, the deeper the blade cuts into the material, the thicker the line on the blade's front side becomes due to the bevel. In this case, the part to be removed is marked on the blade's front side, and the part to be left is marked on the back side.

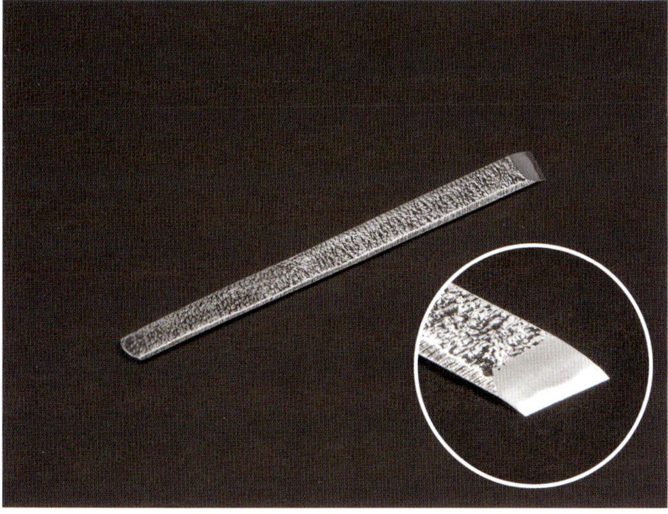

Shiragaki (Marking Knife)

A marking tool shaped like a small utility knife but with a shorter blade. It's used to draw lines against a ruler, allowing for finer and more accurate lines than those drawn with a pencil alone.

Making Accurate Marks with a Shiragaki

Accurate marking is crucial for clean joints without gaps, such as in a dovetail or with tenon joints. The shiragaki is an essential tool for accurate marking, and mastering its use is important for drawing precise lines.

Example of Using a Shiragaki to Mark a Tenon for Dovetail Joints: First, align the blade tip at the marking position, ensuring that the front of the blade is on the part to be removed.

Example of Using a Shiragaki to Mark Part of a Dovetail Joint: Place the blade tip at the edge of the end grain, with the front of the blade on the part to be removed.

Fix the blade tip to the material, align a ruler against it and draw a precise line without any deviation.

Using a Shiragaki with a Bevel Gauge Fixed at a 2-cm (0.79-in) Slope: Align the blade tip of the shiragaki to the end grain and draw a line.

Types of Saws

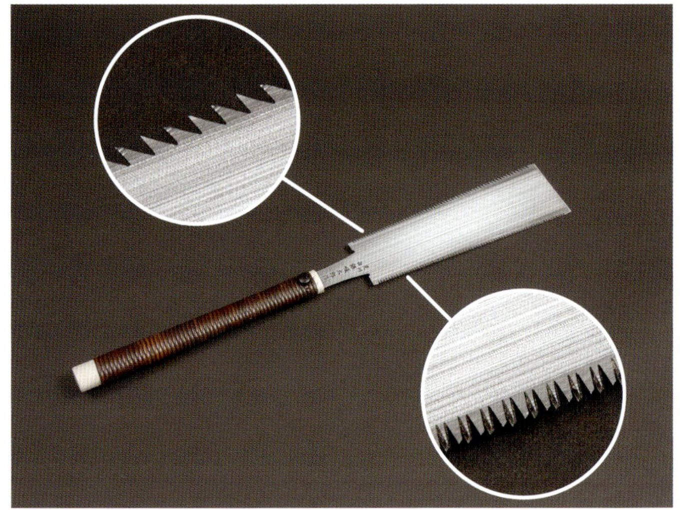

Ryoba (Double-Edged Saw)

A double-edged saw with a rip blade for cutting along the grain and a crosscut blade for cutting perpendicular to the grain. The blade length ranges from approximately 180 mm (7.09 in) to around 360 mm (14.17 in), with 240 mm (9.45 in) being common for fine work and 270–300 mm (10.63–11.81 in) for cutting thick or wide boards.

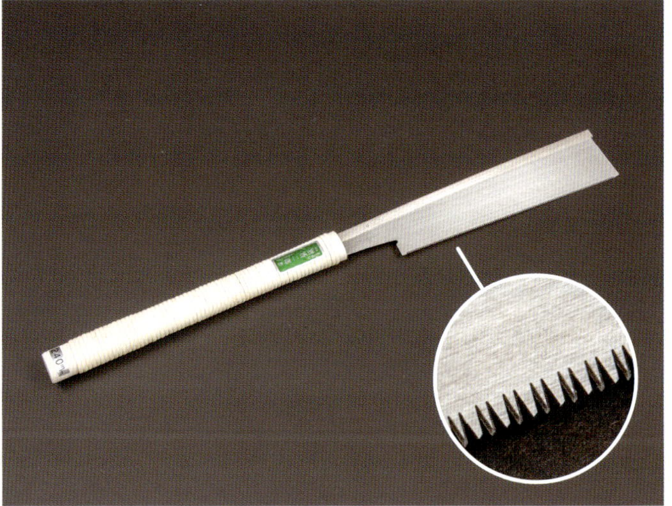

Dozuki Saw

A saw used for precise crosscutting, such as cutting tenons. The blade is thin and pliable, so it's reinforced with a spine. The blade length typically ranges from 180 mm (7.09 in) to about 240 mm (9.45 in). It has fine teeth with minimal set, resulting in a cleaner cut than a regular crosscut saw.

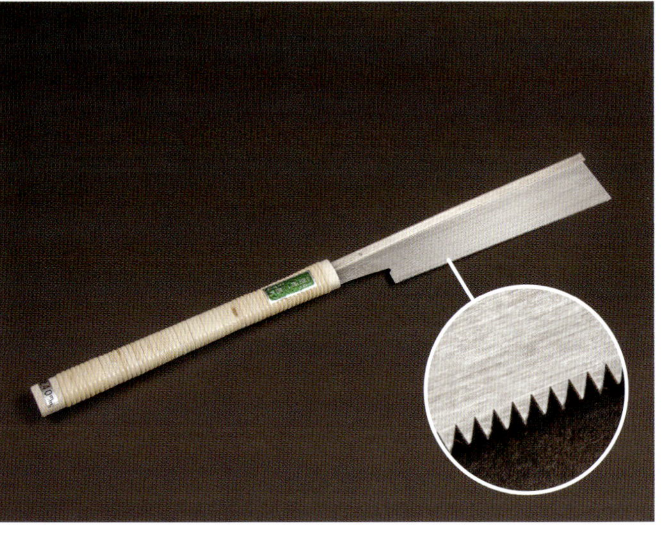

Nokogiri (Tenon Saw)

Similar in appearance to a dozuki saw but with fine rip teeth, it's useful for accurately cutting along the grain when shaping tenons. The blade length is similar to that of a dozuki saw.

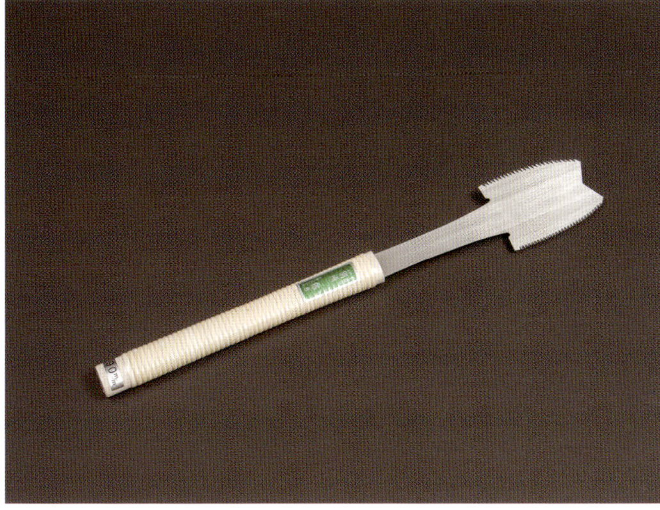

Azebiki Saw

While double-edged and dozuki saws are typically used from the edge of the surface, the azebiki saw features a short, curved blade designed for starting cuts in the middle, such as when creating grooves.

Ranma Saw

A saw used for intricate work like carving transom panels. It has a similar shape to the mawashibiki (turning saw) and the tsukimawashi (push turning saw). The tsukimawashi is used with a pushing motion, while both types are designed for cutting curves.

Crosscut Saw Kerf Width

The teeth of a crosscut saw, designed to cut perpendicular to the grain, are set so that the tips alternate and extend slightly outside the plane of the blade body. This reduces cutting resistance and makes it easier to release sawdust. As a result, the kerf left by the saw is wider than the blade itself, known as the kerf width. When cutting along a marked line, it's important to account for the kerf width to ensure accurate cuts.

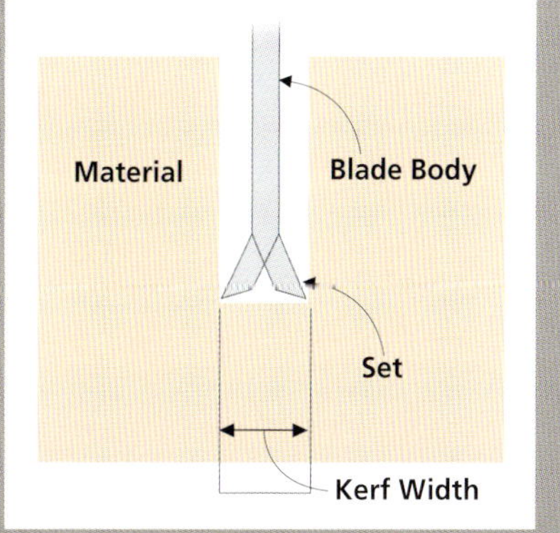

Due to the set of the teeth, make test cuts on scrap wood to determine the exact kerf width of the saw being used.

Types of Planes

Hiragana (Two-Blade Plane)

Since the Meiji era, the two-blade plane, which includes a sub-blade to prevent tearout, has become mainstream and remains unchanged in design. To produce evenly thick shavings across the entire blade width, the bottom of the plane body must be adjusted. Mastering this tool requires experience and skill in both blade sharpening and plane adjustment.

Hiragana (Single-Blade Plane)

Before the advent of the two-blade plane, the single-blade plane was widely used. It's often used as an end-grain plane but can also serve as a regular smoothing plane. However, without advanced skills in adjusting the mouth opening and sharpening the blade, it's challenging to plane without causing tearout.

Dainao-shi Kanna (Sole Planer)

This plane is primarily used to adjust the bottom of a hiragana plane. It has a nearly vertical blade, functioning similarly to a scraper for leveling the sole. Other planes with a blade angle of 45° or more are called standing blade planes and are used for planing hardwoods such as ebony or rosewood.

Kiwaganna (Rabbet Plane, Left-Handed)

A plane used for tasks such as creating rabbet joints or trimming the corners of recesses. It has an angled blade set diagonally, with the blade edge extending to the side of the plane body. There are right-handed and left-handed versions, typically used as a pair. They come in both single-blade and two-blade varieties. The blade must extend evenly from the bottom, with one corner of the blade aligned with the intersection of the side and bottom edges, making it a challenging plane to adjust.

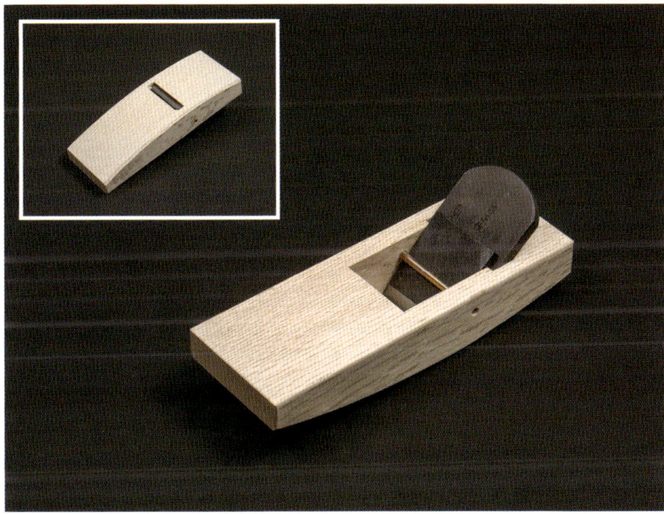

Sori-daikanna (Convex Plane)

A plane with a bottom that curves from the front to the back, used for planing concave surfaces. The bottom is adjusted to match the curvature of the surface being planed. While rarely used in joint making, it can be employed for shaping elements such as chair armrests or back stretchers.

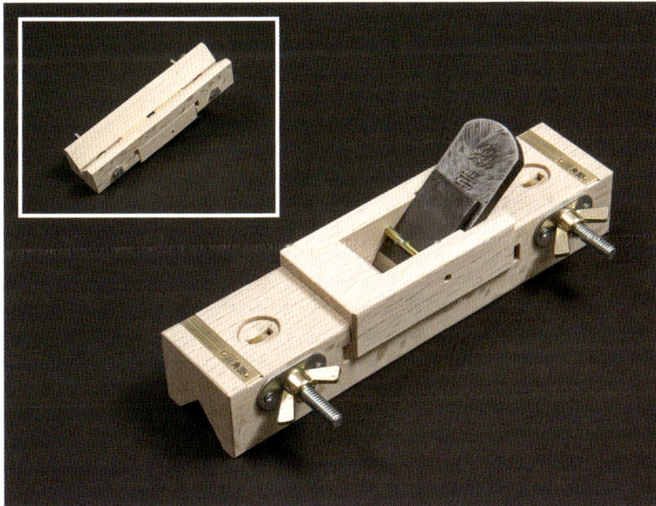

Chamfer Plane

A plane specialized for creating 45° chamfers. By adjusting the width of the guide, you can change the width of the blade's contact with the material, allowing for the adjustment of the chamfer size. It's used for chamfering edges of panels and frames.

Types of Planes

Uchimaru Kanna (Concave Plane)
A plane with a concave bottom surface widthwise, and a similarly concave cutting edge. In construction, it's used for planing round pillars, but in joint making, it's infrequently used, mostly for shaping round rods.

Sotomaru Kanna (Convex Plane)
Opposite the uchimaru kanna, this plane has a convex bottom surface in the width direction, and a similarly convex cutting edge. It's rarely used in joint making, for planing the inside of curved surfaces.

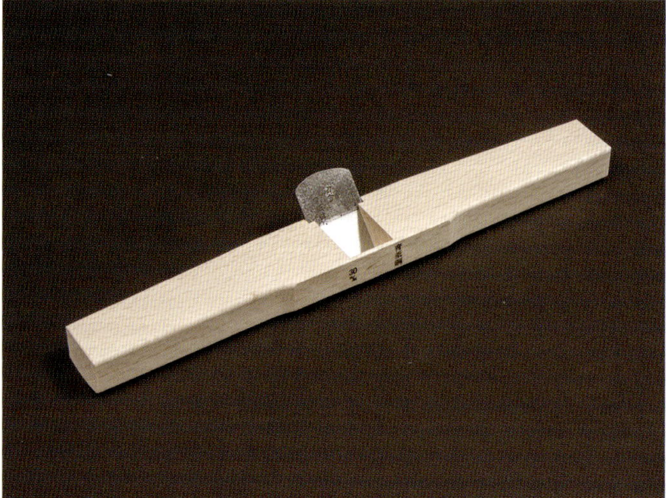

Nankin Kanna (Nankin Plane)
Used for planing strong curves, such as chair legs or curved rails. This plane is rarely used in joint making but is convenient for shaping cylindrical elements like chair spindles. It typically has a single blade and can be used in both pushing and pulling motions.

Adjusting the Bottom of the Hiragana Plane

Among planes, the hiragana plane plays a crucial role in accurately planing the flat surfaces of boards. Depending on the state of the surface, the adjustment of the plane's bottom changes progressively through rough planing, intermediate planing and finishing planing. However, since it's rare nowadays to prepare boards entirely by hand, the finishing plane is most commonly used.

The bottom of the hiragana plane (the surface from which the blade protrudes) serves as a reference, allowing the blade to shave very thin layers from the board. Therefore, the bottom must be accurately adjusted, but because it's made of wood, it can warp or twist due to expansion and contraction. Thus, adjusting the bottom is an essential skill for using a hiragana plane.

The basic adjustment method involves placing a bottom gauge against the bottom surface and observing any gaps to check for warping or twisting, then identifying areas to be planed to remove any unevenness. While traditionally a sole planer is used to remove material, modern methods include flattening the bottom on a thick glass plate with sandpaper and using a scraper instead of a sole planer.

Nevertheless, it's still convenient to use a bottom gauge to check the state of the bottom before and during use. When checking the bottom, retract the blade approximately 2 mm (0.08 in) from the bottom surface. Completely removing the blade won't allow for accurate checking.

Hold the plane with the bottom facing up, place the bottom gauge on top and check for light gaps by facing it toward a light source like a bulb.

How to Use the Bottom Gauge

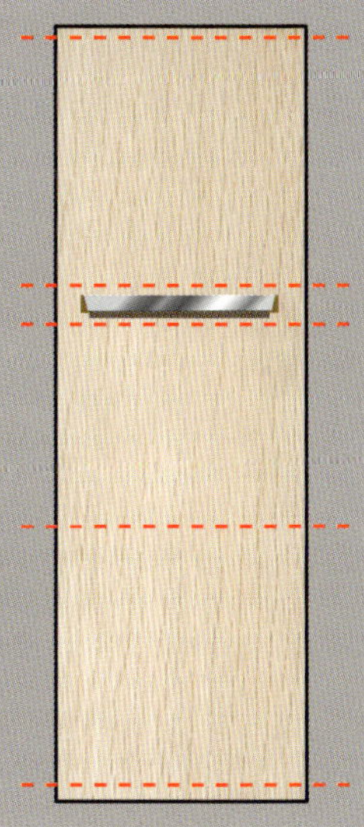

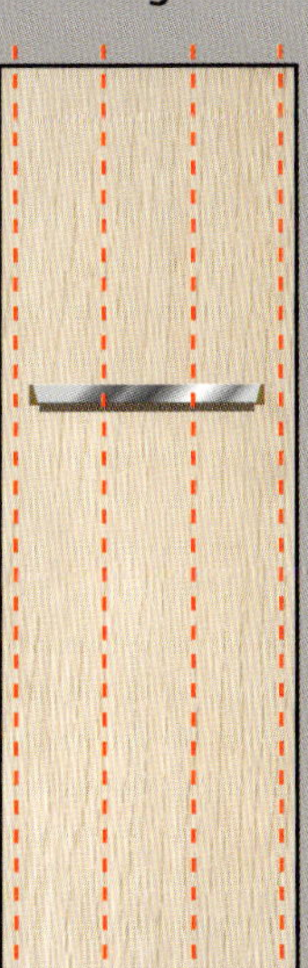

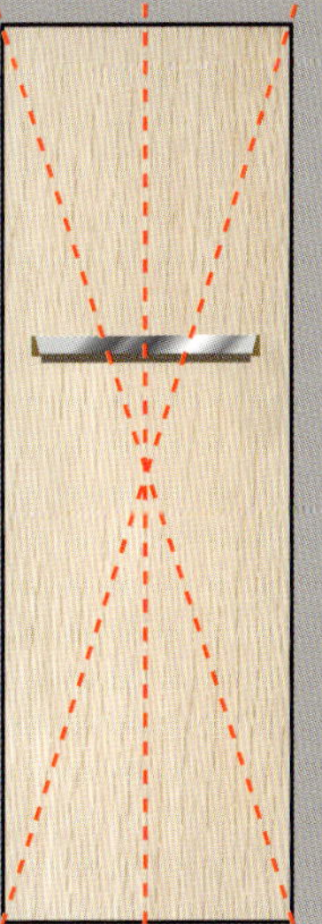

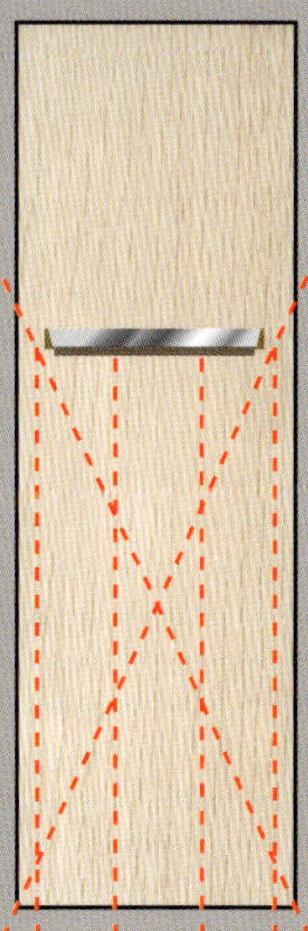

Types of Chisels

Oire Nomi (Mortise Chisel)

A representative striking chisel with a metal hoop called a "kawa" fitted at the top of the handle, which is struck with a hammer. It's the most commonly used chisel, available in widths from 1.5 mm (0.06 in) to 48 mm (1.89 in).

Mukomachi Nomi

A chisel used for digging deep mortises in fittings and furniture. Unlike the oire nomi, which is used for relatively shallow holes, the mukomachi nomi is essential for creating deep, narrow holes. It has a long blade that is thicker than its width.

Usu Nomi (Paring Chisel)

A type of push chisel without a metal hoop at the top of the handle, used by pushing it with the hand. It's used for finishing the edges of marking lines and the sides of mortises. As it relies mainly on arm strength, the handle is longer and has a rounded top compared to striking chisels.

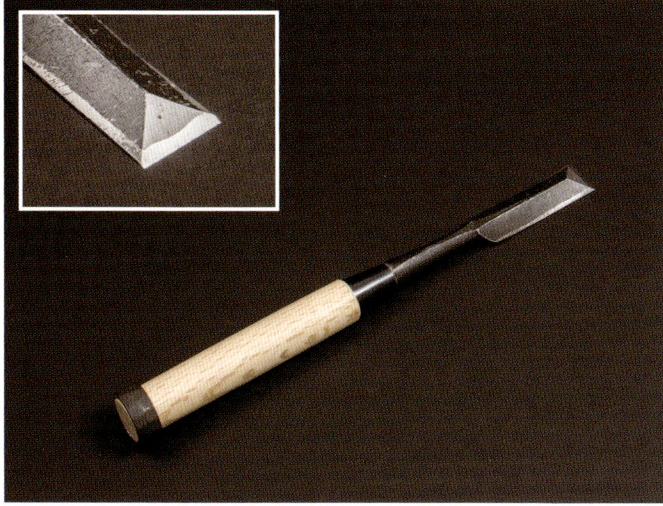

Shinogi Nomi (Triangle Chisel)

Similar to the usu nomi but with a triangular blade when viewed from the front, this modification helps make edges sharper. It's used for finishing the corners of dovetail joints. There are both striking and push varieties.

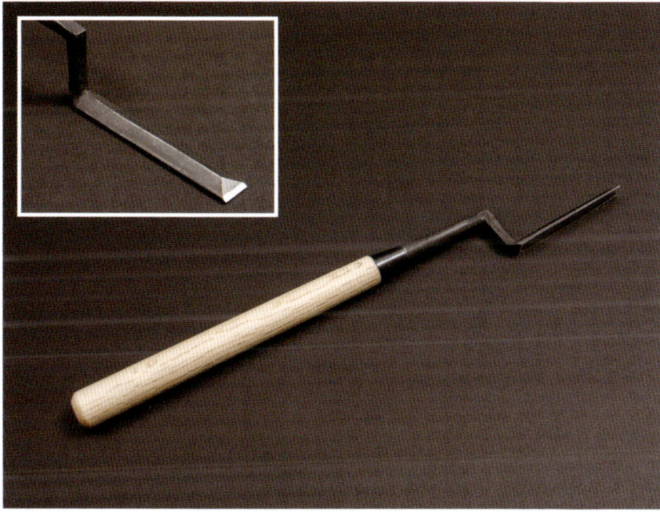

Kote Nomi (Bent Chisel)

A push chisel with a long neck and a bent shape like a trowel. It's used to finish the bottoms of mortises and grooves by pressing the back of the blade against the bottom. This shape comes in versions with either a shinogi (triangular) blade or a standard blade.

Parts of a Chisel

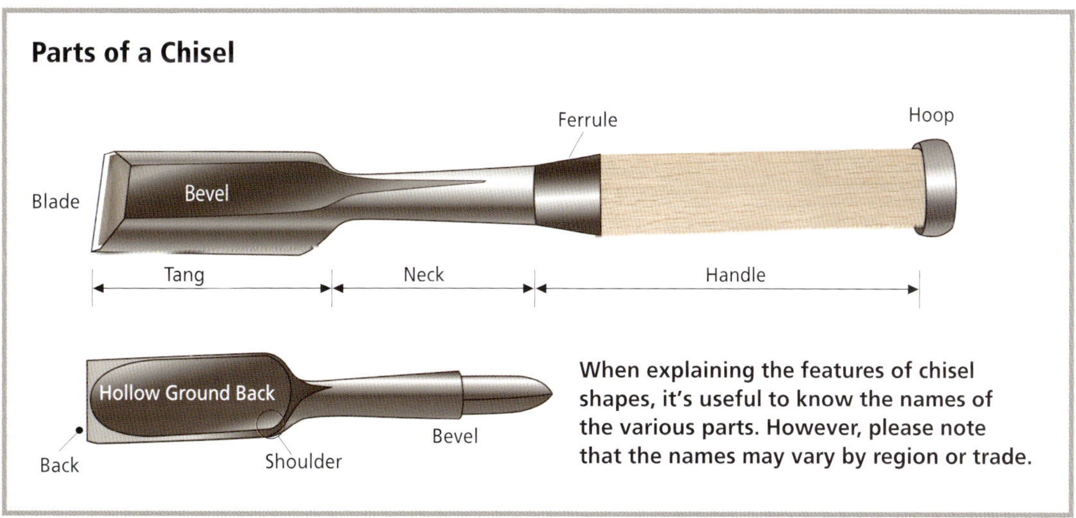

When explaining the features of chisel shapes, it's useful to know the names of the various parts. However, please note that the names may vary by region or trade.

Types of Chisels

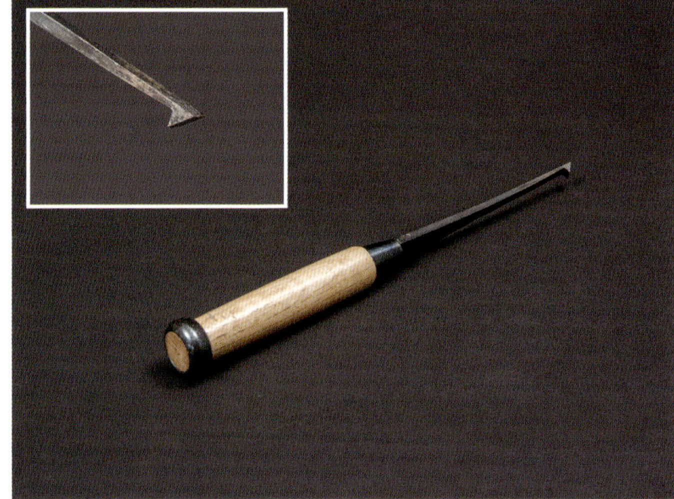

Mori Nomi (Spear Chisel)
A chisel with a blade shaped like a spear. It has a hoop and is used for breaking up and clearing debris from the bottom of holes.

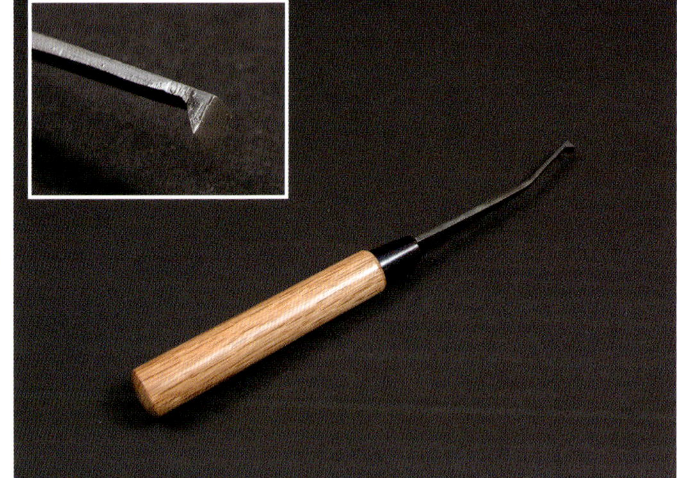

Soko Sarai Nomi (Bottom Cleaning Chisel)
This chisel has a thin section from the ferrule to the blade, with no distinction between the tang and neck, curving along the way. The blade tip is bent into a hook shape, specifically designed to scrape out debris accumulated at the bottom of mortises.

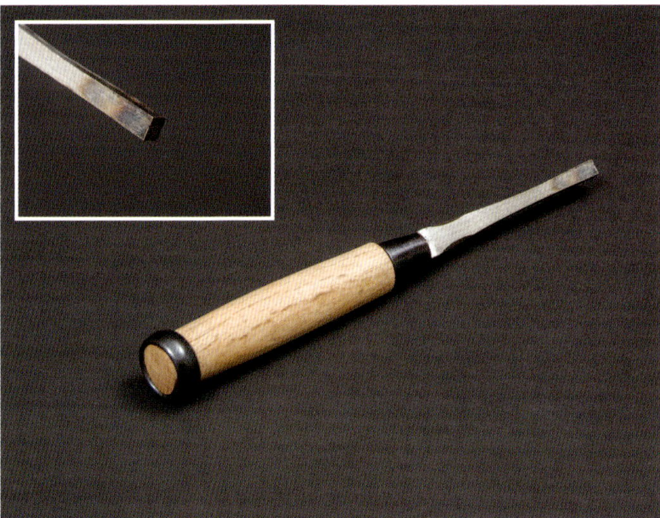

Uchinuki Nomi (Punch Chisel)
A chisel with a square, flat cross-section at the tip and no blade. The flat part has a grid-like groove pattern. After partially excavating a through-tenon from both sides with a mukomachi nomi or a similar chisel, the punch chisel is used to break through from one side to the other.

How to Use Striking Chisels and Hammers

The general method for using a striking chisel involves adding force by hitting the head of the chisel's handle with a hammer. Because of this, the chisel handle is prone to damage, so it's often fitted with a hoop to prevent splitting and chipping.

When excavating a mortise, the chisel blade is lowered perpendicular to the material's surface. The key to striking with a hammer is to hold it near the end of the handle, ensuring the chisel's shaft aligns with the direction of the strike at the moment of impact. The back of the chisel should face the user, and the chisel should be held so that the back is perpendicular to the surface and the sides of the shaft are perpendicular to the surface. When changing the angle of excavation, ensure the strike direction aligns with the chisel shaft.

It's also important to securely fix the material to ensure the force from the descending hammer is efficiently transmitted. The user's posture should be stable and safe, varying slightly depending on whether working at a bench or while seated.

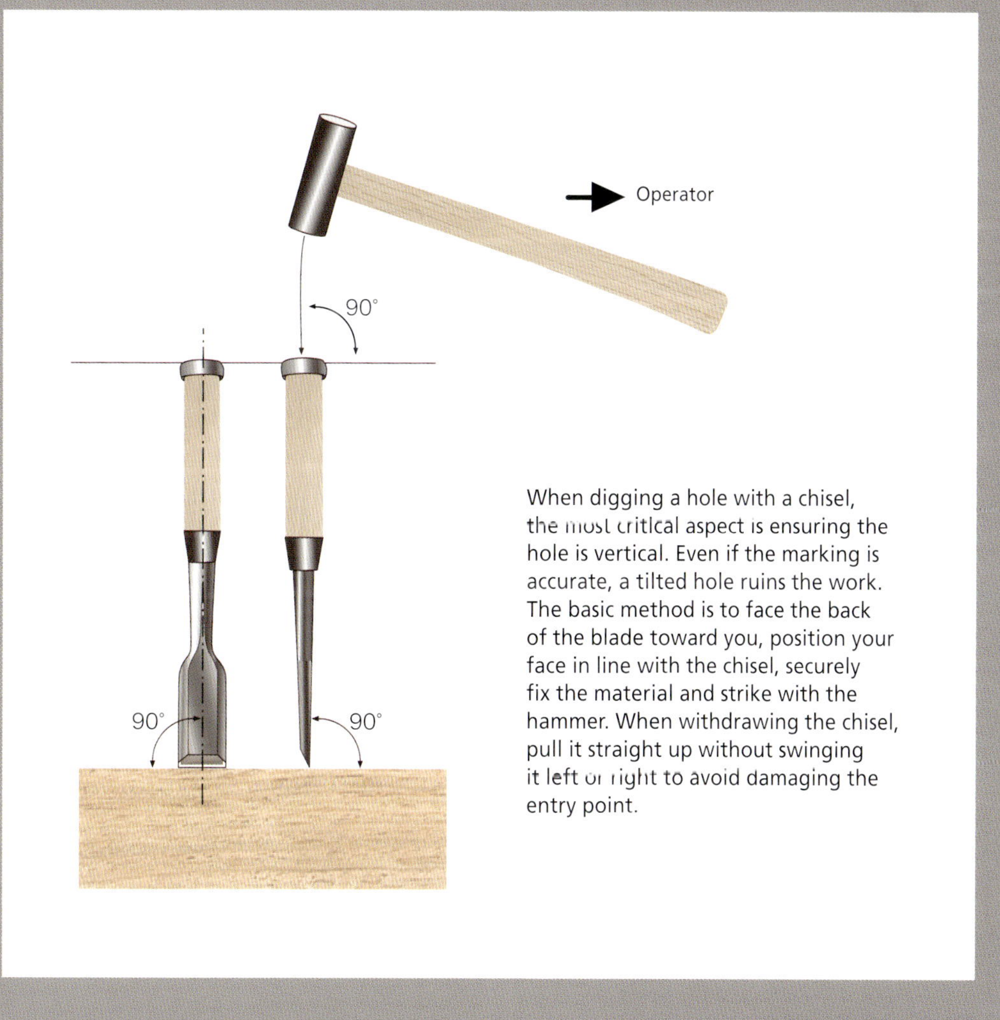

When digging a hole with a chisel, the most critical aspect is ensuring the hole is vertical. Even if the marking is accurate, a tilted hole ruins the work. The basic method is to face the back of the blade toward you, position your face in line with the chisel, securely fix the material and strike with the hammer. When withdrawing the chisel, pull it straight up without swinging it left or right to avoid damaging the entry point.

Hammers & Mallets

Hammer

A mallet made of hard wood such as oak or zelkova is best. It's used for plane blade loading and unloading and for assembly work because it doesn't scratch easily when struck.

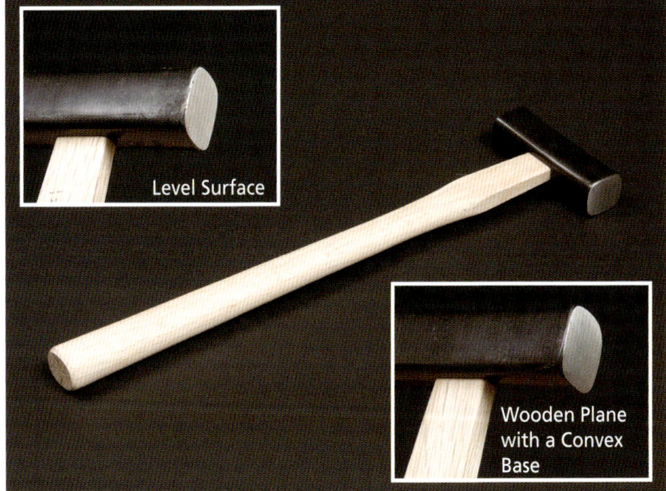

Sledgehammers

There are various sizes and shapes of gennos, ranging from a 90-g (0.2-lb) genno (bean gennos) to a large gennos (about 750 g/1.65 lb). A genno with a slightly spherical surface, called a mokkiri face, and a flat face is generally used in woodworking. The flat side is used when striking the chisel.

Tool Time: The Shape of the Head?

The striking surface of the head (metal part) of the genno is called the koguchi, which has a flat or slightly spherical surface at both ends of the head. There are several different shapes of cross-sections, some of which are mainly used in woodworking. Any shape can be used, but when the chisel is held at various angles, a cylindrical shaped genno called a dharma genno is preferred.

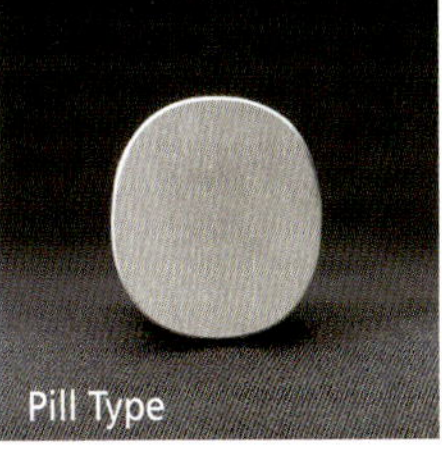
Pill Type

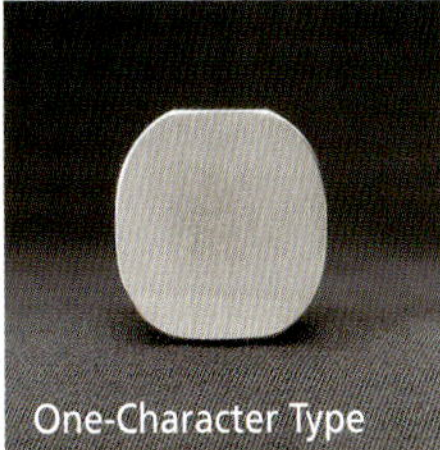
One-Character Type

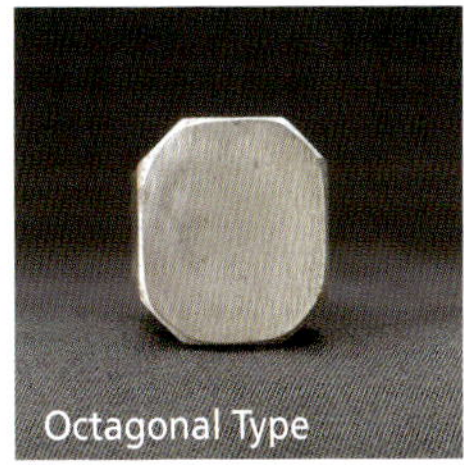
Octagonal Type

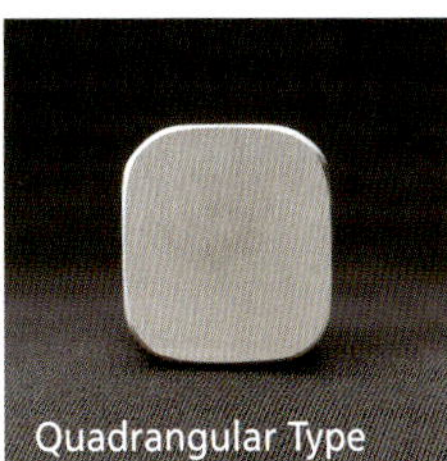
Quadrangular Type

Cutters & Daggers

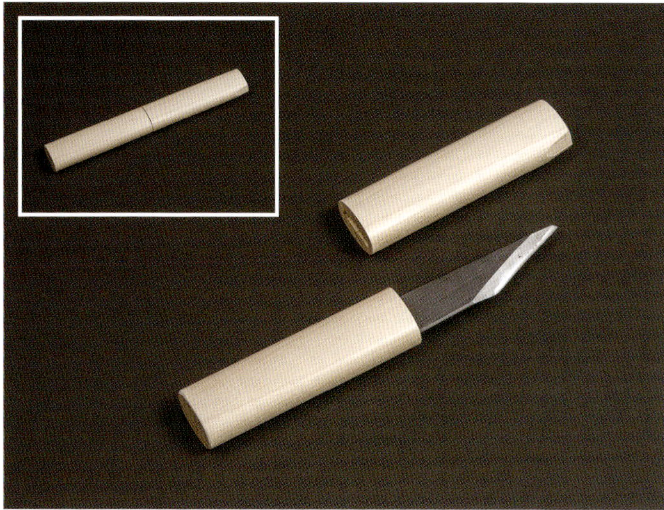

Cutter

A tool that has been used to sharpen wooden or bamboo nails or for everyday cutting tasks. There are ones where a wooden handle is attached and other styles and designs where it's used as is. There are right-handed, left-handed and double-edged tools.

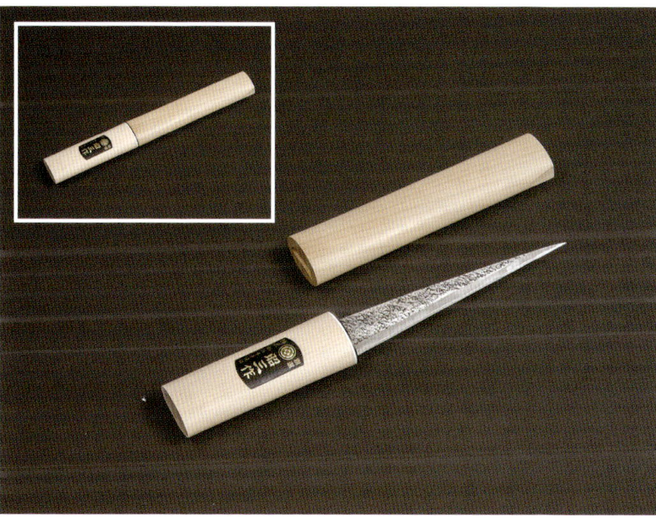

Dagger

The angle between the back and the blade is more acute than that of a kiridashi knife, and the blade length is longer. It's used for cutting curved surfaces and curves. Since the blade is sharp and has a narrower edge than most carpenters' tools, care must be taken not to chip the edge of the blade. There are right- and left-hand ones as well as double-edged blades.

How to Use the Goukuri Knife

The sharp edge of the gouging knife can be very dangerous if used incorrectly. When gouging curved surfaces, don't move the blade using the hand holding the handle, but hold the other hand so that the thumb rests on the back of the blade and press down with the thumb to stabilize the blade edge.

The gouging part of the material can be held and handled as if the thumb is manipulating the cutting edge, allowing safe operation without applying excessive force.

Other Tools

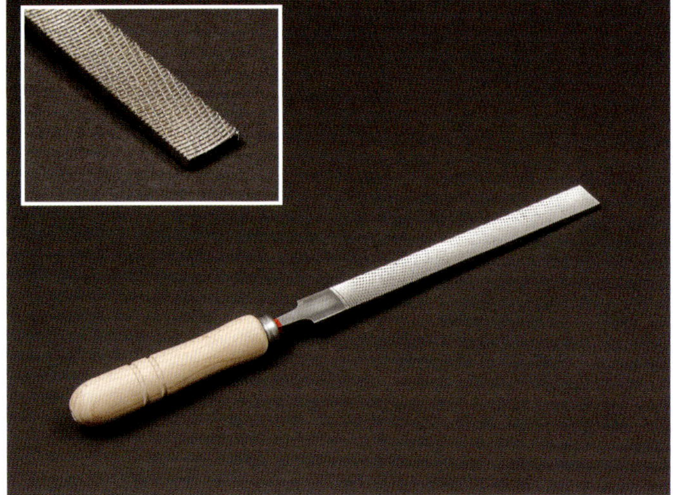

Flat Wood File

Used to manually remove material from wooden components, it's more efficient than sandpaper for shaping curved surfaces.

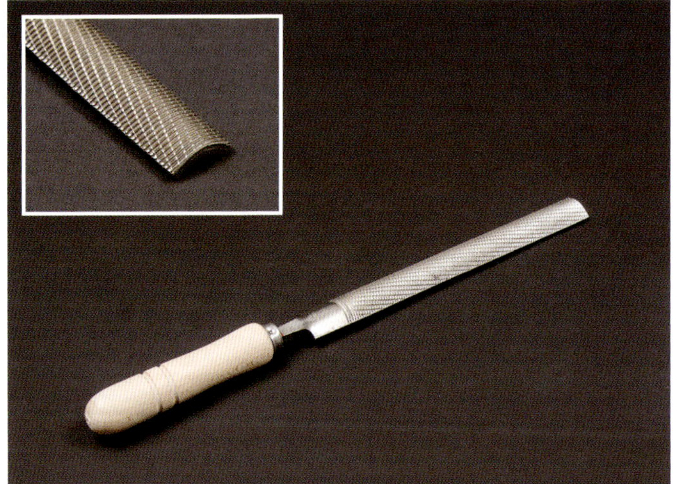

Round Wood File

Used to file concave sections of materials. There are types called "onime" (coarse cut) and "namime" (wavy cut), which are coarser than metal files. Some files have a completely round cross-section.

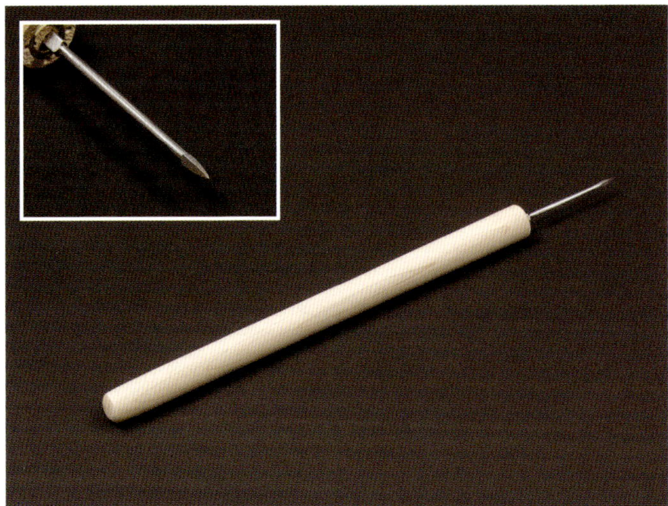

Mitsume-giri (Triangular Awl)

A tool with a triangular cross-section blade, used to make holes by rotating it with the palm. It creates larger holes than the "yotsume-giri" (square awl) and is mainly used for making pilot holes for nails and wood screws.

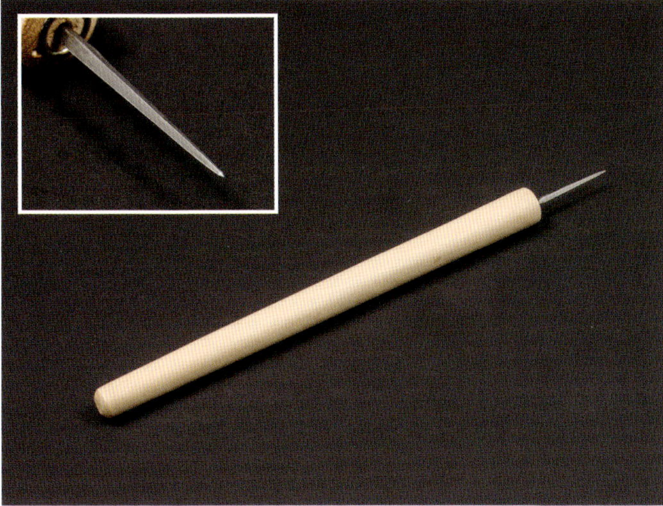

Yotsume-giri (Square Awl)
Used in the same way as the mitsume-giri but for making smaller holes, it's used for making pilot holes for bamboo nails and wooden dowels.

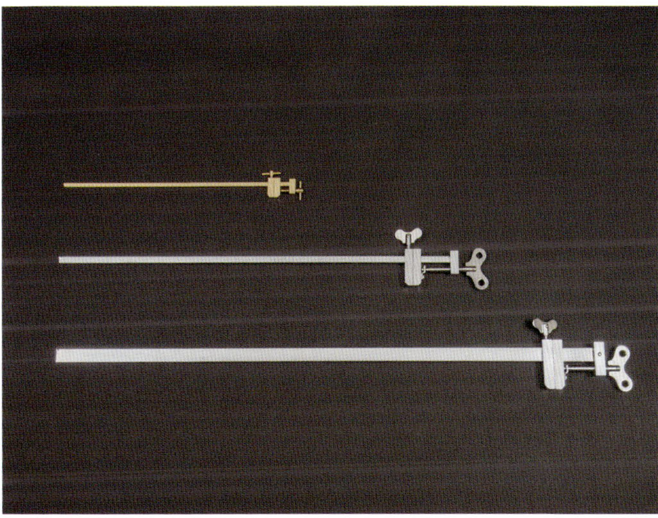

Hagane (End Stop)
Available in iron and brass. Brass ones are usually up to about 300 mm (11.81 in) long, while iron ones are often up to 900 mm (35.43 in) long. Typically used in pairs, they're used to hold boards together after gluing for edge jointing or to secure multiple components together when marking for identical processing.

F-Clamp
A metal clamping tool used for securing materials during gluing or when cutting, filing or performing other tasks. The maximum opening width ranges from about 100 mm (3.94 in) to 1500 mm (59.06 in). There are various other types of clamps, such as C-clamps, three-way clamps and corner clamps, used depending on the size and purpose of the task.

Other Tools

Woodworking Vise

A tool used to clamp and hold materials in place during processing. The handle is rotated to move the clamping plate, securing the material between the fixed plate and the clamping plate. Typically, protective pads are attached to the fixed and clamping plates to prevent damage to the clamped material. It's used by being fixed to a workbench or similar surface.

Metal Plate

A tool used for flattening the backs of plane blades and chisels. A perfectly flat back is essential for straight cuts. This process, known as "uraoshi," involves placing a small amount of abrasive grit on the metal plate, adding a few drops of water and grinding the back of the blade until it is completely flat. The metal plate itself has no abrasive power; the abrasive grit provides the necessary grinding action. A thicker metal plate is preferable, especially since significant downward force is applied using a push rod to hold the blade during the uraoshi process.

Sharpening Stone Holder

Artificial sharpening stones can be used on a cloth or similar surface because they're flat on both sides. However, natural stones may not have a flat back, so they should be secured to a holder or a wooden base for stable sharpening.

Types of Grinding Stones

Finishing Stone

A stone used for the final honing of blades. Generally, stones with a grit number of #3000 or higher are considered finishing stones. However, even stones of the same grit number can vary in characteristics, and some can have grit as fine as #10000 or more. The effectiveness depends on the type of steel and the user's technique, so it's important to try different stones to find the one that suits you best. This principle applies to medium and coarse stones as well.

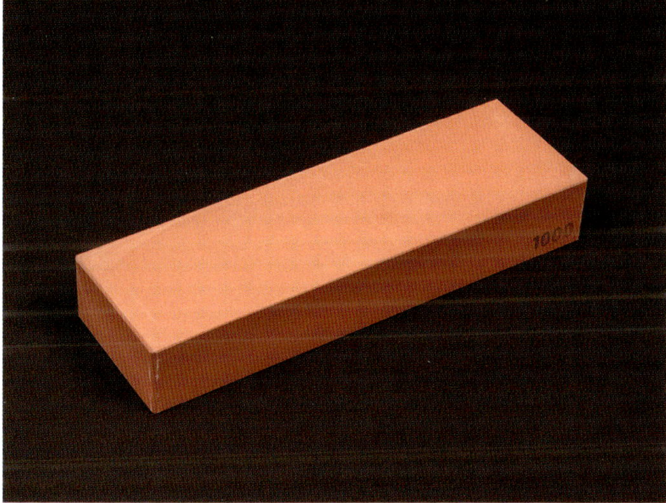

Medium Stone

Stones with a grit number ranging from about 800 to 2000 are generally considered medium stones. Like finishing stones, medium stones of the same grit number can have different cutting abilities and hardness. Typical sharpening starts with a medium stone. Due to variations in manufacturing, it's essential to try different stones to find one you prefer.

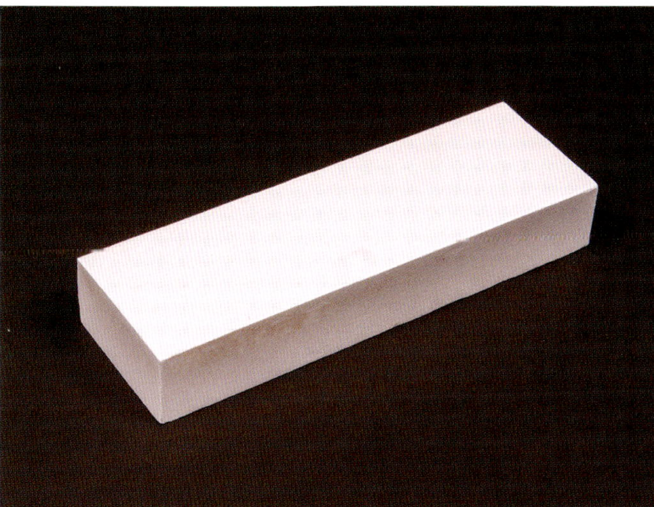

Coarse Stone

Stones with a grit number lower than medium stones are called coarse stones. They're mainly used for significant grinding, such as repairing chipped blades. Because they remove material quickly, they can leave deep scratches on the blade, so they should be used sparingly in regular sharpening.

Joints and Fixtures for Furniture and Woodwork

Essential Fixtures for Accurate Joint Making

To join wood pieces without gaps, the cutting and shaving processes must be precise. Even for simple joints like butt joints or dowel joints, the surfaces to be glued must be cut at exact angles and smoothly shaved. To perform these tasks efficiently, it's recommended to use appropriate fixtures.

Fixtures are auxiliary tools that hold materials in place and maintain a consistent path and angle for cutting tools, ensuring stable processing. While they're also used in metalworking, common woodworking fixtures include a shooting board for planing board edges at right angles, a miter shooting board for planing end grain at 45° angles for frames and a miter jack (a box-shaped miter shooting board) for planing board edges at 45° angles for box construction.

These fixtures are usually prepared before starting the work and are typically homemade. Depending on the shape of the materials being processed, new fixtures may need to be created. Furthermore, to ensure a stable work space when using these fixtures, it's important to use a workbench made of thick planks or laminated wood with minimal warping, maintaining a flat surface for accurate work and a consistent process. Here, we'll cover the basic elements for creating essential fixtures.

Sitting and Standing Sliding Table

In woodworking, including joint making, it's common to work either seated or standing at a workbench. Fixtures are used to stabilize the materials being processed.

If there's no designated place for the workbench, a simple workbench purchased from a home improvement store can be used, but it is preferable to work on a sturdy surface. Workbenches typically have pegs for securing materials. For joinery work, a bench stop, called "ate-dome," is often used. On workbenches, pegs are inserted into square holes and hammered into place from underneath the tabletop to act as stops. Some standing workbenches come with preinstalled woodworking vises.

Most workbenches are made of wood, and many woodworking enthusiasts prefer to make their own. This involves choosing materials and ensuring that the tabletop is made of thick, stable boards. For specific joinery work, very thick boards, around 100 mm (3.94 in), are used. Solid wood boards can be expensive and hard to find. Practical alternatives include using laminated wood or lumber core with a natural wood veneer or using hardwood laminated boards.

Standing workbenches have a table-like structure with legs, rails, shelves and a tabletop. You can add woodworking vises and pegs at convenient positions as you work.

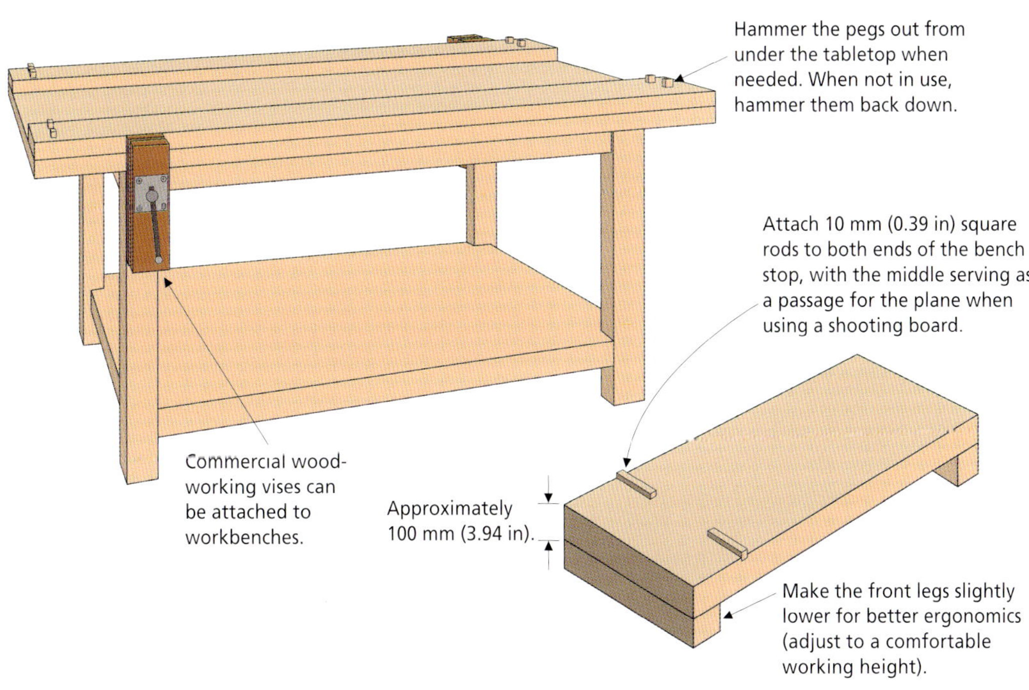

Sewing Block

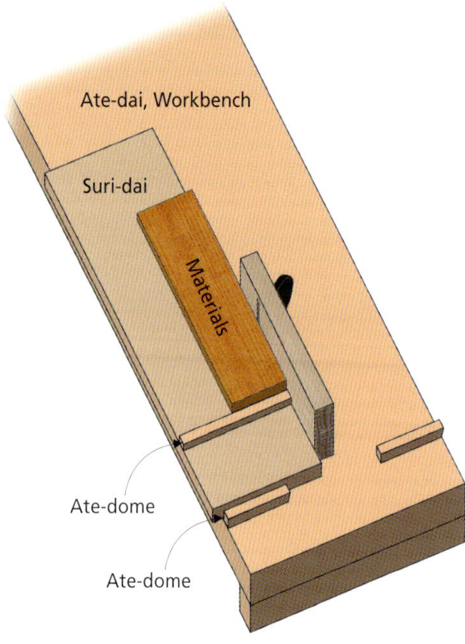

The suri-dai used for planing the ends of materials at right angles is placed on a flat workbench or surface and fixed with ate-dome. The material is then placed on top of it and planed. It's important that the top and bottom surfaces of the suri-dai are parallel, and that the bottom of the plane and the ends of the material are at right angles.

The length of the suri-dai should be the length of the material to be planed plus 10–15 cm (4–6 in) on the side where the material is placed from the ate-dome. The portion of the suri-dai in front of the ate-dome should be large enough to stabilize the base when the plane is drawn and the planing is finished (when the blade reaches the ate-dome).

The board used for the base should be made of well-dried straight-grain wood such as cypress, ash or zelkova. If other materials are used, they should be as warp- and twist-free as possible. If the width is insufficient, it can be glued together, or laminated wood can be used from the start.

The ate-dome (koma-dome) should not be too high, as it becomes difficult to use when planing thin boards flat. Use square sticks about 12–14 mm (0.5–0.6 in) thick, with half of them embedded in a groove carved in the suri-dai. Hardwoods such as cherry or zelkova should be used for the ate-dome to prevent it from coming loose. The width of the groove for the ate-dome should be about 0.3 mm (0.01 in) narrower than the square stick used, and the ate-dome should be driven in with wood.

The key point in making a suri-dai is that the top and bottom surfaces are parallel. If these two surfaces are not flat and parallel, the ends of the material being planed on them will not be finished at right angles. If you're not getting a good right angle, recheck the parallelism of these two surfaces.

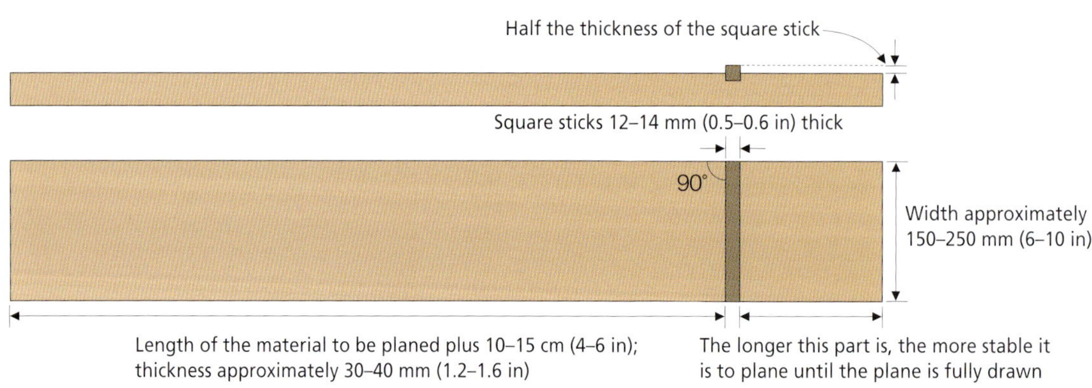

Cutting Block

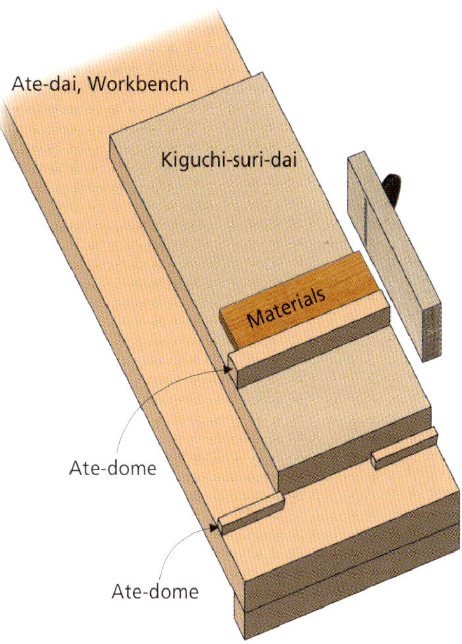

The kiguchi-suri-dai, used for planing the ends of materials at right angles, is placed on |a workbench or similar surface and fixed with an ate-dome. The material is placed on top of it, and the part that protrudes from the base is planed.

The board used for the base should have all adjoining edges meeting at right angles, and the ate-dome should be attached perpendicular to the long edge of the base. Since it's used to plane the ends of square sticks and board materials, the base doesn't need to be as long as the suri-dai. Using the ends of the base and the ate-dome as guides, the ends of the materials are planed at right angles with a plane. Since the ate-dome is held by hand together with the material, it's easier to use if it's of a thickness that is easy to hold; 3–5 cm (1.2–2 in) thick square timber is typically used.

The board used for the base should be as free from warp as possible, just like the suri-dai. Hardwoods are used for the ate-dome, but since the corners can easily chip and the right angles with the base can be misaligned, it's acceptable to initially attach them a bit longer. In such cases, the ate-dome shouldn't be glued to the base, but rather placed in a groove 3–5 mm (0.12–0.2 in) deep and fixed from the back of the base with screws.

Also, since the ends of the base can be planed and the right angle with the ate-dome can be misaligned, the ends of the base should be corrected using the ate-dome as a reference.

To make it easier to understand the state of the ends of the base, drawing a few lines with a pencil will make it easier to check since the lines will disappear from the planed parts.

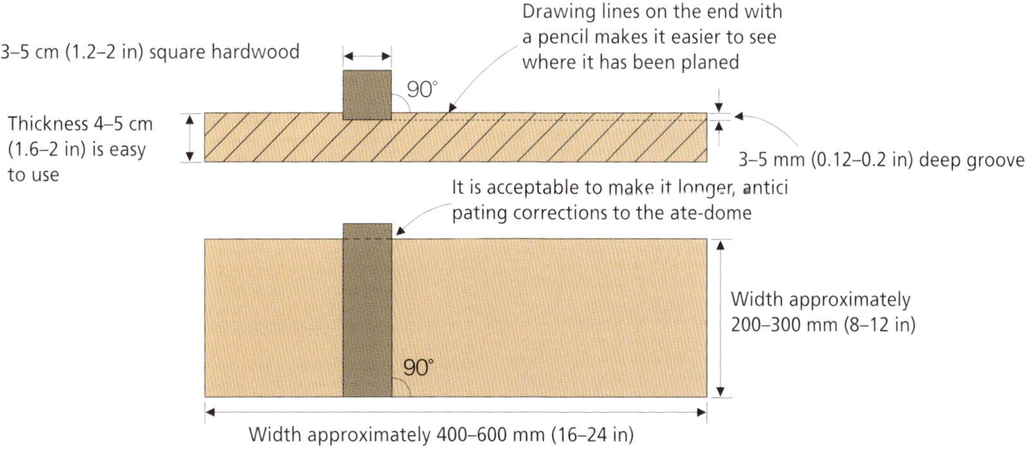

Clamping Wood Gouged Shaving Table

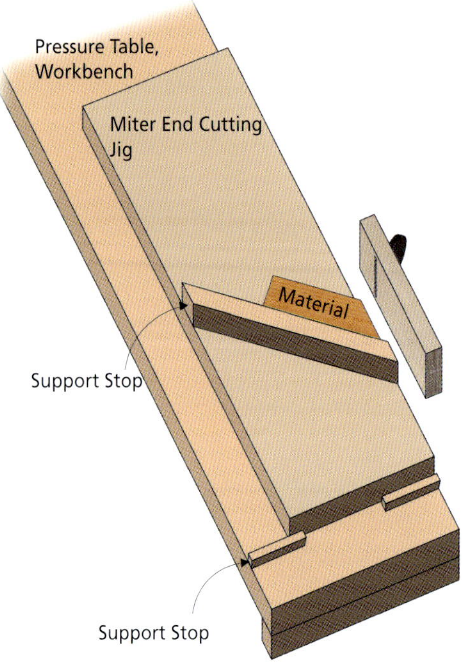

The miter end cutting jig used to cut the ends of materials at 45° (miter) is used for tasks such as making frames or assembling rails where the ends need to be cut at a 45° angle. Simply put, you just need to fix the support stop of the end cutting jig at 45°, but because it is mounted at an angle to the jig, if the jig expands or contracts, the angle of the support stop can become misaligned.

Generally, materials such as well-dried straight-grained hinoki, tamo or keyaki are recommended for jigs, but natural wood is not entirely free from expansion and contraction. Therefore, it's also an option to use non-natural boards, such as lumber core material, for the support stop. The size of the material used for the support stop should be about the same as the end cutting jig. Since it may need adjustment over time, it's O.K. to start with a longer length. The support stop is fixed with screws for easy removal, but since it can shift during fixation, carve an accurate 45° groove with a depth of 3–5 mm (0.12–0.20 in) in the edge of the jig to ensure more precise attachment.

The materials cut at a miter will fit together at a right angle, but if you want to create hexagonal or octagonal frames, you can change the angle at which the stop is attached to create a dedicated jig.

The jig doesn't need to be very long since it's mainly for cutting end bars, but it should be made long enough to accommodate the angle at which the stop is attached.

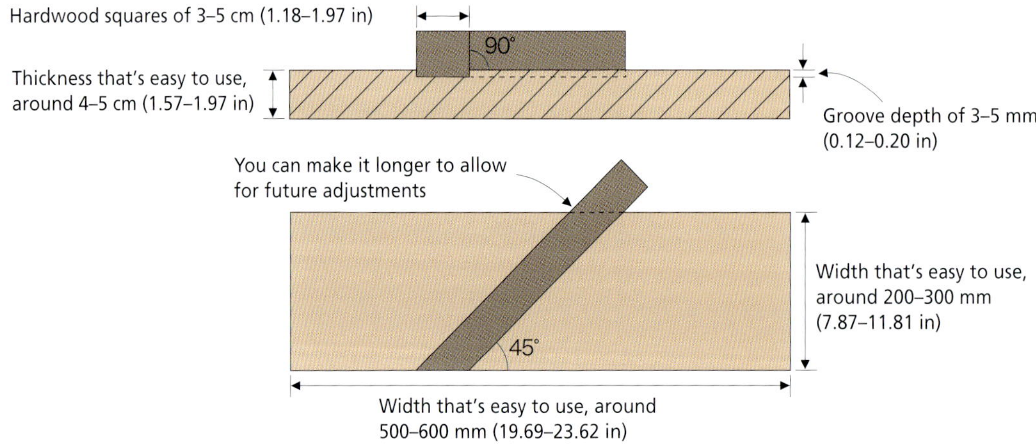

Unlike the miter end cutting jig used for cutting end bars for frames, the miter board cutting jig is used for cutting the ends of wider boards used for the side panels of boxes. It's also known as the box miter end cutting jig, but to avoid confusion with the previously mentioned jig, it's referred to as the miter board cutting jig here.

Both the base plate and the support stop should be cut so that the cutting surface faces the end grain, and the support stop should be fixed at a right angle to the base plate. If you want to make it simple, you can use just a fixed support stop and base plate, but as shown in the right diagram, you can add another board of the same height as the support stop to the opposite edge of the jig, and place another board across both sides to stabilize the plane's bottom edge during use. In this case, since the plane's bottom edge is attached to both the base plate's guiding surface and the board above, the thickness of the board material to be cut is limited, so the height of the support stop should be decided based on the intended use and the width of the plane used.

Since the end grain of the jig base is cut at 45°, the lower edge is sharp and prone to chipping upon impact. There's also a risk of injury such as cutting your hand, so chamfer the edge about 3 mm (0.12 in) for safety.

This jig is also made in narrower versions for use when cutting dovetail miter joints, where the back of a chisel is pressed against the jig.

The types of materials used are the same as those for the end cutting jig or sliding jigs.

Clamping Board Shaving Table

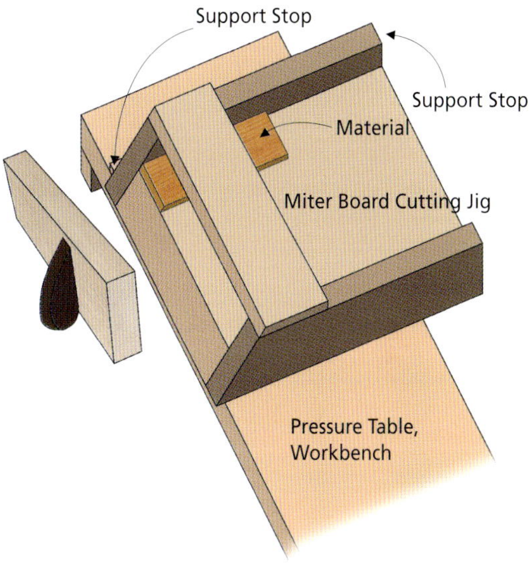

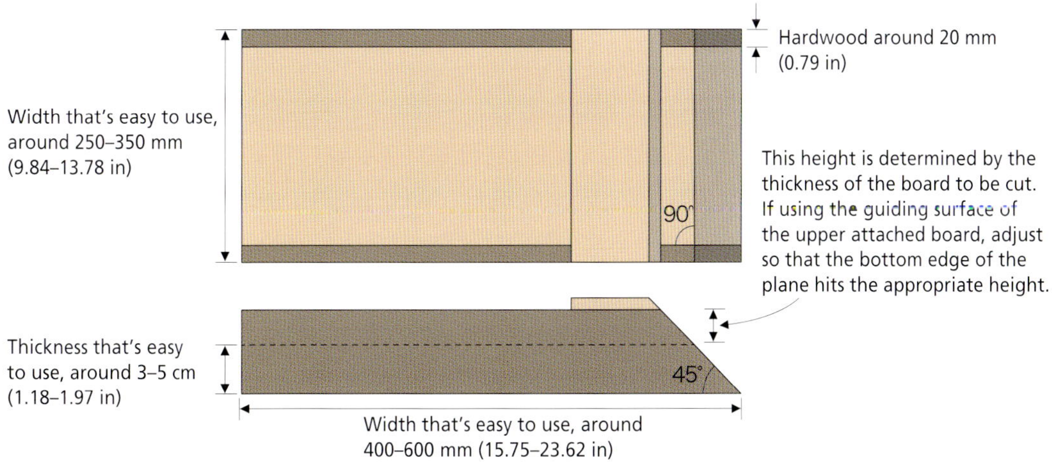

Types of Joints Used in Furniture and Cabinetry

Japanese Joints for Beginners

There are various types of joints used in furniture and cabinetry. These include joints for connecting boards at right angles or other angles, joints for connecting the edges of boards to widen the material, joints for connecting boards to timbers and joints for connecting timbers to each other. It's essential to choose the most suitable joint from among the various types, depending on the materials and the purpose of the connection.

Additionally, there are joints that, despite being complexly crafted, become hidden and invisible once assembled, and joints that are designed to be clearly visible and serve an aesthetic purpose. The choice of joint can also depend on the maker's preference. However, for items such as chairs or large furniture, where the effect of loading must be considered, it's crucial to select joining methods that ensure high strength and durability for safe use.

Here, we'll introduce the representative types of joints used in furniture and cabinetry with illustrations, focusing on the most common and important joints, and look into the manufacturing process of each.

First, let's look at the structure and names of the parts of commonly used household items like chairs, desks and wardrobes as examples. These are general examples meant to help explain the applications of joints.

Furniture Parts

To understand where joints and connections are used, let's review the names of various parts of chairs, desks and wardrobes.

■ Names of Parts of a Small Chair

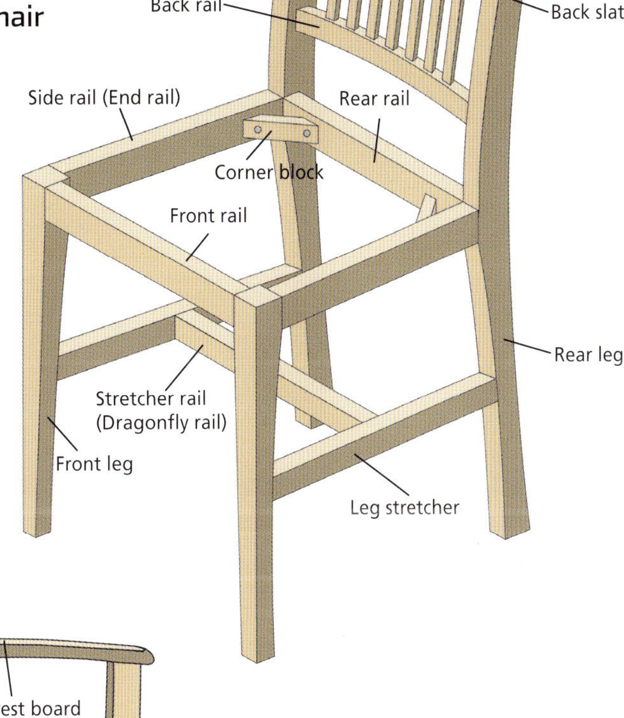

■ Names of Parts of an Armchair

For parts not visible under the seat board, refer to the small chair.

■ Parts of a desk

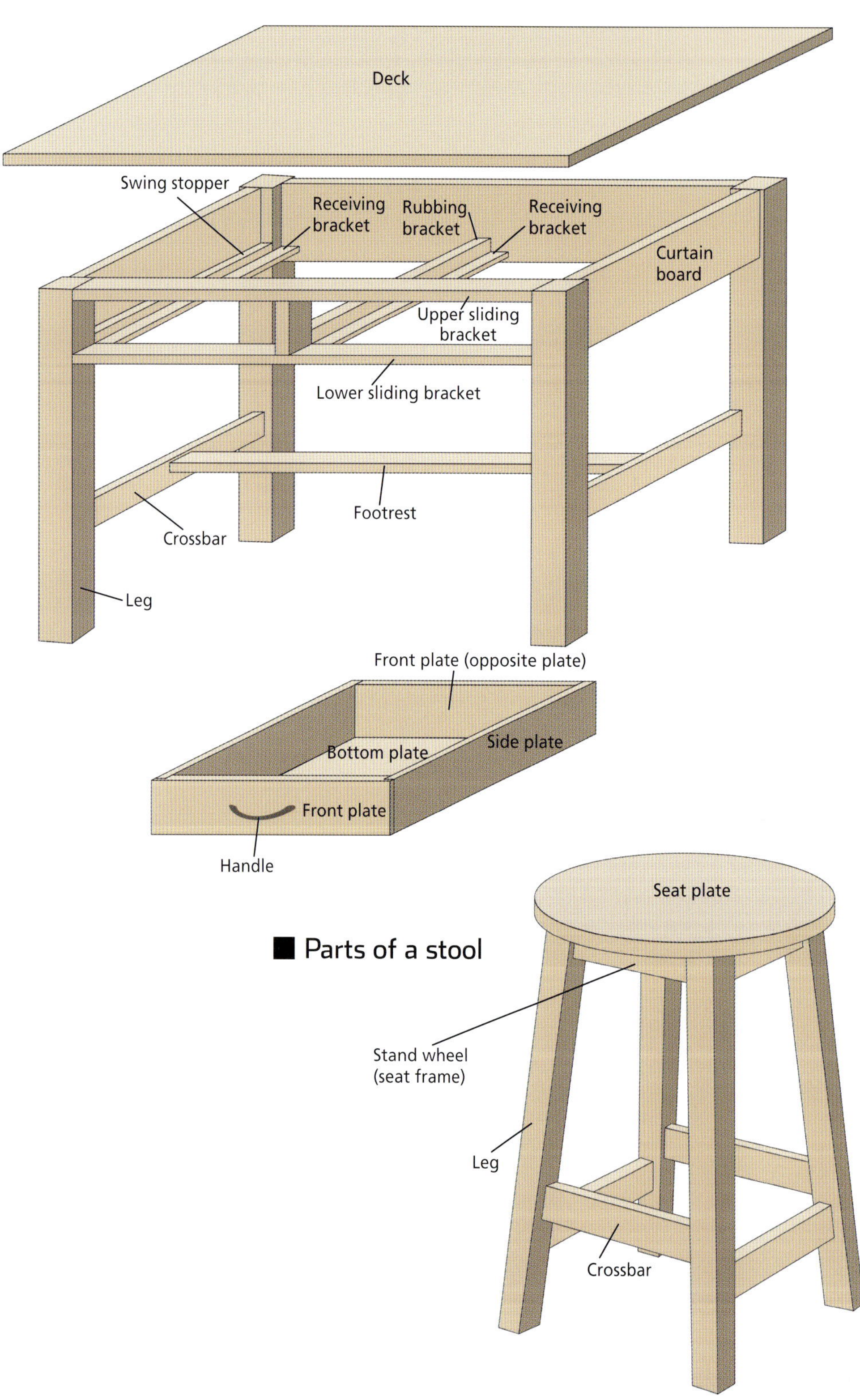

■ Parts of a stool

Parts of a dresser

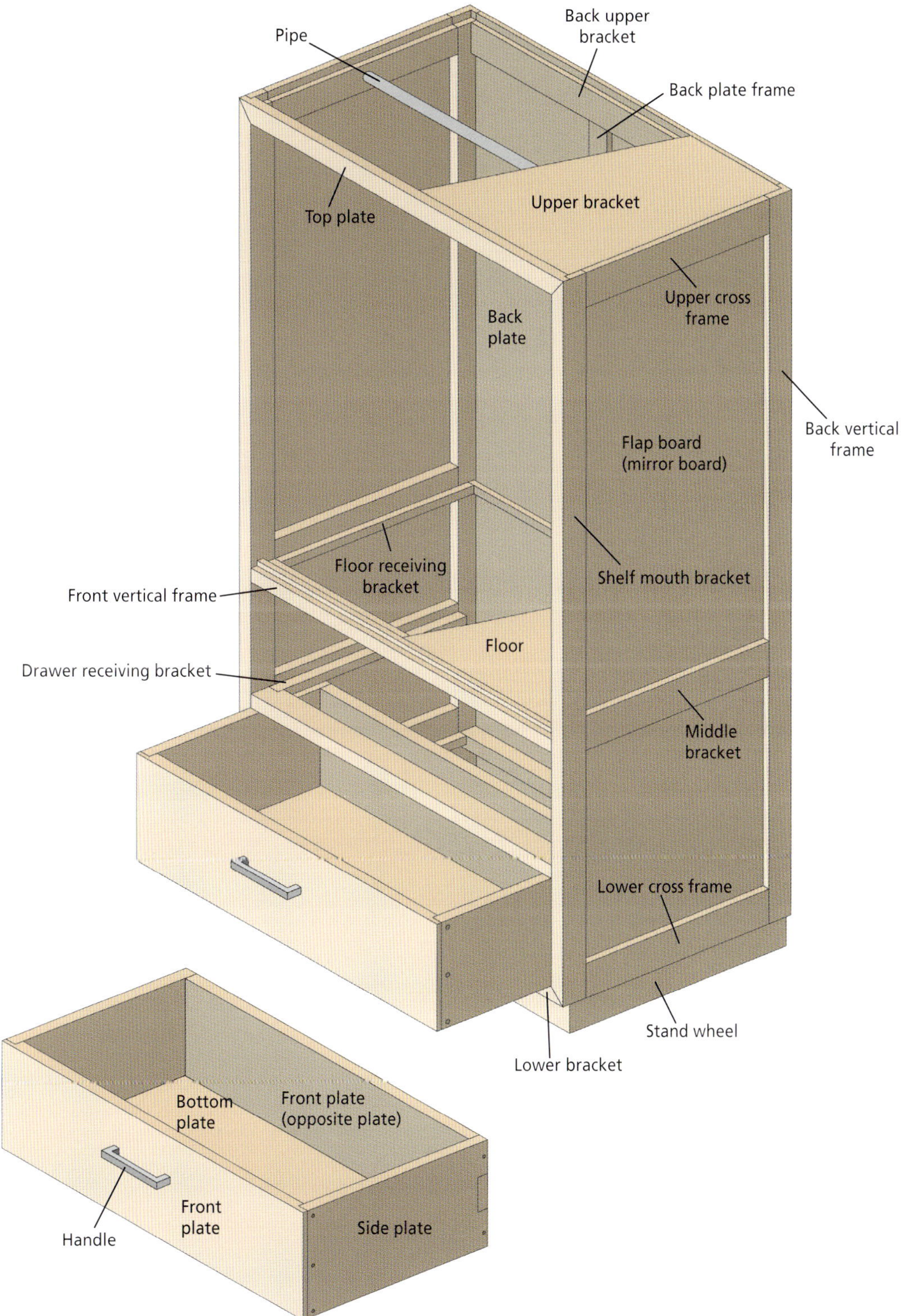

Types of Joints

When classifying joints based on the shape of the components, we can categorize them into three types:

1. Joining boards with boards
2. Joining boards with beams
3 Joining beams with beams

The choice of these joints depends on the purpose of the connection. In general, for furniture and cabinetry sold as products, the selection of joints considers factors like strength, appearance and cost-effectiveness. However, even if using hand tools to create joints isn't considered efficient, there's an appeal to crafting with one's own skills and tools. Even when hand tools are the only option, prioritizing the enjoyment of the work over efficiency can be a rewarding approach, especially if the goal isn't to sell the products.

Let's take a look at the types of joints commonly used in furniture and cabinetry. There are many other types of joints beyond those introduced here. There are countless variations, such as irregularly shaped dovetail joints or a combination of different methods. Understanding the purpose of the joint and choosing a method that ensures the necessary strength is crucial. For items that don't require much strength, like small boxes, using joints with a strong design aspect can be part of the fun of crafting.

The table below shows the types of joints and their main purposes. Some joints may be unsuitable for certain applications due to strength considerations, so check the description of each joint for appropriate uses.

1. Joining Boards with Boards

There are joints designed to widen the board by joining the edges, to connect the outer parts of boxes or shelves at right angles,or to join at angles other than right angles.

2. Joining Boards with Beams

These joints are primarily used to prevent warping or twisting of the board, or in furniture that can be assembled and disassembled.

3. Joining Beams with Beams

These joints, like frame joints that allow for lightweight or strong boards as inserted panels, are used in large pieces like dressers and cupboards, as well as in movable elements like sliding doors, fusuma and regular doors. They're also frequently used in the legs and stretchers of tables and chairs.

TYPE OF JOINING	PURPOSE OF JOINING	MAIN USES
Joining plates and plates	Widen the board	Desk decks, cupboards, chest of drawers, etc.
	Joining at right angles and other angles	Side panels of boxes and drawers, joining of top and side panels of shelves and chests of drawers, partitions of drawers and shelves, etc.
Joining of board and square timber	Prevent warping and twisting	Prevents warping and twisting of single boards and wood boards such as table decks, box lids, doors, etc.
Joining of square timbers and square timber	Joining at right angles and other angles	Joining of frames, joining of legs and cores of chairs and desks, etc.

Joining Boards with Boards

Types of Joints

■ Butt Joint (Edge Joint)

Used to join the edges of boards to widen them. This method is used for making wide materials from large items like tables to thin boards used in cabinetry. Longer materials are often joined this way, requiring the skillful use of planes. The high performance of modern adhesives makes accurately made butt joints essential.

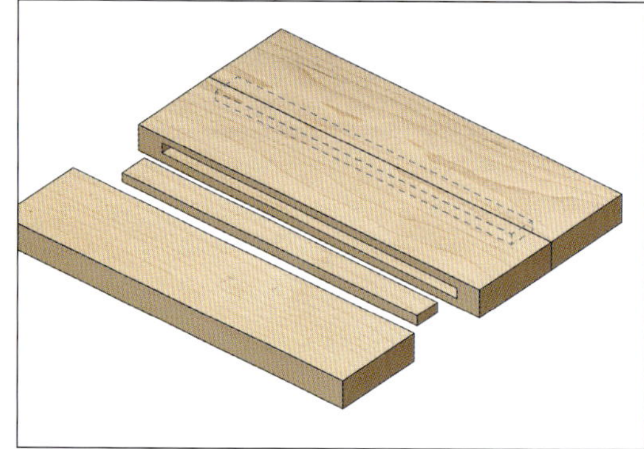

Housed Butt Joint

The core's thickness is about ⅓ to ¼ of the board's thickness being joined, and the width is about four times the core's thickness. Plywood is often used for the core, hidden without reaching the ends, or solid wood is used for the ends.

Rubbed Joint (Plain Butt Joint)

The most basic type of joint. Creating a slight hollow in the gluing surface increases adhesive strength. With the improved performance of adhesives, this joint provides sufficient strength.

Spline Joint

The core's thickness is about ⅓ of the board's thickness, and the width is about twice the core's thickness. Commonly used for joining solid wood boards.

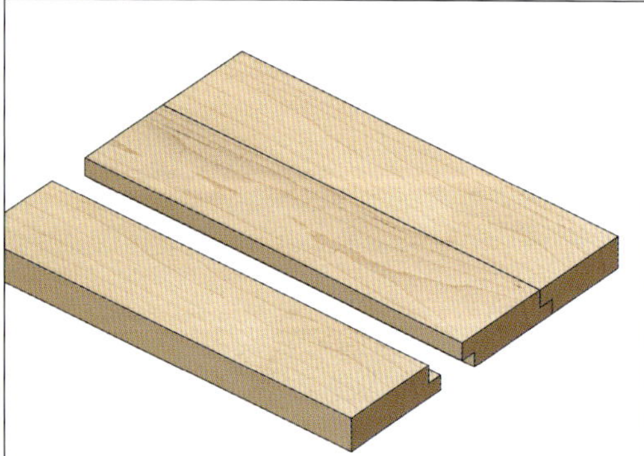

Lap Joint

Half the thickness of each board is removed to join them. This method is suitable for thin boards and is frequently used in cabinetry.

Dowel Joint

Added strength with dowels replacing tenons. Besides round dowels, bamboo pegs can also be used, suitable for joining boards with boards, boards with beams, and beams with beams.

About Rubbed Joints (Plain Butt Joints)

Joining the edges of boards to widen them is done with thick boards for tables, medium-thickness boards used in furniture like shelves and thin boards used in cabinetry. Here, we'll look at the most basic rubbed joint (plain butt joint). Due to the improved performance of adhesives, this joint method can achieve sufficient strength. Even when using other methods like the spline joint or the dowel joint, it's necessary to precisely process the mating surfaces (the surfaces being joined).

The joining method is the same for both thin and thick boards, but the planing work on the mating surfaces differs slightly. For boards used in tables, which are often made of hard wood and are wide, it's easier and more stable to plane the edge with the board standing upright, allowing for better control.

For thin boards, planing the narrow edge while the board is standing is less stable. Therefore, use a planing jig called a suri-dai, laying the board flat for more precise work (see page 57, rubbed joint for thin boards). Boards between 3–6 mm thick can be planed this way, while boards up to about 20 mm thick can be planed directly on a workbench. Boards around 3–6 mm thick may be planed in layers, but for thicker boards, it's more accurate to plane them one at a time due to the difficulty in securing them.

Starting with an 18-mm-thick board, the key point, regardless of thickness, is to create a slight hollow in the mating surface to form a glue reservoir. Additionally, use the plane properly to ensure the edge is square to the board's surface.

Place the plane horizontally on a flat platform, and check the right angle between the plane's bottom edge and the board's edge.

Assuming the top and bottom surfaces of the board are flat and parallel, and the board is placed on a flat platform, place the plane with its edge facing down on the platform. Use a try square to check that the plane's bottom edge is perpendicular to the board's top surface or the platform. The plane used here, called a long plane, has one side of its platform wider to accommodate sliding on the suridai. If you don't the plane or the board isn't very long, a standard flat plane can also be used.

For rubbed joints, since no grooves are cut into the mating surfaces, even if the plane isn't perfectly square, the joint can still be aligned by reversing the top and bottom orientations of one of the boards being joined. There's also a joint method called the bevelled butt joint that initially takes a wider surface area for joining, so it's not incorrect, but it's important to understand the condition of the plane's bottom edge relative to the platform.

Even if the plane's bottom edge isn't square to the board's edge, flipping one board upside down and planing it can align the joint surfaces.

Procedure for Medium-Thickness-Board Butt Joint

1 Place the plane sideways on a flat surface and shave the edge of the board to be joined.

2 After shaving the joint edges of two boards, place one board below and one above, align the joint edges, and move the upper board side to side.

3 If the middle part is high, as shown in the left picture, the pivot point will be in the center, so shave it so that the pivot point comes to the opposite edge being swung.

4 Create a gap of about 0.1–0.2 mm in the middle to form a glue pocket. The photo shows a slightly larger gap.

5 Use a single sheet of copy paper as a guide for the gap size of the glue pocket.

6 After processing all joint surfaces, apply adhesive and spread it with a brush.

7 Fix it with end clamps. The first one is stopped in the center with enough force to prevent the end clamp from falling off even if flipped.

8 Attach end clamps from the opposite side to both ends. If glue has oozed out, wipe it off to prevent the end clamps from sticking.

9 After securing both ends with end clamps, tighten the center clamp strongly.

10 Use a ruler to check if the joined boards are flat.

11 Leave it for at least a day until the adhesive dries.

Thin Board Butt Joint

Thin boards used in joinery are also butt-jointed when a wider board is needed. In joinery, thin boards around 5mm are often used, and a fixture called a suri-dai is used to shave the edge at a right angle to the board surface (see page 44).

For authentic joinery work done while seated, the suri-dai is placed on an ate-dai to plane the board. Even when working standing, the suri-dai can be placed on a flat workbench and planed on it.

To plane, press the thin board's edge slightly protruding from the suri-dai, hold the plane sideways and slide it along the workbench. The bottom of the plane and the edge contacting the workbench must be at right angles, and the suri-dai must have perfectly parallel top and bottom surfaces, and the workbench must be flat.

After butt-jointing the thin boards, fix them to maintain flatness until the adhesive dries. In addition to end clamps, clamp the boards between square timbers from above and below, wrapping the timbers in plastic wrap to prevent them from sticking to the adhesive.

Procedure for Thin Board Butt Joint

1 For this procedure, we will join three thin cypress boards, so first mark them.

2 Place the suri-dai on the workbench, set the material on it, and plane so that the board surface and edge are at right angles.

3 Align the surfaces to be joined, stack the three boards, and apply adhesive. Apply adhesive to the opposite side of the middle board as well.

4 Use a brush or paintbrush to apply adhesive evenly. This is the same for thick boards.

5 Check the marks and align the three boards.

6 Use two pressure plates, wrapping them in plastic wrap to prevent adhesive from sticking.

7 Clamp the middle area of the three joined thin boards with the two pressure plates.

8 Fix both ends with end clamps about 3 cm (1.18 in) from the edge.

9 Once everything is fixed, ensure the boards do not wobble with the middle pressure plate.

PRO TIP 1

Board Order

For furniture boards, it's common to use the inner side (wood back) as the visible surface. For thick boards like tabletops, which are prone to warping, it's standard to use the wood back as the top surface and consider anti-warping measures on the underside. However, for narrower and thinner boards with less warping, such as drawer bottoms or box sides and tops, it's acceptable to prioritize appearance over using the wood back as the visible surface. In the photo below, all boards have the wood back on top, but since knots are visible, the wood front is used as the visible surface, and the grain of other boards is matched accordingly.

1 First, line up all boards with the wood back facing up. If there are knots, use the wood front as the visible surface.

2 Arrange the boards to ensure the grain appears natural.

3 Decide the joining order based on appearance rather than using the wood back as the visible surface.

4 To know the front and back of the joined boards, mark a matching symbol at the front or back according to your own rule.

Thick Board Butt Joint

For larger pieces such as tables, thicker boards are often used, typically made of hard woods like zelkova. When planing thick boards, using the plane sideways as with thin boards doesn't apply sufficient force.

When planing thick boards, set the joint edge upward and fix it in place. Use the plane in the usual manner, with the bottom edge facing downward. Since the surface to be joined is wide, the plane remains stable. However, unlike sliding the plane edge along a guide, maintaining accuracy can be challenging. The plane blade's position can easily shift, so to stabilize the plane, use your fingers as a guide.

In the photo on the next page (PRO TIP 2), photo 3 shows the position of the right hand without holding the plane. The middle and ring fingers are touching the material. By maintaining this position while holding the plane, you can use the same part of the plane blade consistently. Using different parts of the blade intentionally can sometimes yield different results, but unintended blade slippage generally leads to poor outcomes. Planing thick, hard board edges to be at right angles to the surface requires a certain level of skill and experience.

Additionally, it's important to understand the state of shavings when planing with your plane using the full width of the blade. Generally, the plane blade is sharpened so that the middle part is slightly higher than the edges. This means that when shavings are taken across the full width, the edges will be thin, and the middle will be thicker.

Thick Board Butt Joint Procedure

1 Fix the edge of the board to be joined facing up on the workbench and plane the edge at a right angle to the surface.

2 After planing both boards, align the joint surfaces and move the top board side to side to check the pivot point.

3 Apply adhesive to the aligned surfaces of the two boards.

4 Use three clamps to secure the boards, starting from the center.

5 Wipe off any excess adhesive with a damp cloth.

6 Flip the boards and clamp about 3 cm (1.2 in) from the edge on the opposite side of the center clamp.

PRO TIP 2

Planing Thick Board Edges to a Right Angle

When planing thick board edges, standing the board makes it easier to apply force and ensures stability. For long materials, use a jointer plane, or a standard plane if unavailable. Planing edges to a right angle to the surface requires skill and experience. Plane blades are usually sharpened so that the center is slightly higher than the edges. This means that the shavings will be thicker in the center and thinner at the edges. It's essential to keep this in mind and be conscious of which part of the blade is shaving the desired area.

1 Clamp a piece of timber to the workbench, then clamp the material to be planed with the surface facing up.

2 Position the right hand on the plane with the middle and ring fingers touching the surface, adjusting the blade's contact with the edge.

3 Without holding the plane, ensure the middle and ring fingers touch the surface.

4 Use a square to check the right angle of the edge. Here, the side near the square's heel is slightly higher.

5 Align the center of the blade with the desired planing area, using the middle and ring fingers of the right hand as a guide.

6 The shavings produced will be thin at the front and thicker towards the back.

To plane the edge and surface at a right angle, it's essential to adjust by shaving the high parts slightly. Understanding which part of the blade is shaving the desired area is crucial.

To check the high parts of the joint surface, place one board below and one on top, and move the top board side to side, just like with medium-thickness boards. Adjust so that the pivot point forms at the opposite end from the hand holding it, creating a gap of about 0.1–0.2 mm in the middle.

Board widths can range from about 61–91.5 cm (24–36 inches), so prepare strong, wide-jawed clamps like pony clamps.

PRO TIP 3

Creating Glue Pockets

When making a butt joint, the joint surfaces are slightly recessed in the middle to create glue pockets (nakasuki). The gap created is about 0.1–0.2 mm (0.004–0.008 in), just enough for a faint sliver of light to pass through when a ruler is placed against the shaved edge. To confirm this, place a ruler against the shaved edge and check for light leakage. Alternatively, place the boards to be joined on top of each other and move the front edge of the top board side to side to check the pivot point. If the pivot point is near the opposite edge, there is a gap in the middle. If the pivot point is in the middle, there is no gap. When finishing the shaving, slightly lift the plane to avoid lowering the edges (photo 4).

1 Shave the edge of the joint surface with a plane and check for straightness with a ruler.

2 A gap should be visible in the middle. If the gap is too wide, shave a bit more from both ends.

3 Stack the boards to be joined and move the front edge of the top board side to side to check the pivot point.

4 When finishing with the plane, slightly lift it to avoid over-shaving the ends.

■ Butt Joint (Butt End Joint)

This method involves joining boards in an L or T shape, commonly used in box or frame construction. While simple, this method typically lacks strength, so nails, screws, and adhesives are often used in conjunction. It's a fundamental joint but not typically used when aesthetics are a priority.

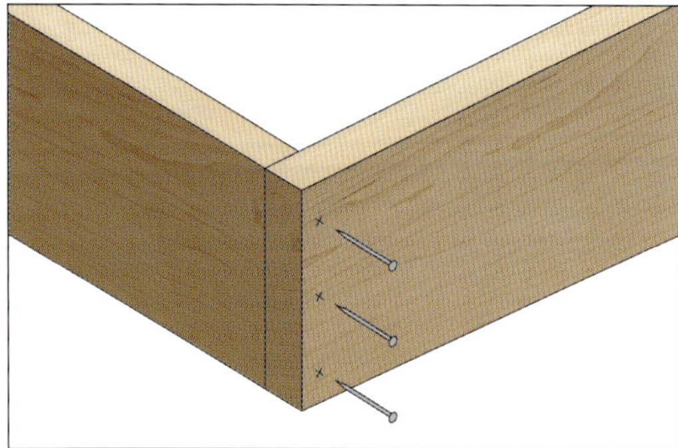

Corner Butt Joint

The simplest joint for joining two boards. Often used in areas where appearance is not critical, such as packing boxes.

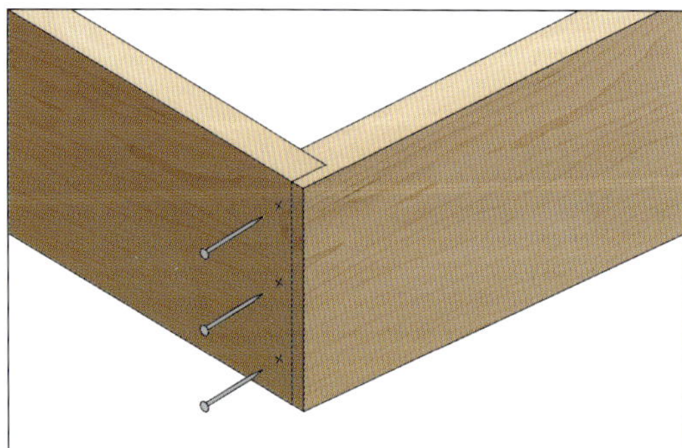

Wrapped Butt Joint

Used for joining drawer fronts and sides or corners of baseboards. Glue is used along with nails or screws, which are countersunk and concealed with dowels.

Single Groove Mortise and Tenon Joint

One board has a groove on the inside face, and the other has a tenon on the edge. Commonly used for attaching bottom boards.

Shouldered Single Groove Mortise and Tenon Joint

Similar to the single groove mortise and tenon joint but with the groove hidden, providing a cleaner look. Used for slightly more premium box constructions.

Butt Joint

Boards are joined and fixed with nails or screws. It's a straightforward method used for dividing shelves.

Mortise and Tenon Joint
One board has a groove the same width as the thickness of the joining board. Used for partitioning boxes.

Shouldered Mortise and Tenon Joint
A mortise and tenon joint with a shoulder for a cleaner appearance. Used for box partitions.

Dovetail Mortise and Tenon Joint
A dovetail-shaped tenon and groove. Used for shelves, baseboards, and higher-quality box partitions.

Combination Joints

Used frequently in box constructions, these joints involve creating interlocking parts. They're more durable and aesthetically pleasing than butt joints, often used in high-end boxes. Some types can only be made by hand.

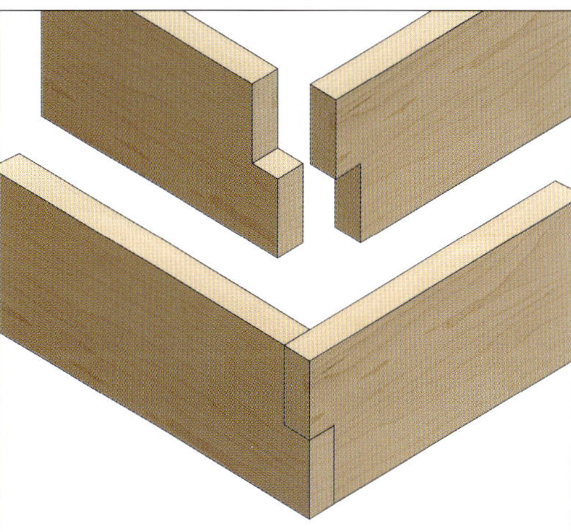

Double Tenon Joint
The simplest and most basic combination joint. Both top and bottom ends are cut to the same width.

Triple Tenon Joint
The board is divided into thirds, with one side cut into a male part and the other into a female part. Used for strong box joints.

Pin (Checkerboard) Joint
A generic term for joints with numerous evenly spaced interlocks, where the tenon width is smaller than the board width. Used for high-end boxes.

Mitered Double Tenon Joint
A combination joint with both top and bottom ends mitered. The number of interlocks in between can vary. Used for high-end box joints.

Mitered Seven-Pin Joint
A combination joint with the top end mitered. Used for strong and aesthetically pleasing box joints.

Dovetail Joint
Tenons are dovetail-shaped and interlock in one direction only. Combines strength and aesthetic appeal.

Balance Joint
Similar to the dovetail joint but with one dovetail tenon narrower. Used for high-end box constructions.

Wrapped Dovetail Joint

The end of the male tenon wraps around the dovetail joint. Used for high-end drawer front and side joins.

Hidden Mitered Dovetail Joint

Often used in joinery for box constructions. Appears like a simple mitered joint but has intricate internal interlocks, used for the highest quality boxes.

Hidden Dovetail Joint

Both male and female tenons wrap around and conceal the joint. It looks like a wrapped butt joint but prevents warping of the front board.

Angled Joint

Both male and female tenons are angled. Requires advanced skill, and when rounded, it becomes a "net joint."

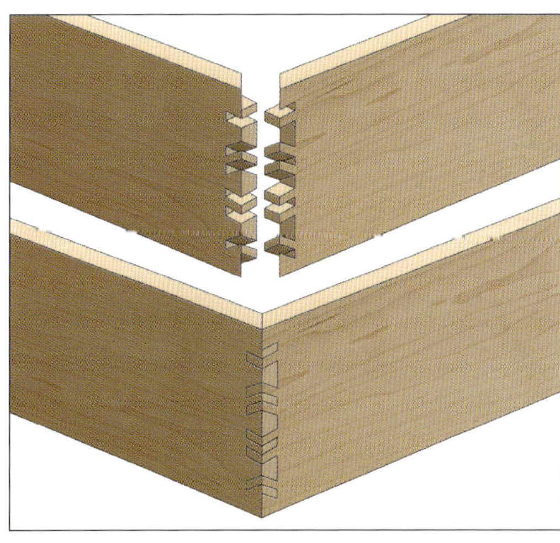

Twisted Joint

Also called a water joint, it's one of the most challenging joints.

Mitered Joint

This method is used in box constructions to hide the end grain of the wood. While not as strong as combination joints, it provides a clean finish. Also used for joining timber pieces.

Large Mitered Joint (Butt Miter Joint)
Used for joining boards in box constructions or timber for frames and panels. Relies on adhesive strength, not suitable for high-strength joints.

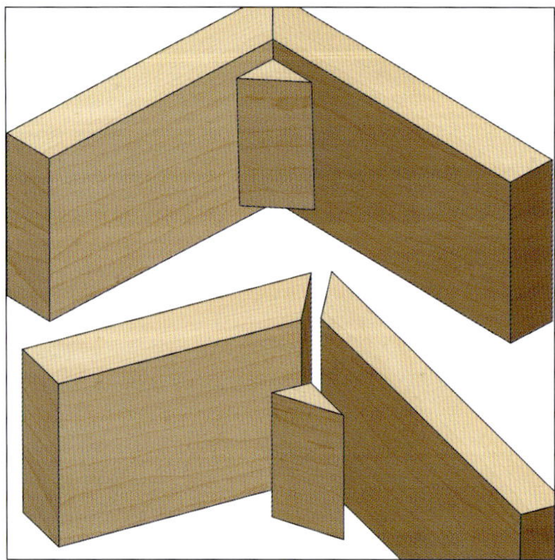

Flat Mitered Joint
A simple method to reinforce the weak strength of the large mitered joint by using corner blocks. Provides moderate strength.

Sawed Mitered Joint
Reinforces the large mitered joint by cutting a slot at the corner and inserting a thin board to increase the adhesive surface. Different wood species can be used for the thin board for a decorative finish.

Inserted Large Mitered Joint
Inserts a thin board called an "inserted core" into the adhesive surface of the large mitered joint to increase strength. Used when the large mitered joint alone does not provide sufficient strength, such as in decorative frame constructions.

Joining at Right Angles and Other Angles

When joining boards, there are methods for both edge-to-edge joints to widen the board and for joints meeting at various angles, including right angles. The fundamental method involves joining boards at right angles to create square or rectangular box shapes. These joining methods can be categorized into butt joints, combination joints, miter joints, and dowel joints.

The primary consideration when choosing a joining method is the required strength. For boxes that don't require aesthetic appeal and only need to be strong enough to hold objects, simple butt joints with nails or screws will suffice. This method is commonly used for shipping crates. However, different types of boxes require different levels of strength. A box meant to carry heavy items needs to be stronger than a small decorative box. For decorative boxes that don't require much strength, the joining method can be chosen based on appearance.

The most challenging aspect is selecting a joint that balances both strength and appearance. For professional furniture making, considerations such as the complexity of the process and the product cost are important. However, in the context of enjoying the craft, we'll prioritize the process and appeal of creating pieces this way and disregard economic factors when discussing joining methods.

Right-angle joints are essential in box making. The examples provided range from simple to complex, and while the shapes may be similar, the production processes can vary significantly. The commonly used joints selected here focus on practicality.

The descriptions of the joining methods might be similar due to the similarities in joint types, but each step is necessary for the process. Detailed points of the tasks are explained with more photos in some joint types, while others have more summarized steps.

For examples of joints, we'll look at the checkerboard joint, mitered seven-pin joint, balance joint, dovetail joint, wrapped dovetail joint, hidden mitered dovetail joint, and sawed mitered joint in that order. Since the mitered seven-pin joint involves many steps, we'll delve into that first. The dovetail joint and balance joint, which have almost identical processes, will be explained with fewer photos. Detailed chisel techniques can be confirmed in the steps for the mitered seven-pin joint.

It is fundamental to have an odd number of tenons for checkerboard and dovetail joints. The basic principle is to have evenly spaced tenons, so here we will use 7 or 9 evenly spaced tenons.

PRO TIP 4

Designating Each Part's Surface

The various surfaces of boards and timber pieces are referred to as end grain, edge grain, face grain, and back grain. When marking out the processing lines on the material, it's fundamental to designate a reference surface from which the names of the other surfaces are determined. The method of determining the reference surface can vary between individuals. In this book, for box construction, the inside surface is designated as the first reference surface, and the top edge as the second reference surface. The back of the first reference surface is called the third surface, and the back of the second reference surface is called the fourth surface. When considering the top and side panels of a chest of drawers or a shelf, the first reference surface is the inside, and the second reference surface is the visible surface (the surface seen from the front).

For timber pieces, the inside surface is often the first reference surface, and the visible surface the second reference surface. However, in some cases, the visible surface is designated as the first reference surface. Therefore, each surface is marked on the layout drawing accordingly. When marking out, dimensions are fundamentally measured from the first or second reference surface to ensure accurate processing.

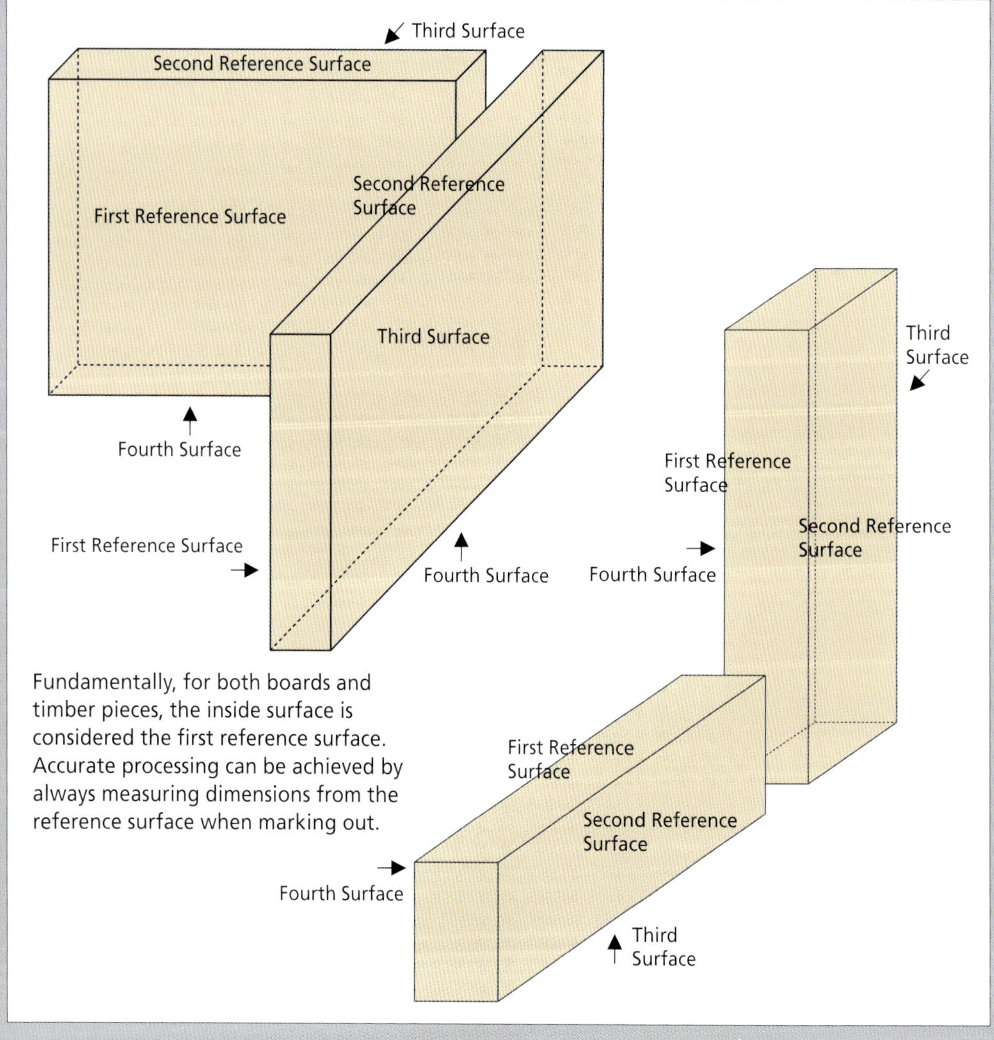

Fundamentally, for both boards and timber pieces, the inside surface is considered the first reference surface. Accurate processing can be achieved by always measuring dimensions from the reference surface when marking out.

Processing of Cobblestone Assembly Joints

The tenon width is made narrower than the thickness of the board for cobblestone assembly joints. It is also known as "arai joint" or "kizami joint." Here, it is assembled with nine pieces, but the number of tenons will change depending on the width of the board. The board thickness for both male and female joints is the same. The tenons are made 1–2 mm (0.04–0.08 in) longer than the finished size (to allow for trimming), and after assembly, they are finished with a plane.

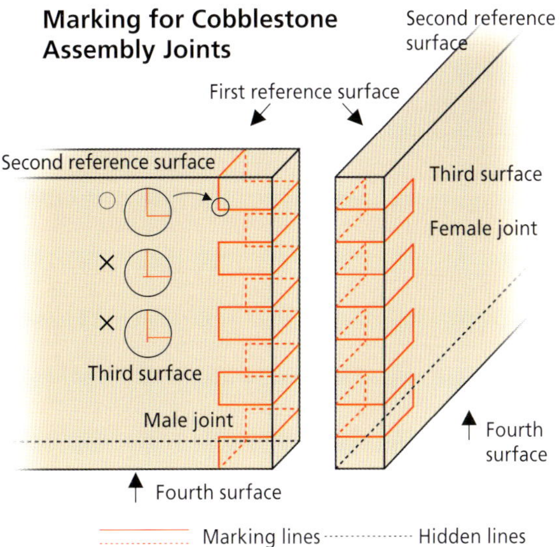

The marking line on the inner side of the body may be drawn from end to end, but the lines that come out should not leave ink on the uncut parts. Refer to page 74, PRO TIP 6 for the layout method.

Cobblestone Assembly Joints

1 Use a marking gauge to mark the position on the first reference surface where the bottom of the tenon will be (board thickness +1–2 mm/0.04–0.08 in) for trimming.

2 Align the scale of the carpenter's square with a number divisible by 9 and make marks to divide it into 9 equal parts.

3 Align the scale of the carpenter's square with a number divisible by 9 and make marks. Align the carpenter's square with the marks made for the 9 equal parts and mark the positions where the tenons will be cut, to divide it into 9 equal parts.

4 Transfer the lines marked for the 9 equal parts to the other piece of material. Here, a pencil is used for better visibility.

5 Align the carpenter's square with the transferred marks and draw lines up to the position of the shoulder line.

6 Before turning the piece over to mark the front, draw a guide line with a pencil at the position of the shoulder line (see next page, PRO TIP 4).

7 Draw marking lines from the guide line to the end grain; marking is now complete.

8 To avoid mistakes, mark the parts to be cut and those to be left with circles or other symbols. Do this on the end grain and the third surface as well.

9 Deepen the shoulder lines of the parts to be cut with a marking gauge. Be careful not to mark the parts to be left.

10 Use a fine-toothed saw to cut along the boundary between the parts to be cut and those to be left.

11 Make cuts with a vertical saw along the tenons. If a vertical saw is not available, use a rip saw.

12 Once all the cuts for the tenons are made, the parts to be left will still have ink lines on them.

PRO TIP 5

Finger-Assisted Guide Lines

Since the shoulder lines have parts to be cut and parts to be left, drawing lines with a fine marking knife from end to end will leave lines on the parts that are not cut. Therefore, first draw guide lines with a pencil, and after drawing lines for the parts to be left and cut, draw the shoulder lines only on the parts to be cut with a fine marking knife. While it's possible to carefully draw the lines with a ruler, the guide lines are drawn freehand to save time. When drawing these lines, you can draw parallel lines by resting the middle or ring finger of the hand holding the pencil against the end grain or edge of the material.

When drawing guide shoulder lines, rest the middle or ring finger of the hand holding the pencil against the end grain.

The finger resting against the end grain acts as a guide, allowing you to draw nearly parallel lines. For a guide, this level of accuracy is sufficient.

13 Hold the chisel with the back facing up and align the blade about 1 mm (0.04 in) before the ink line. The chisel width is 4 bu (approximately 12 mm or 0.47 in).

14 Hold the chisel vertically and tap it with a mallet.

15 With the back of the chisel facing up, tilt the handle toward you and chisel at an angle to create a triangular cut.

16 Chisel to a depth of about half the board thickness, leaving the parts near the end grain.

17 The tenons chiseled from the back side. The ends will be cut off later with a saw.

18 Next, turn the piece over and chisel from the front side. Since the parts near the end grain are left as shown in photo 16, it is stable for chiseling.

19 Chisel vertically until you reach the depth chiseled from the back, and the part to be cut out will come off.

20 With the back of the chisel facing up, align the blade with the shoulder line.

21 Hold the chisel vertically and carefully remove the bottom of the shoulder that was left about 1 mm (0.04 in) before.

22 The part cut out with a rip saw and chisel. From here, finish the corners and bottom.

23 Rest the back of the chisel against the tenon wall and remove the debris left in the shoulder corners.

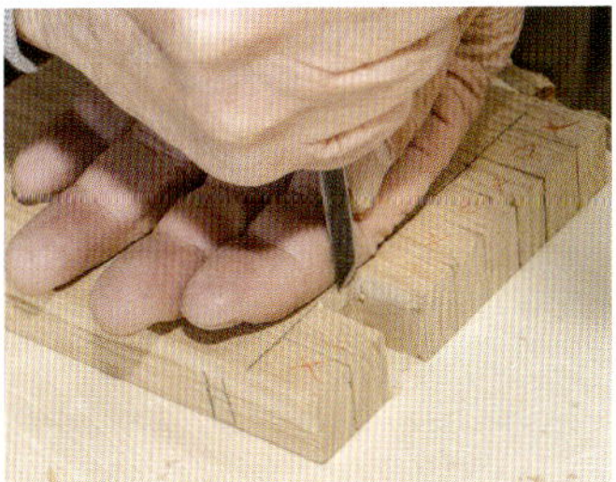

24 Also, shave the corners from the bottom of the shoulder. Use a narrow chisel to avoid shaving off extra parts.

25 You can see that the marked line indicated by the blue arrow to the right forms a step. Shave the bottom by the height of this step.

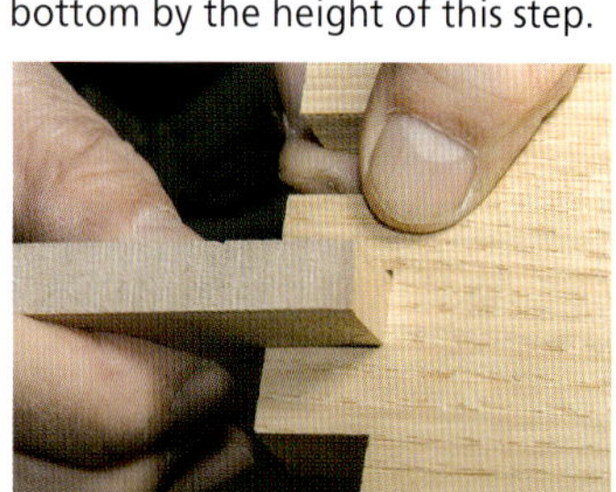

26 Shave the step seen in photo 25. Use a sharp chisel to shave very thinly.

27 Prepare a ruler with right angles and a flat surface, and check the flatness and right angles by placing it against the shoulder and tenon wall.

28 Cut off the parts to be removed at both ends with a shoulder saw. At this time, cut off about 1 mm (0.04 in) before the ink line.

29 Shave the bottom and corners of the shoulder and adjust to ensure there are no gaps, using a ruler as needed.

30 Lightly crush the corners of the tenon with a mallet to insert it into the female joint.

31 Process the female joint in the same way as steps 13–30, and check the fitting.

32 Use a mallet to tap the tenon in with a block of wood. When it doesn't go in anymore, the sound will change, so adjust without forcing it in.

33 If it doesn't go in, the part that hits strongly will appear shiny, so shave off that part little by little.

34 After several trial assemblies and adjustments to ensure it fits without force, apply adhesive and proceed with the final assembly.

35 Apply adhesive to the entrance side of the female joint's shoulder and the left and right walls.

36 Place a block of wood and insert the tenon with a mallet. When it goes all the way in, the sound will change and the rebound on the mallet will increase.

37 Since the tenon is made 1–2 mm (0.04–0.08 in) longer than the board thickness, finally tighten with a clamp until there are no gaps in the shoulder part.

38 Check the right angles with a square.

39 The assembled cobblestone joint. Shave the protruding parts flush.

40 Remove any press marks caused by clamps or debris, and completely eliminate gaps in the joint by applying moisture with a wet cloth and ironing.

41 Steam causes swelling, making the end grain easier to shave, and it becomes easier to remove any misalignment with a plane.

Completed cobblestone assembly joint.

PRO TIP 6

Marking for Cobblestone Assembly

The tenons for cobblestone assembly are generally marked at equal intervals. The number of tenons is typically odd, and the basic method involves using a try square or straightedge rather than measuring the board width. For example, if you want to make a seven-tenon joint with a board width of 10 cm (3.94 in), use a try square or straightedge to divide it into seven equal parts. First, align the 0 mark of the ruler with edges A and B, then align a number divisible by 7 (here 14 cm or 5.51 inches) with edges C and D. Mark the positions at multiples of 2, and use a carpenter's square to draw lines from these marks to the end grain of the wood. It is essential that edges A and B are parallel to edges C and D.

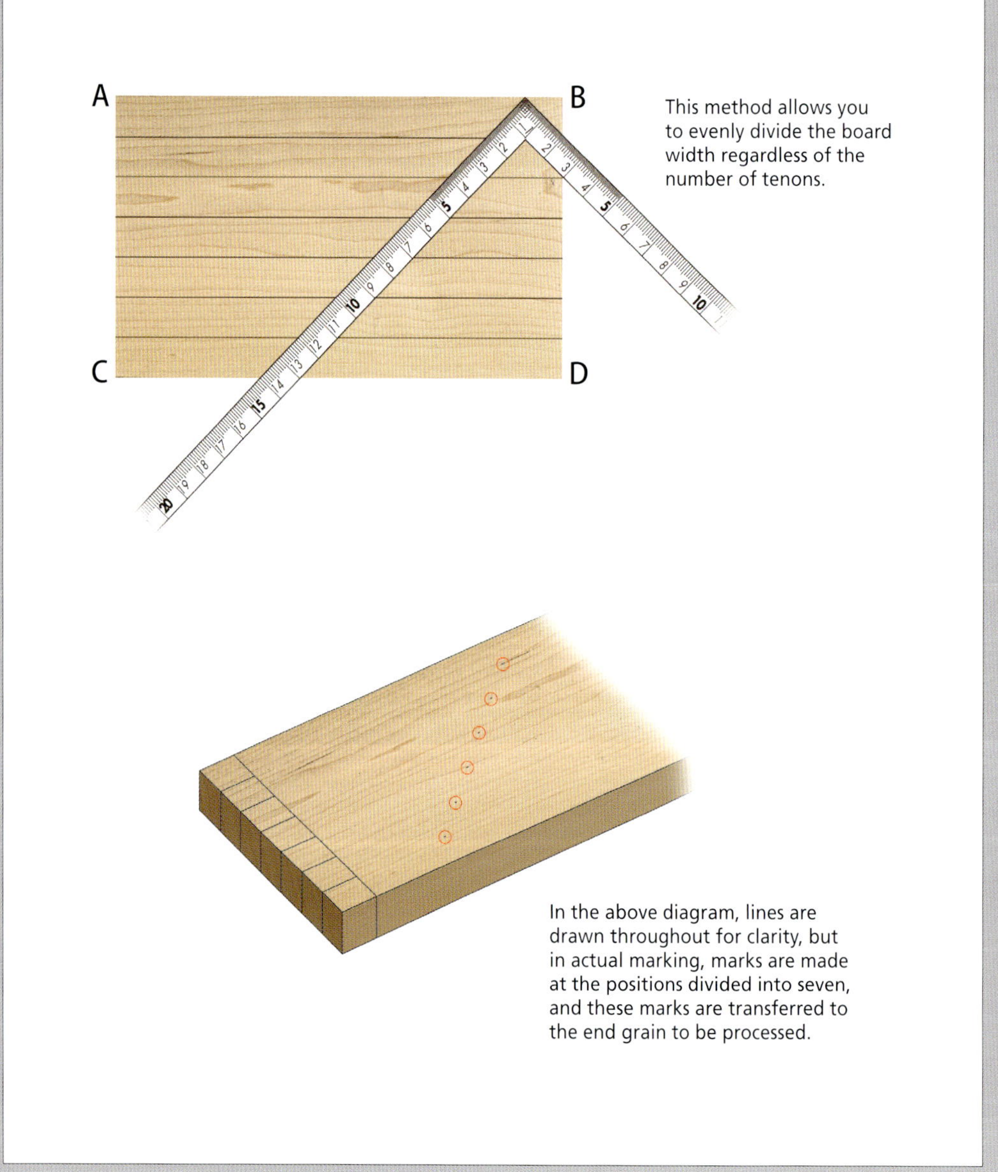

This method allows you to evenly divide the board width regardless of the number of tenons.

In the above diagram, lines are drawn throughout for clarity, but in actual marking, marks are made at the positions divided into seven, and these marks are transferred to the end grain to be processed.

Processing of Seven-Tenon Dovetail Joint with Top End Stop

Using chestnut wood with a thickness of 18 mm (0.71 in) and a width of 120 mm (4.72 in), make a seven-tenon dovetail joint with a top end stop. The dovetail slope is set at 2 cm (0.79 in), and the tenons are divided into seven equal parts from the center of the tenon length. Generally, the dovetail slope is 2–3 cm (0.79–1.18 in). Adjust the slope to your preference when processing. Since the joint is finished with a plane after assembly, leave an extra 1 mm (0.04 in) for trimming.

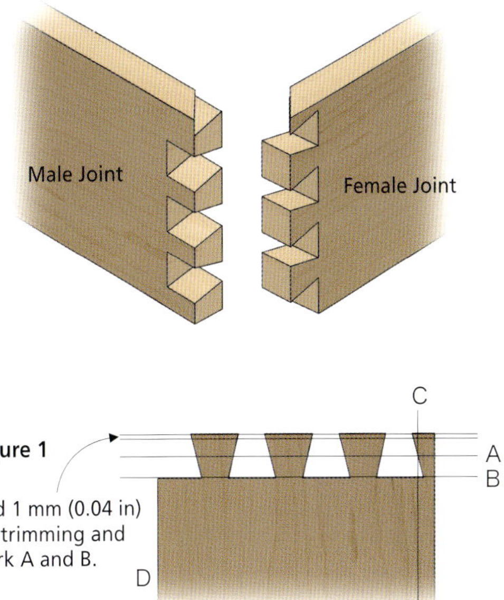

Marking for Seven-Tenon Dovetail Joint with Top End Stop

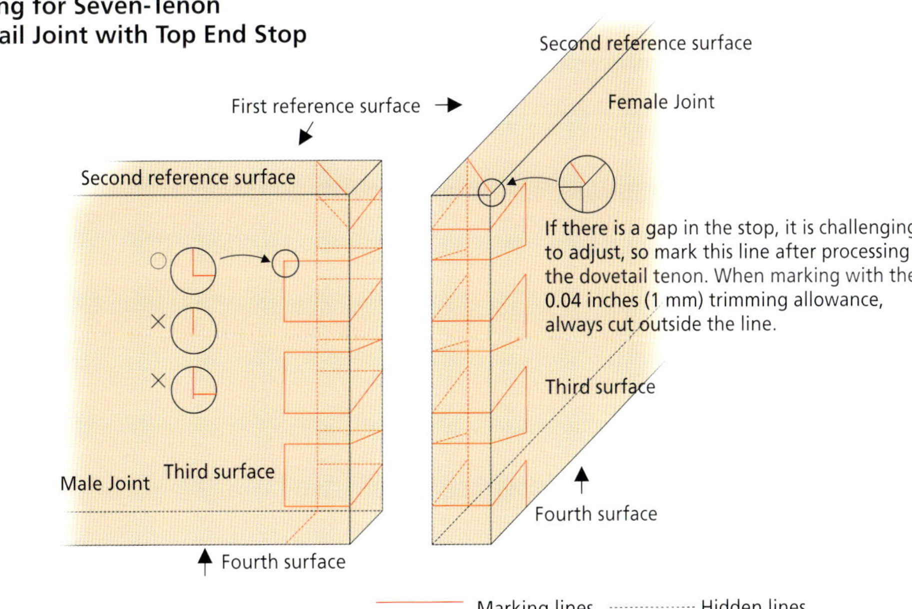

Example of marking for a seven-tenon dovetail joint with a top end stop on an 18 mm (0.71 in) thick board. The dovetail slope is set at 2 cm (0.79 in). Divide the space between the top end stop line (C) and the edge to be divided (D) into seven equal parts and align with the center line (A). Since the center line (A) is drawn with an extra 1 mm (0.04 in) for trimming, it is located 10 mm (0.39 in) from the end grain. For marking the dovetail tenons, refer to page 82, PRO TIP 8. Since there is a trimming allowance for the top end stop, mark it after processing the dovetail tenon.

Procedure for Seven-Tenon Dovetail Joint with Top End Stop

1 Adjust the marking gauge to the board thickness, then add 1 mm (0.04 in) for trimming and fix the width.

2 Using the fixed marking gauge in Photo 1, draw parallel lines (shoulder lines) on the female joint's end grain to the first reference surface.

3 Since the marking gauge has an additional 1 mm for trimming, also add 1 mm to the centerline, marking a position 10 mm from the end grain (see Figure 1).

4 Lightly draw the centerline with the marking gauge.

5 Measure 9 mm (0.35 in) for the top end stop width and draw lines using a carpenter's square. Use a pencil to make the lines more visible.

6 Divide the distance from the 9 mm (0.35 in) top end stop mark to the edge where the dovetail will be made into seven equal parts.

7 Transfer the marks for the seven equal parts to the tenon centerline.

8 Fix a sliding bevel gauge to a 2 cm (0.79 in) slope and align it with the marked positions on the tenon centerline, then draw the dovetail tenon lines with a marking knife.

9 Mark the parts to be cut and the parts to be left with circles or other symbols to avoid mistakes.

10 Draw the tenon lines on the end grain. Since these are vertical lines, use a carpenter's square.

11 With the third surface facing up, align the marking knife with the end grain marks and draw the dovetail tenon lines.

12 Use the marking knife to mark the parts to be cut from the tenon shoulders.

13 Make cuts on the tenon with a rip saw, leaving a slight amount of the line. It is convenient to prepare a gauge processed to a 2 cm (0.79 in) slope.

14 Make vertical cuts on the parts to be removed from the end grain. Roughly cut, stopping before the shoulder lines.

15 With cuts made in the parts to be removed, add auxiliary cuts to make it easier to chisel out the dovetails.

16 Use a chisel with a blade width close to the width of the vertical cuts and chisel vertically, leaving about 1 mm (0.04 in) from the shoulder lines.

17 Once chiseled halfway, chisel diagonally to remove a triangular piece.

18 Turn it over and chisel vertically to remove the part to be cut out.

19 Use a chisel with a width close to the shoulder and remove the remaining part, leaving about 1 mm (0.04 in) from the shoulder lines.

20 With the back of the chisel facing away, chisel vertically into the shoulder lines to remove the remaining 1 mm (0.04 in).

21 Since only 1 mm (0.04 in) is being removed, use the weight of the mallet rather than force to tap.

22 Use a narrow chisel to shave the corners of the tenon, avoiding shaving extra parts.

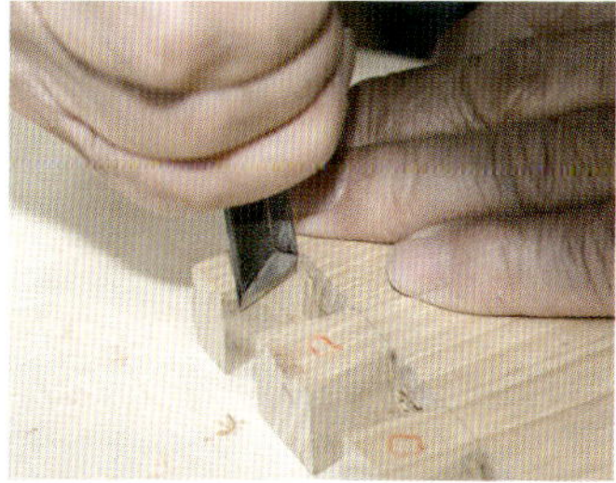

23 Continue to shave the corners from the side of the tenon and the convex part in the center of the side.

24 Check if the shoulder is flat by placing a ruler against it.

25 Cut the lower part to be removed with a shoulder saw. For accuracy, use a square ruler when cutting.

26 Shave the corners of the shoulder with a chisel to finish.

27 The female joint with the parts to be removed. The leftmost tenon will be the stop.

28 Fit the female joint against the end grain of the male joint and mark the parts to be removed with a trial fit.

29 Using a sliding bevel gauge fixed at a 2 cm (0.79 in) slope, draw the dovetail tenon lines on the end grain and extend the lines to the first and third reference surfaces.

30 As the tenons on the male joint viewed from the end grain are trapezoidal, use the 2 cm (0.79 in) slope gauge and make cuts with a tenon saw.

31 Make cuts and vertical end grain cuts as with the female joint. The leftmost cut is shallow and angled for the stop.

32 Remove the vertical cuts with a chisel. Use the same method as in Photos 16–18.

33 Carefully remove the remaining angled parts without damaging the tenon.

34 Finish the shoulder corners with a narrow chisel.

35 For the stop at the top end, use a stop gauge to mark a 45° angle. For accuracy, use a marking knife.

36 Use a wooden gauge to cut the stop to avoid damaging the saw blade. This is the stop on the female joint.

37 Use a shoulder saw to cut at a 45° angle. Be careful not to cut the tenon as it is connected to the male joint.

38 Make saw cuts from the end grain gradually, avoiding cutting too much.

39 Use a stop jig to finish the stop with a chisel.

40 Ensure the stop is cut straight.

41 Lightly crush the corners of the male tenon with a mallet before fitting into the female joint.

PRO TIP 7

Jigs Used for Fastening with Chisels

When using a plane for stop processing, use a stop end grain shaving platform or stop board shaving platform. However, for parts like the top end stop that are difficult to plane, use a chisel. A convenient tool is the stop end grain shaving jig, which is made by cutting the end grain of a board glued in an L-shape at a 45° angle, as shown in the photo below. Press the back of the chisel against this surface while finishing the stop.

A jig for chisel stop processing. While a simple one can be made, for frequent use, make one from well-dried wood to minimize distortion.

It's useful for the final finishing of the top end stops and hidden dovetail stops. Press the back of the chisel firmly against the jig while shaving.

42 Initially, press the joint by hand to check the fit. If there are tight spots, adjust them at this stage.

43 If the fit seems good, use a block of wood and tap it in with a mallet.

44 Since there is a 1 mm (0.04 in) allowance for trimming, once it is partially in, secure it in a vise, and use wooden blocks to tap it without hitting the trimming allowance.

45 Assemble until the sound changes when tapping with a mallet, indicating full insertion, but if there are still gaps between the shoulders and the tenon, adjust to remove these gaps.

46 The outer corner of the top end stop is also slightly open. Adjust this part to eliminate any gaps completely.

47 If clamping with a vise removes the gaps, proceed to assembly. If gaps remain, locate and adjust the tight spots.

48 To disassemble, place the female joint down, use a block of wood, and tap it out with a mallet.

49 Identify tight spots by looking at the color where it is strongly contacting, especially the inner corners.

50 The machining is complete. Now proceed to assembly.

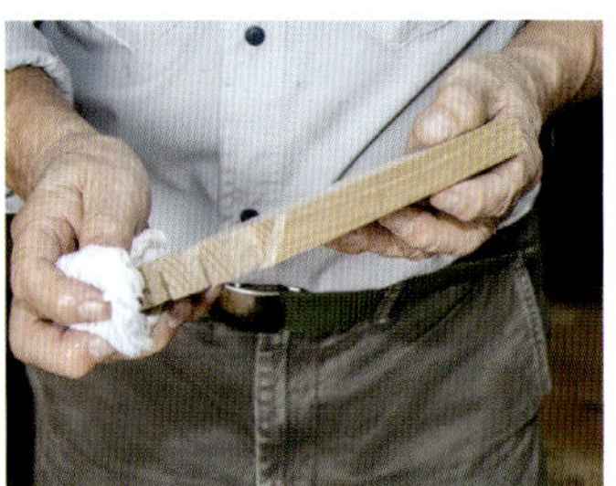

51 Finish the inner side before assembly. Wet a cloth, wipe around the end grain to make it easier to plane.

52 Finish the inner side with a plane. Since it cannot be finished after assembly, be sure to finish it first.

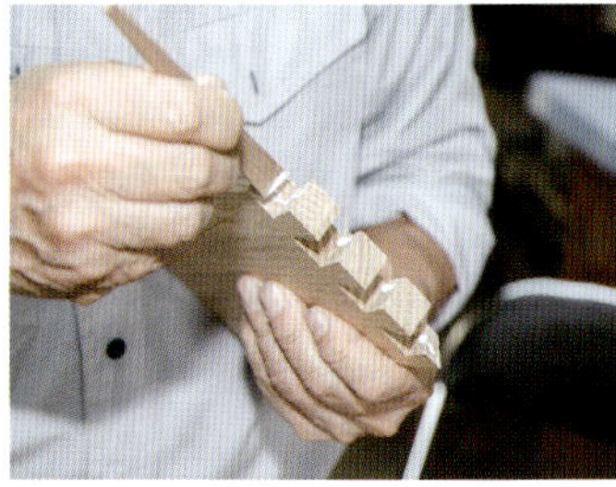

53 Apply adhesive to the joint surfaces. Apply near the inner side considering the insertion of the male joint.

54 Use a block of wood and tap in with a mallet.

55 Use a block of wood avoiding the trimming allowance and clamp it with a vise to eliminate gaps.

56 Check the right angle with a square before the adhesive dries.

57 Wipe off excess adhesive with a wet cloth or brush.

58 Once the adhesive has dried, a 1 mm (0.04 in) trimming allowance is visible.

59 Finish with a plane. To avoid chipping the end grain, plane from the direction the parts are assembled toward you.

The completed seven-tenon dovetail joint with top end stop.

PRO TIP 8

Marking the Dovetail Tenon

The female joint has the board surface, and the male joint has the end grain in a dovetail shape. There are several methods for marking, but generally, a line is drawn at the center of the tenon's length for the female joint, which is then divided equally. For the male joint, a centerline is drawn on the end grain.

For example, when marking a seven-tenon dovetail joint on a 10 cm (3.94 in) wide and 18 mm (0.71 in) thick board, the process up to dividing it into seven equal parts is the same as for the cobblestone assembly joint. In the case of the dovetail joint, a line is drawn at the center of the tenon's length for the female joint, which is then divided into seven equal parts. The dovetail slope is generally 2 to 3 cm (0.79 to 1.18 in), and the marking is done at a preferred angle within that range.

For the male joint, since the end grain is in a dovetail shape, draw a centerline on the end grain and then divide it into seven equal parts. It is easier to shave the slightly protruding tenon with a plane after assembly, rather than aligning the male joint's end grain flush with the female joint during processing. Therefore, the male joint's tenon should protrude by about 1 mm (0.04 in), and mark the shoulder part at 19 mm (0.75 in).

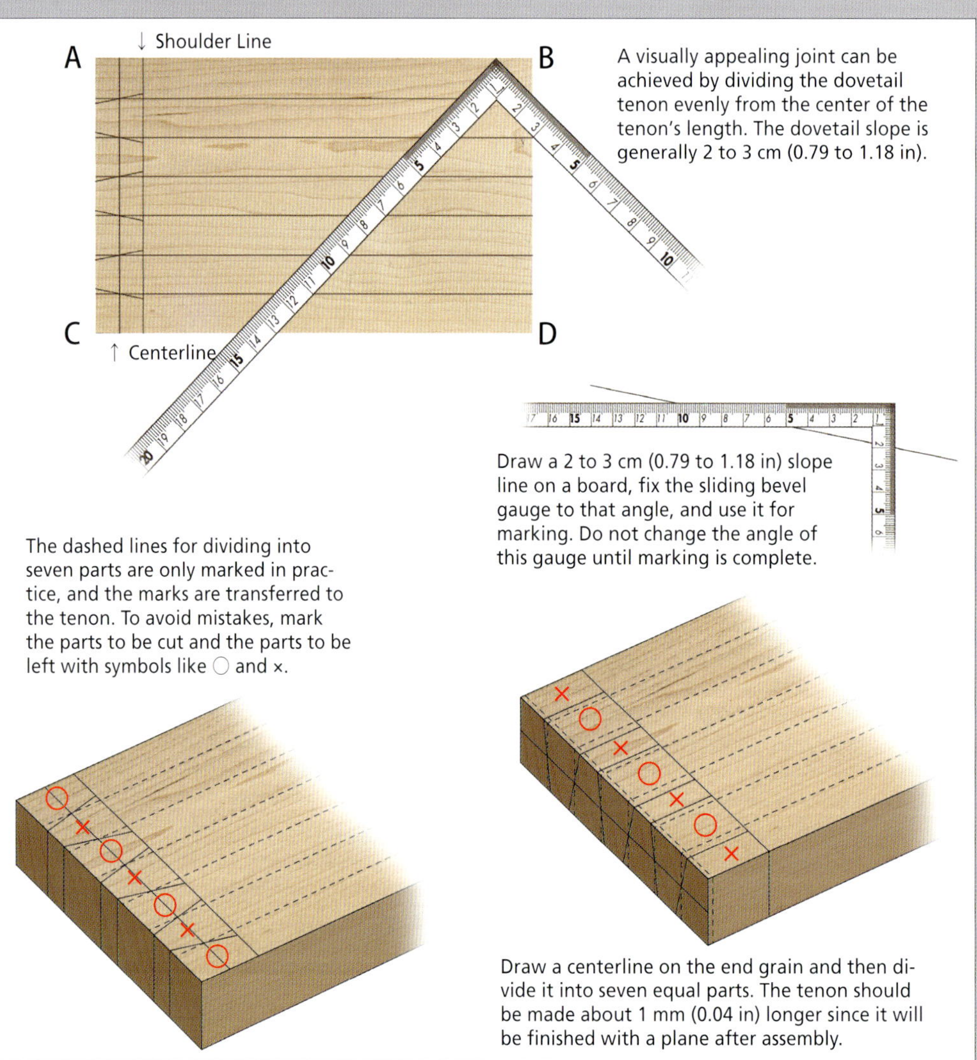

A visually appealing joint can be achieved by dividing the dovetail tenon evenly from the center of the tenon's length. The dovetail slope is generally 2 to 3 cm (0.79 to 1.18 in).

Draw a 2 to 3 cm (0.79 to 1.18 in) slope line on a board, fix the sliding bevel gauge to that angle, and use it for marking. Do not change the angle of this gauge until marking is complete.

The dashed lines for dividing into seven parts are only marked in practice, and the marks are transferred to the tenon. To avoid mistakes, mark the parts to be cut and the parts to be left with symbols like ○ and ×.

Draw a centerline on the end grain and then divide it into seven equal parts. The tenon should be made about 1 mm (0.04 in) longer since it will be finished with a plane after assembly.

Processing of Seven-Tenon Dovetail Joint

This is the most basic procedure for dovetail joints. The board thickness is 18 mm (0.71 in) with an additional 1 mm (0.04 in) for trimming. Start by drawing the tenon centerline 10 mm (0.39 in) from the female joint's end grain, similar to the top end stop seven-tenon dovetail joint. By dividing equally from this centerline, all dovetail tenons will be evenly distributed, creating a visually appealing joint. While this example shows a seven-tenon dovetail joint, the same method applies for nine-tenon, eleven-tenon, etc. Refer to the top end stop seven-tenon dovetail joint processing for saw and chisel techniques.

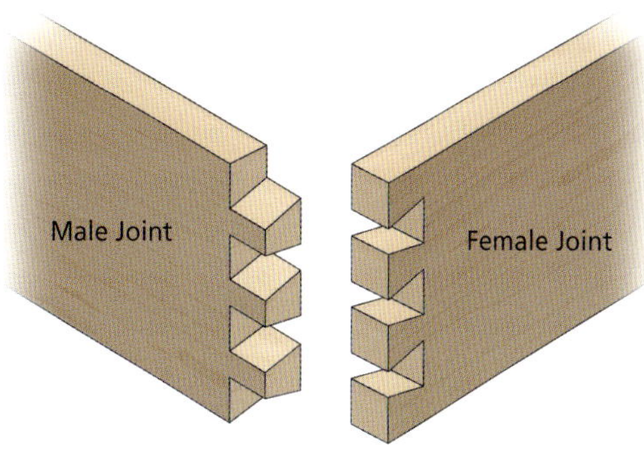

Marking the Seven-Tenon Dovetail Joint

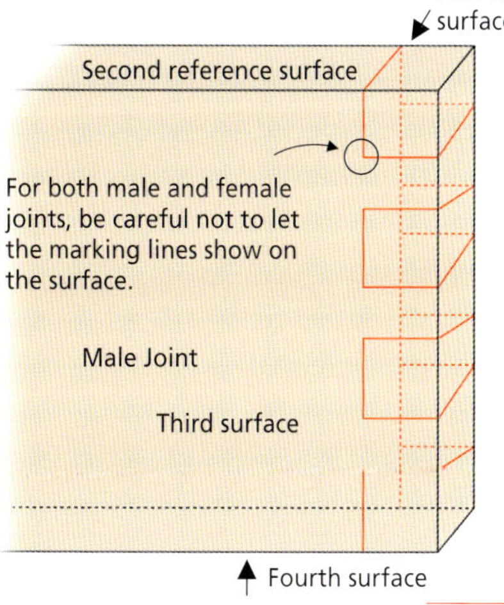

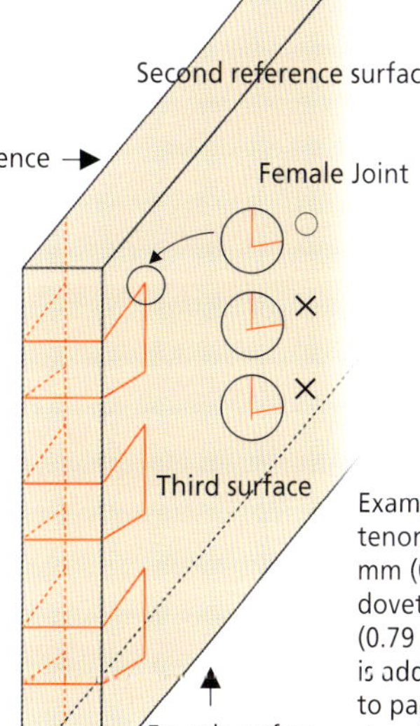

Example of marking a seven-tenon dovetail joint on an 18 mm (0.71 in) thick board. The dovetail slope is set at 2 cm (0.79 in), and 1 mm (0.04 in) is added for trimming. Refer to page 82, PRO TIP 8 for dovetail marking.

Marking lines ······ Hidden lines

Steps for Dovetail Joint

1 Adjust the marking gauge to the board thickness.

2 Draw the shoulder lines on the first reference surface of the female joint.

3 Fix the width of another marking gauge to 10 mm (0.39 in) and draw the centerline on the first reference surface of the female joint.

4 Divide the board width into seven equal parts, and from the points where they intersect with the centerline of the female joint, mark the dovetail lines using a sliding bevel gauge set at a 2 cm (0.79 in) slope (refer to page 81).

5 Draw the centerline on the end grain of the male joint and mark the dovetail lines from there.

6 Saw inside the marking lines for the parts to be removed from the tenon.

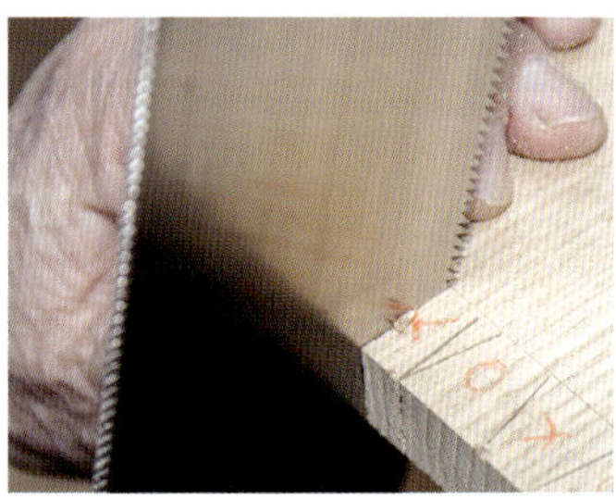

7 Once the cuts along the marking lines are made, make vertical cuts from the end grain (refer to page 90, PRO TIP 12).

8 Chisel the shoulder parts, removing the portions to be cut out (refer to photos 16–27 on pages 77–78).

9 For the male joint, use a 2 cm (0.79 in) slope gauge and a tenon saw to make the cuts from the end grain (refer to photos 30 and 31 on page 78).

PRO TIP 9

Making Jigs for Accurate Cuts

For joints like dovetail and box joints, precise cuts with a saw are required to fit the male and female tenons together. It is recommended to use jigs aligned with the marking lines to stabilize the saw and ensure accurate cuts. Prepare jigs for vertical cuts and those matching the angles of dovetail joints.

A jig for cutting dovetail tenons. Prepare jigs to match angles such as 2 cm (0.79 in) or 3 cm (1.18 in) slopes.

Align the jig with the marking lines on the material. Make the jigs out of wood to avoid damaging the saw blade.

10 Complete the processing of the male and female joints. Perform a trial assembly and make any necessary fine adjustments.

11 Apply adhesive to the tenon and shoulder parts of the female joint.

12 Use a block of wood and tap the joint together with a mallet.

13 Check the right angles with a square.

14 Secure with a vise. In the photo, the end grains are avoided, but it is convenient to have blocks of wood with grooves to fit the uneven parts.

15 Final planing. As with other joints, wet the end grain and use an iron before planing to make it easier.

The completed seven-tenon dovetail joint.

Processing of Tenbin-Dashi Joint

The tenbin-dashi joint is a narrower version of the dovetail tenon joint. In tenbin-dashi joints, the spacing between tenons can vary for decorative purposes. Here, two tenons are placed close together, with a small gap before two wider tenons. You can create unique joints by varying the spacing and the number of tenons, but be careful not to make the tenons too narrow, as it can weaken the joint.

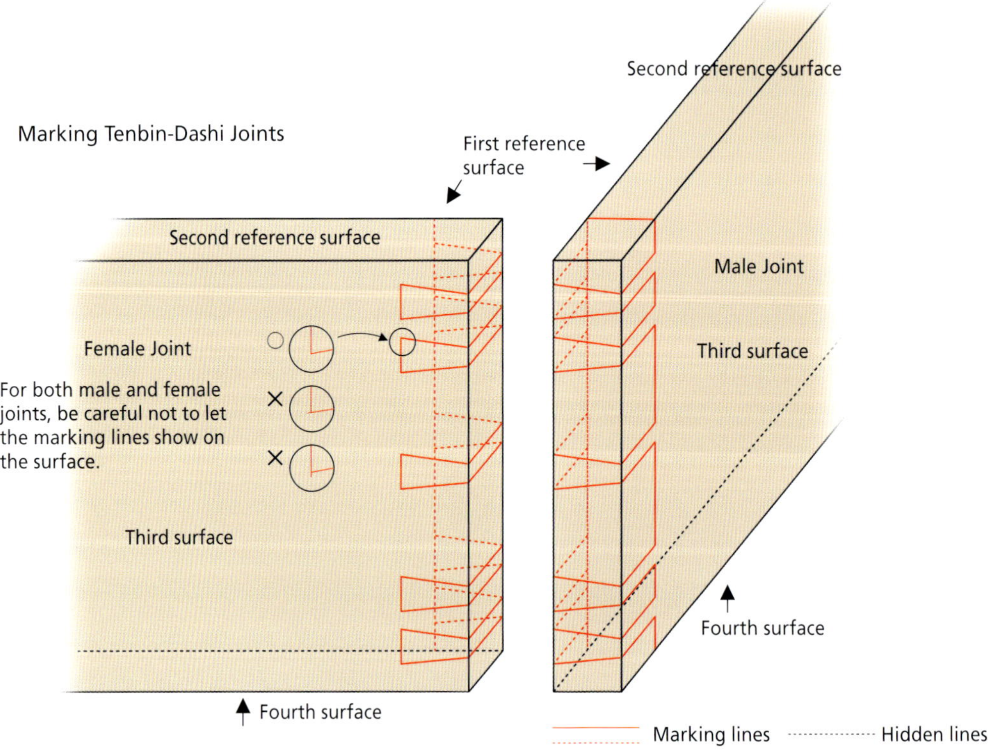

Example of marking a tenbin-dashi joint on an 18 mm (0.71 in) thick board. While the usual dovetail slope is 2–3 cm (0.79–1.18 in), tenbin-dashi joints often have a slope of 1–1.5 cm (0.39–0.59 in). In this joint, both the male and female joints have an additional 1 mm (0.04 in) for trimming.

Procedure for Tenbin-Dashi Joint

1 First, draw the shoulder and center lines on the first reference surface of the female joint using a marking gauge.

2 Divide the board width into 13 equal parts and mark them with a pencil.

3 Transfer the 13 equal parts to the centerline.

PRO TIP 10

Balancing the Tenons in Tenbin-Dashi Joints

The tenons in a tenbin-dashi joint are usually marked with a 1–1.5 cm (0.39–0.59 in) slope, and the spacing between tenons can vary. To achieve a balanced joint, first divide the board equally, then vary the tenon spacing. Here, the board is divided into 13 equal parts, creating five tenons for the female joint and four tenons for the male joint, forming a nine-tenon joint. The diagram shows the centerline splitting the tenons, but if you are adding trimming, draw the lines so the tenon extends about 1 mm (0.04 in) outward.

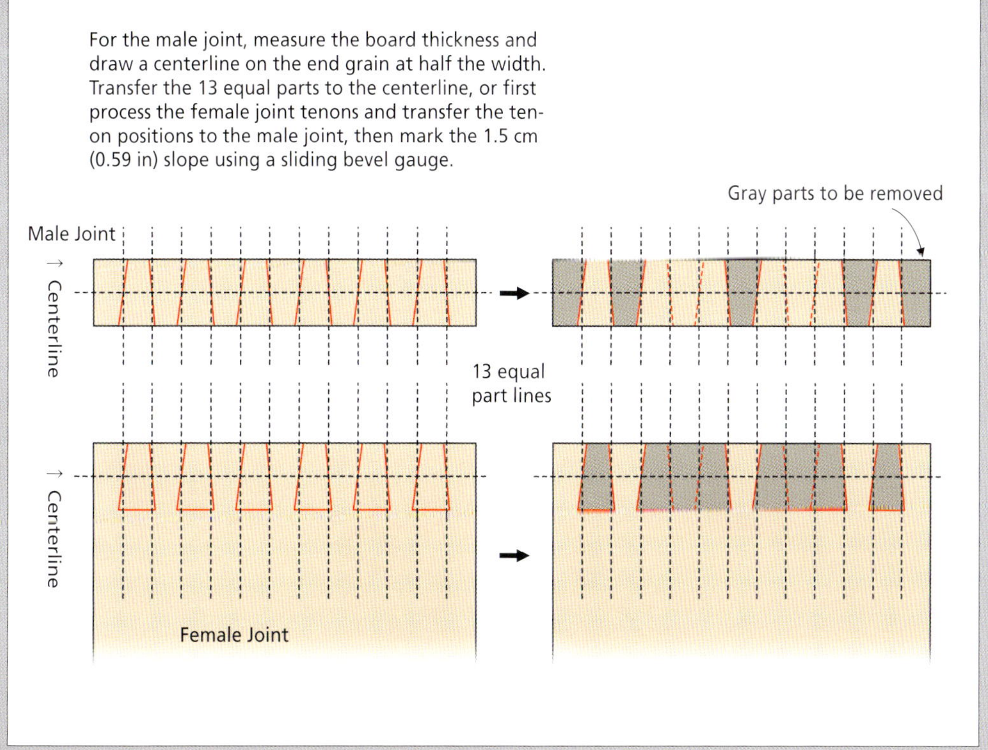

4 From the marks on the centerline, use a sliding bevel gauge set at a 1.5 cm (0.59 in) slope to draw the tenon lines.

5 Extend the tenon lines drawn on the first reference surface to the end grain.

6 Draw the shoulder lines on the third surface with a pencil.

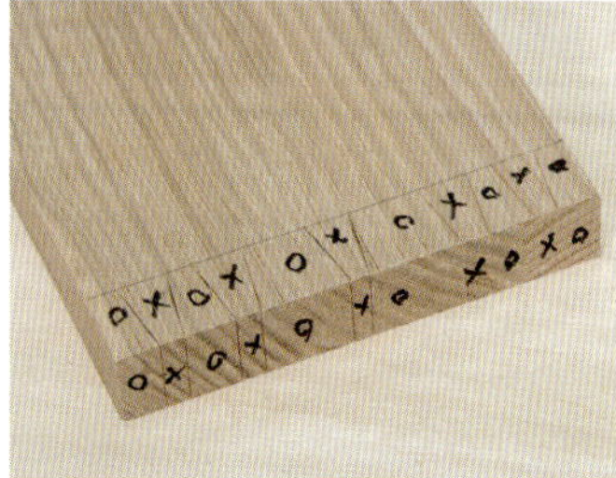

7 Extend the tenon lines to the third surface and mark the parts to be cut and left.

8 Redraw the shoulder lines on the third surface with a marking knife.

9 Use a rip saw to make cuts along the tenon lines, leaving a small margin.

10 After making diagonal cuts along the tenon lines, make vertical cuts from the end grain to make chiseling easier.

11 Use a 1-bu (3 mm/0.12 in) chisel to remove the vertical cut sections.

12 Use a chisel with a width close to the tenon width to remove the remaining parts, leaving about 1 mm (0.04 in) from the shoulder lines.

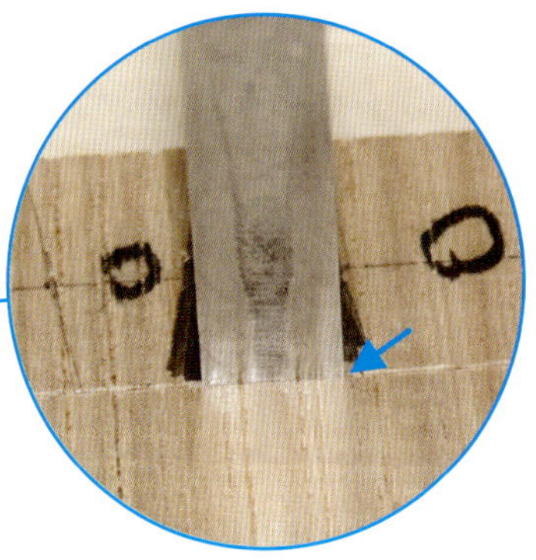

13 Once the parts to be removed are taken out with a 1 mm (0.04 in) margin left, place the chisel blade on the lines and remove the remaining parts.

14 After removing the tenons, gradually chisel out any remaining parts in the inner corners.

15 The female joint is now processed. Transfer the bottom part of the tenon to the male joint.

16 With the first reference surfaces of the female and male joints facing inward, transfer the shoulder parts of the female tenon to the male joint.

17 From the transferred marks, use a sliding bevel gauge to draw lines on the end grain of the male joint.

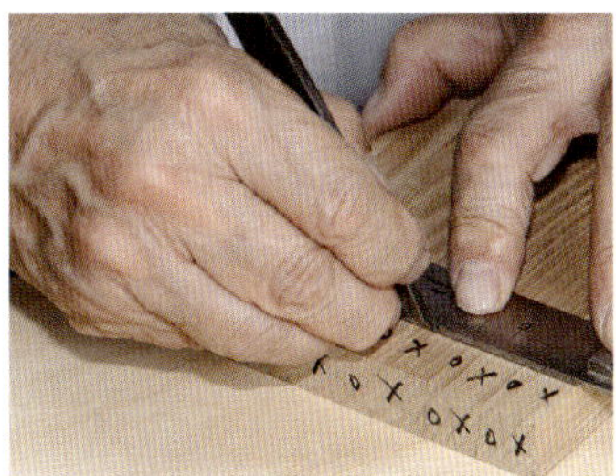

18 Extend the lines on the end grain to the first and third surfaces, and also draw the shoulder lines.

19 Use a rip saw to make vertical cuts along the tenon lines, leaving a margin, then make auxiliary cuts from the first reference surface (refer to page 90, PRO TIP 12).

20 From the third surface, use a chisel to remove the parts along the auxiliary cuts.

PRO TIP 11

Adjusting Tenons with the Left Hand

In joint assembly, the tenons may be too tight. In such cases, make fine adjustments with a chisel. The corners, especially those adjacent to the third surface, shouldn't have gaps after assembly. Control the chisel with your left hand to avoid overcutting. Depending on your posture, place the back or palm of your left hand between the material being cut and the right hand holding the chisel to control the force and to avoid overcutting.

Adjusting the tenon walls for a snug fit. Control the force with the left hand when shaving.

Similarly, control the chisel force with the left hand, with the palm facing up, adding lifting force.

21 Similarly, control the chisel force with the left hand, with the palm facing up, adding lifting force.

22 Use a shoulder chisel to remove and finish the inner corners of the tenon.

23 The male and female joints are now processed. Proceed to fine adjustments for finishing.

24 Before trial assembly, lightly crush the tenon ends with a mallet.

25 Use a block of wood and a mallet to test the fit. If too tight, remove and adjust as needed.

PRO TIP 12

Adding Auxiliary Cuts for Dovetail Tenons

For dovetail tenons, make diagonal cuts on the female board surface and male end grain. When chiseling the shoulders, add parallel cuts as auxiliary cuts about 1 mm (0.04 in) before the shoulder lines. This reduces resistance and allows for more accurate chiseling.

Male dovetail tenon. Make saw cuts just leaving the marking lines, then add parallel cuts close to the shoulder lines.

Female dovetail tenon. The face with the dovetail slope is different, but the auxiliary cuts are similarly oriented. These cuts don't need to be precise as long as they don't overcut.

26 Adjustment for tightness. In this case, the penciled parts are shiny, indicating tight spots that need to be shaved.

27 Be careful not to overcut, which could create gaps during assembly. Control with the left hand (refer to page 89, PRO TIP 11).

28 Once properly adjusted, apply adhesive and join.

29 Use a block of wood and a mallet to assemble. For final assembly, switch to a narrower block to avoid the trimming allowance.

30 Wet the assembled parts with a damp cloth to soften the end grain for easier planing.

31 Finish planing. As with other joints, plane from the assembled direction towards yourself.

The completed tenbin-dashi joint.

Processing the Wrapped Dovetail Joint

The wrapped dovetail joint hides the joint from one side by covering the end grain of one tenon with the other, making it suitable for joining drawer fronts and sides. For an 18 mm (0.71 in) thick board, the covering part is 4.5 mm (0.18 in) thick. While the processing takes slightly more effort than a regular dovetail joint, the hidden joint is more forgiving of minor gaps. The joint is created by marking and processing the female joint first, then transferring the marks to the male joint.

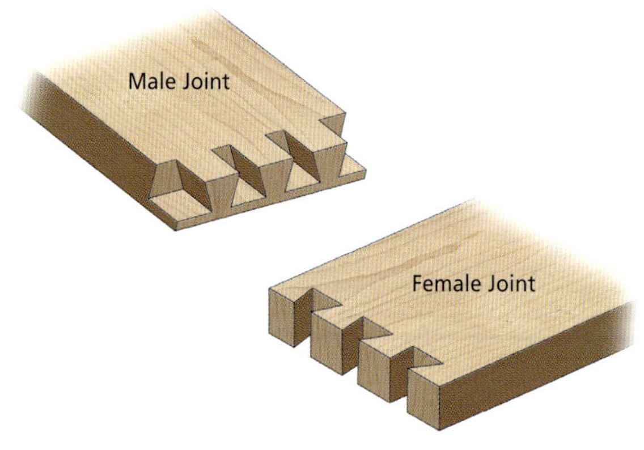

Marking Wrapped Dovetail Joints

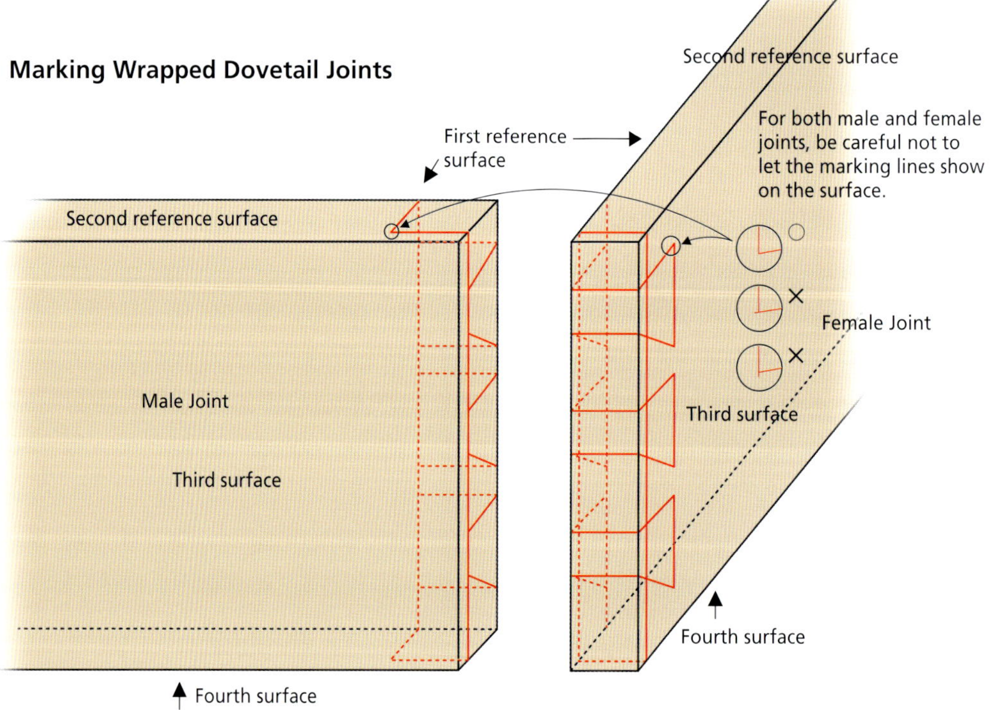

Example of marking a wrapped dovetail joint on an 18 mm (0.71 in) thick board. Mark the dovetail slope at 2–3 cm (0.79–1.18 in). In this joint, the tenon is wrapped, so no trimming allowance is added. The wrapping thickness is generally ⅓ to ¼ of the board thickness.

Marking lines Hidden lines

Steps for Processing Wrapped Dovetail Joint

1 Use a marking gauge to draw the shoulder line and the centerline on the first reference surface of the female joint, 9 mm (0.35 in) from the end grain.

2 Draw a line 4.5 mm (0.18 in) from the end grain. After processing, this line will be used to trim the end grain and adjust the wrapping.

3 Use a square to divide the board width into seven equal parts and transfer these marks to the centerline.

4 From the marks on the centerline, use a sliding bevel gauge set at a 2 cm (0.79 in) slope to mark the dovetail tenons.

5 Use a carpenter's square to extend the lines to the end grain and then to the third surface with the sliding bevel gauge.

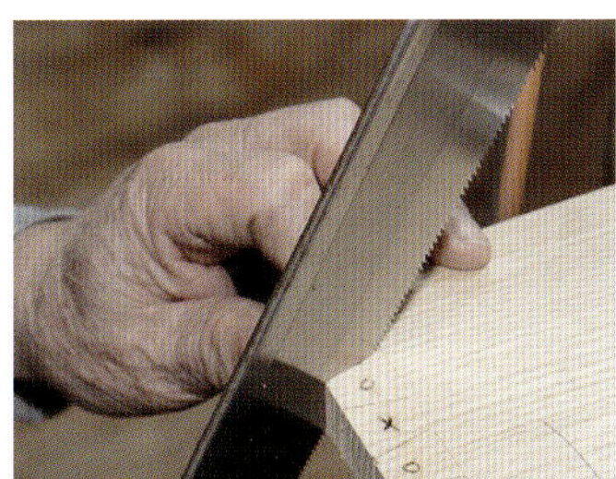

6 Use a tenon saw to make cuts in the tenons and remove the waste with a chisel (refer to page 90, PRO TIP 12).

PRO TIP 13

Establish Rules for Marking

When marking joints, decide in advance which surfaces will be the inside and how to orient the top and bottom. Avoid drawing unnecessary marking lines on the outer surfaces as they will remain visible after finishing. To prevent mistakes, establish your own marking rules. For example, mark the inside and bottom surfaces.

Marking with established rules helps avoid mistakes. In this example, markings are made on the inside and bottom edge.

Marking starts from the inside surface.

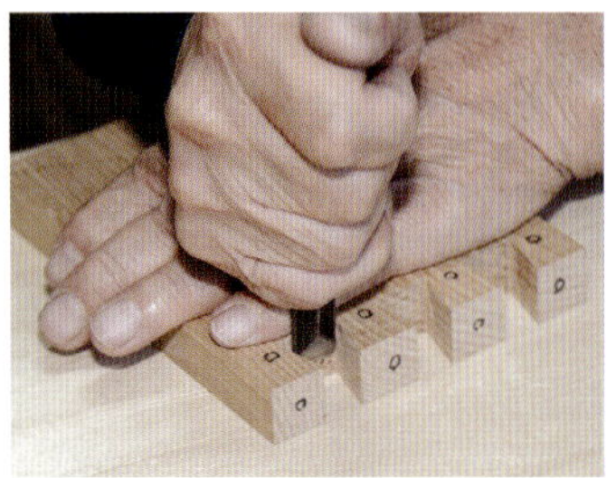

7 Finish the female joint to a certain extent so the marks can be transferred to the male joint.

8 Place the male joint's end grain facing down on the female joint and mark the bottom position of the tenons.

9 From the marked positions, use a carpenter's square to mark the first reference surface.

10 Use a marking gauge fixed at 4.5 mm (0.18 in) to draw the wrapping lines.

11 From the marks made in step 8, use a sliding bevel gauge set at a 2 cm (0.79 in) slope to mark the dovetail tenons on the end grain of the male joint.

12 Mark the parts to be removed and the parts to be left.

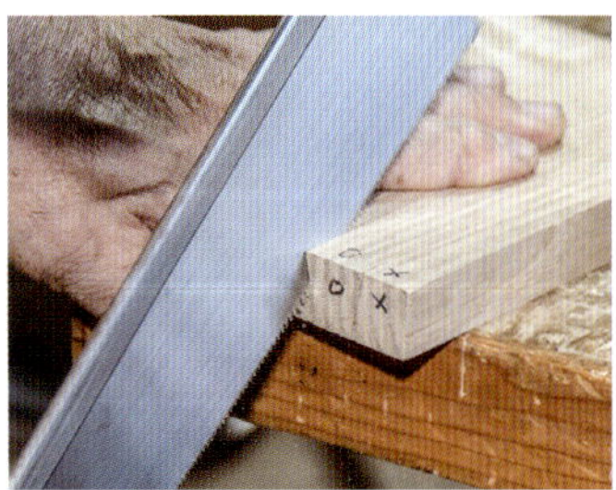

13 Use a tenon saw to make cuts in the tenons, avoiding the wrapping part.

14 Make triangular cuts in the tenons and remove the waste with a chisel, leaving the marked side.

15 Chisel about 1 mm (0.04 in) before the shoulder line on the first reference surface.

16 After chiseling 2–3 mm (0.08–0.12 in) deep, chisel from the end grain side to remove the waste easily.

17 Chisel from the tenon sides, gradually approaching the wrapping line.

18 Clean out the inner corners of the wrapping from the end grain side.

19 Use a shoulder saw to cut the outermost shoulder part at an angle, following the wrapping line.

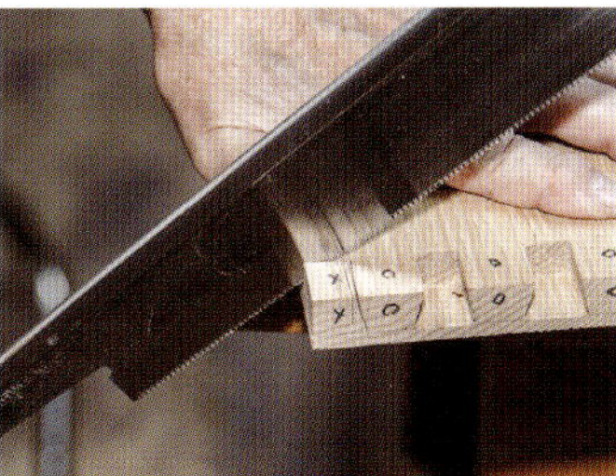

20 Lay the saw blade slightly flat and cut along the tenon line, leaving the marked part.

21 Chisel from the end grain to remove the waste.

22 Clean the inner corners of the wrapping and shoulder with a chisel.

23 For the female joint, cut off the waste parts along the 4.5 mm (0.18 in) marking line drawn on the end grain.

24 Do a trial assembly and check for any tight spots.

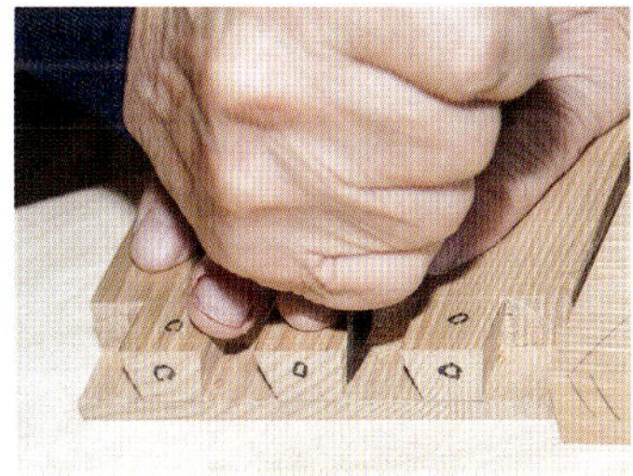

25 Ensure there is no debris in the wrapping and shoulder inner corners as it can create gaps, clean them with a chisel.

26 The processing is complete. Proceed to the final assembly.

27 Apply adhesive to all joining surfaces, including the inside of the wrapping and the shoulder bottom.

PRO TIP 14

Make Assembly Blocks

In joints like cobblestone and dovetail joints, an allowance is often added, and the trimming is done after assembly. With the allowance, clamping directly with a block may not secure the desired part due to interference from the end grain. Therefore, use a block with a convex shape to avoid the allowance and ensure proper clamping.

Blocks with a convex shape, to avoid the allowance, are useful for clamping.

28 Place the female joint down, position the male joint's end grain, and use a block of wood to tap it in with a mallet.

29 As the wrapped part can warp easily, there might be a small gap, but secure it with clamps for adhesive bonding.

30 If the wrapping warps, use a block to control the warp while clamping.

31 Check the right angle with a square on the inside.

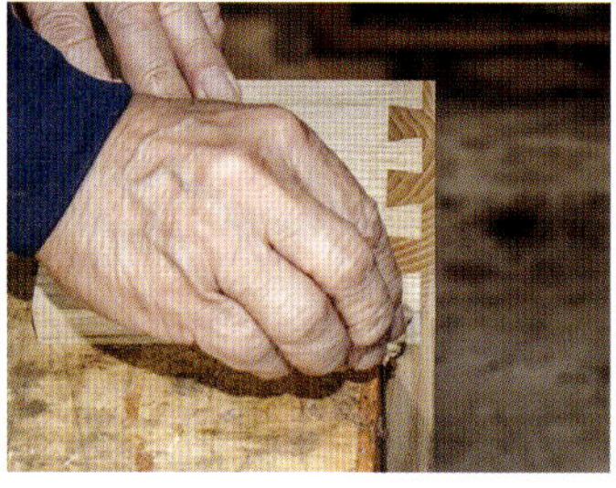

32 Once the adhesive dries, soften the end grain by wiping with water to remove the grain pattern.

33 Finish planing to remove any misalignment on the joint surface.

Completed wrapped dovetail joint.

Processing the Stopped Hidden Dovetail Joint

The stopped hidden dovetail joint, often used in joinery for small boxes or Kanto-style hibachis, is a type of joint that conceals the joinery from view after assembly. During the dry fit, mark the male and female joints to avoid confusion about the direction of insertion. For this example, we use an 18 mm (0.71 in) thick board, creating seven tenons with a stop width of 6 mm (0.24 in). Divide the entire width into seven equal parts and then mark the stop width. When trimming the stop, you will need a chamfer plane and a stop end grain trimming platform.

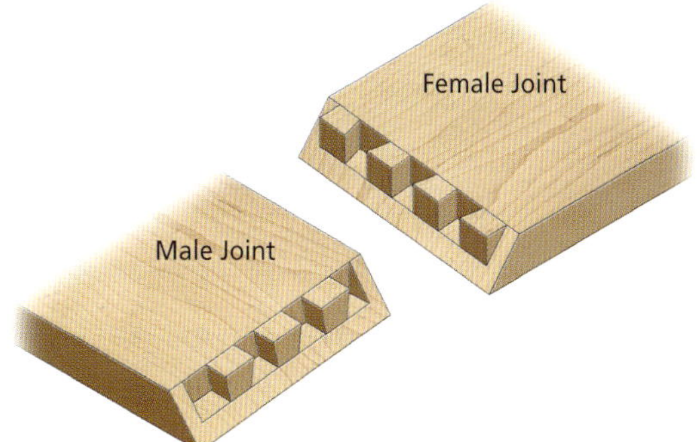

Example of marking a stopped hidden dovetail joint on an 18 mm (0.71 in) thick board. The dovetail slope is marked at a 2–3 cm (0.79–1.18 in) slope. This method conceals all the joinery after assembly, so you don't need to worry much about visible marking lines. Additionally, no trimming allowance is taken for the tenons. Use a marking gauge set at 6 mm (0.24 in) to draw the stop lines. However, draw the end grain lines from the third reference surface instead of the first, as the marking gauge width would need to change.

Marking lines ----------- Hidden lines

Marking Stopped Hidden Dovetail Joints

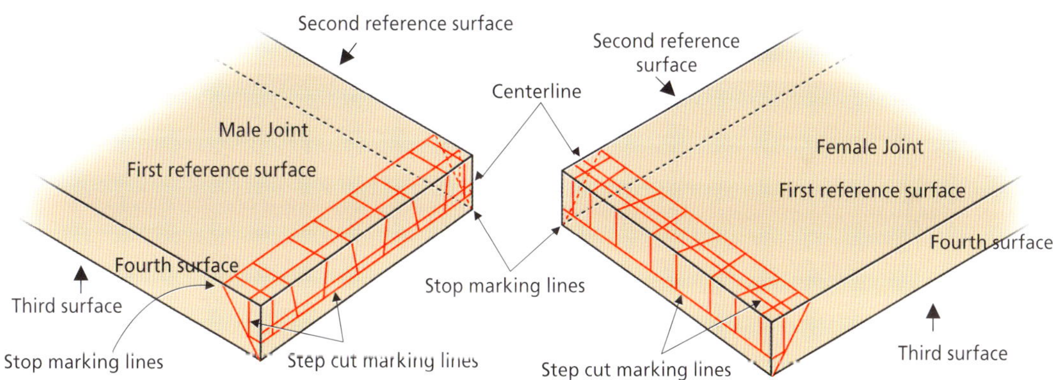

Steps for Processing Stopped Hidden Dovetail Joints

1 First, set the marking gauge to the board thickness. This width will be used to mark the bottom position of the tenons.

2 Draw the shoulder line from the end grain on the first surface of the female joint. Then, use a marking gauge set to a width of 9 mm (0.35 in) to draw the centerline from the same surface.

3 Divide the board width into seven equal parts and transfer these marks to the centerline drawn in step 2 (refer to page 82, POINT 8).

4 Based on the seven equal marks transferred to the centerline, use a sliding bevel gauge set at a 2 cm (0.79 in) slope to draw the dovetail tenon lines.

5 From the third surface, use a marking gauge set to a width of 6 mm (0.24 in) to draw lines on the end grain. These lines will be on the inside of the stop and will be removed.

6 Use a stop gauge to draw 45° lines on the second reference surface and the fourth surface.

7 Use a marking gauge set to a width of 6 mm (0.24 in) to draw lines on the end grain from the second and fourth surfaces. They mark the step cut.

8 The end grain with step cut and stop marking lines.

9 Mark the parts to be removed and the parts to be left on the dovetail tenons.

10 Align the end grain of the female joint with the third surface of the male joint, and transfer the centerline from the female joint to the end grain of the male joint.

11 From the third surface of the male joint, use a marking gauge set to a width of 6 mm (0.24 in) to draw the step cut lines.

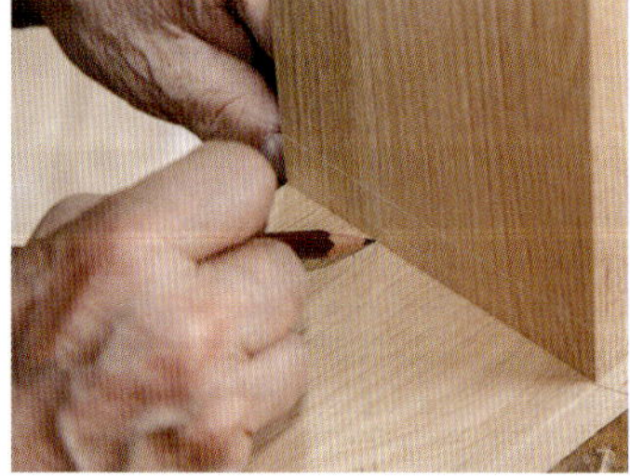
12 Transfer the positions from the female to the male joint. It should have the same steps as photos 1–7, the centerlines drawn on the end grain.

13 Draw the lines from the bottom position of the tenons to the end grain on the male joint based on the transferred positions.

14 Use a sliding bevel gauge set at a 2 cm (0.79 in) slope to draw the dovetail tenon lines on the end grain of the male joint.

15 Both the male and female joints with all the markings completed. Mark the parts to be removed.

16 Based on the stop line and the bottom tenon line shown in photo 8 on page 98, make cuts with a saw.

17 After making cuts along the dovetail marking lines, make vertical cuts from the end grain to facilitate removal.

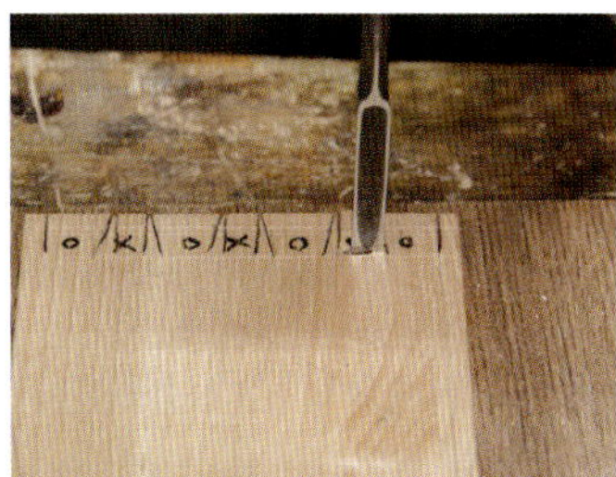

18 Use a chisel to remove the waste from the tenon. Do not chisel too deeply at once; start by removing the waste from the vertical cuts.

19 Once chiseled from the first reference surface, secure the board in a vise and continue chiseling from the end grain.

20 Use a chisel close to the width of the tenon bottom to remove the remaining waste in the corners.

21 Use a shoulder chisel to clean the bottom corners that are difficult to reach.

22 Do not chisel from one direction all at once; gradually shave from the tenon sides, bottom, and end grain.

23 Once you can barely see the tenon bottom line, move on to processing the male joint and finish by fitting them together.

24 Make cuts in the tenons of the male joint. Although the male joint's end grain is cut at an angle, make vertical cuts as well.

25 Similar to the female joint, first remove the waste from the vertical cuts with a chisel.

26 After chiseling from the first reference surface, remove the waste from the vertical cuts, leaving the angled sides of the tenon.

27 As with the female joint, chisel gradually from the end grain and the inside of the board alternately.

28 Once both the male and female tenons are chiseled, proceed to the step cut processing.

29 Along the 6 mm (0.24 in) line drawn on the end of the male tenon, make cuts with a shoulder saw.

30 Chisel from the end grain to remove the waste up to the saw cut.

31 Similar to the female joint, gradually shave from the tenon sides, bottom, and end grain.

32 After finishing the tenon processing, use a shoulder saw to cut off the stop. As the stop is pointed, it is prone to chipping and should always be processed last.

33 Before trimming the stop with a chamfer plane, roughly remove the waste with a chisel.

34 Since trimming the stop end cannot be corrected later, proceed to finish with the chamfer plane after rough chiseling.

35 Use a stop end grain trimming platform and finish the stop with a chamfer plane.

36 Adjust the blade depth of the chamfer plane to produce thin shavings like those shown in the photo.

PRO TIP 15

Points for Trimming the Stop

In the stopped hidden dovetail joint, the top and bottom stops can't be trimmed with a chamfer plane due to interference from the tenons. Trim these parts with a saw or chisel, ensuring to leave the marking lines, and adjust while trimming with the chamfer plane to make them flush. In the photo, the top stop is not yet trimmed, leaving a gap. Adjust this part to be level.

The top stop appears lighter in color as it hasn't been trimmed with the chamfer plane yet. Trim until it's flush.

37 Press the stop against a flat board to check for gaps.

38 Finish the stop ends of the female joint similarly to the male joint.

39 With the male and female joints processed, proceed to fine-tuning.

40 Before a trial assembly, use a mallet to chamfer the corners of the tenon ends.

41 Perform a trial assembly. Check for any tight spots and make fine adjustments as needed. Mark the male and female joints to avoid confusion.

42 Fine-tune by shaving the tight spots gradually, checking frequently.

PRO TIP 16

Marking the Stop

For the stopped hidden dovetail joint and other stopped joints, it's crucial that the ends of the two stops fit perfectly. Therefore, precise marking is essential, but if the stops are too short, it will affect the overall dimensions. It's safer to mark them slightly longer and adjust later. When marking with a stop gauge, ensure the back of the marking knife blade is perpendicular to the board and align it with the line drawn inside for the board thickness. Proper marking is especially critical for stops.

Ensure the back of the marking knife blade is perpendicular to the board and aligned with the line drawn inside for the board thickness.

Align the edge of the stop gauge with the marking knife. Handle the stop gauge carefully to avoid damaging this crucial part.

43 Align the edge of the stop gauge with the marking knife. Handle the stop gauge carefully to avoid damaging this crucial part.

44 Secure with a vise. The vise is clamped on the male joint. Pay attention to the direction of tightening.

45 Check the right angle of the inner corners with a square.

46 Use a damp cloth to moisten and iron the joint to eliminate gaps.

47 Finish with a plane.

48 Remove any misalignment on the end grain with a plane.

Completed stopped hidden dovetail joint.

Joining Board and Timber

Types of Joints

End Lap Joint

This method uses timber across the grain to join the end grain of a board or glued-up panel to prevent warping or twisting. It's commonly used for tabletops and shelves. The timber needs to be harder and more stable than the board to be effective.

Nailed End Lap Joint

The simplest form, where the cross timber is nailed to the board. The end lap material is secured with adhesive and nails, and the nail heads are hidden with wood plugs.

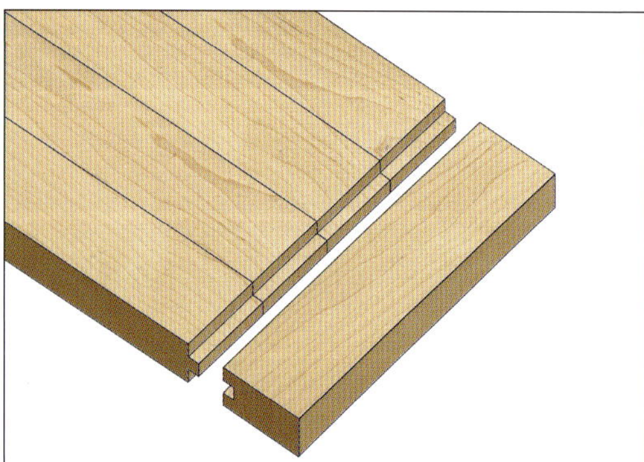

Main Core End Fitting Joint

A core is created at the end of the board and grooves are created in the crosspiece to increase the degree of joint. Do not use adhesive; if you use wood screws, drill long holes to accommodate expansion and contraction.

Dovetail End Lap Joint

This is a dovetailed version of the basic end lap joint. It provides strength and prevents the cross timber from coming off without using adhesive.

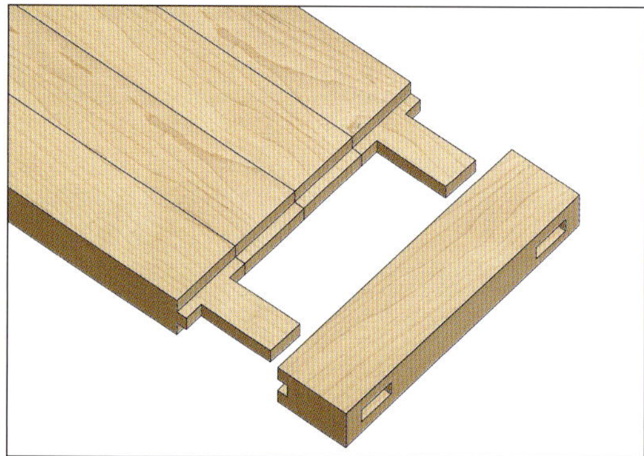

Through Tenon End Lap Joint

A secure end lap joint where a through tenon is added to the basic end lap joint. This method is used for wider pieces.

Mitered End Lap Joint

To conceal the end grain of the cross timber, the ends are mitered. Nails or wood screws are used for the joint.

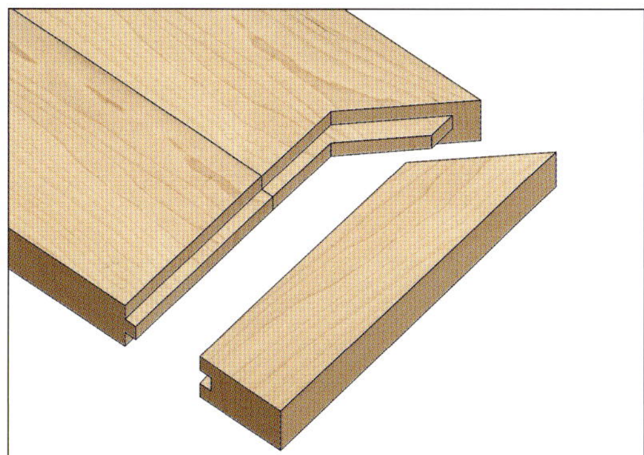

Basic Mitered End Lap Joint

A strong and aesthetically pleasing joint where a tongue is created on the end grain of the board, and the end grain of the cross timber is concealed. It's used for decorative lids and similar items.

Through Tenon Basic Mitered End Lap Joint

An advanced version of the basic mitered end lap joint where a tenon is added.

■ Sliding Batten Joint

This method uses a timber batten called a sliding batten on the backside of a board to prevent warping or twisting. It's used for wide boards like tabletops, and adhesive is not used on the joint to accommodate board expansion and contraction.

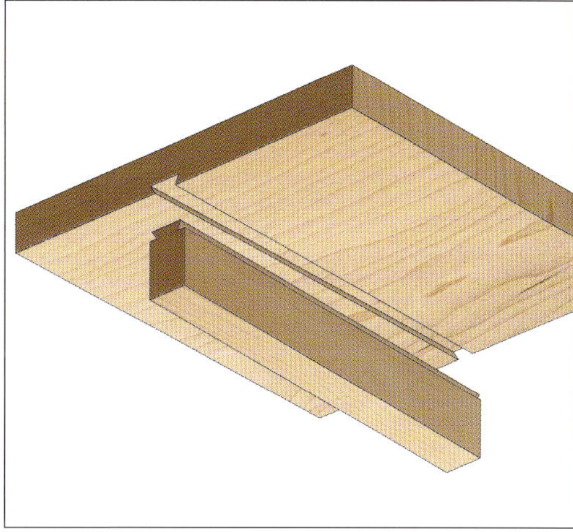

Dovetail-shaped suction joint

Dovetail grooves are dug on the back side of the board, and dovetail handles are installed on the crosspieces to prevent warping and twisting. In order to strengthen the joint without using adhesives, create a tightening slope of about 1 mm (0.04 in) across 30 cm (11.8 in) of dovetail grooves.

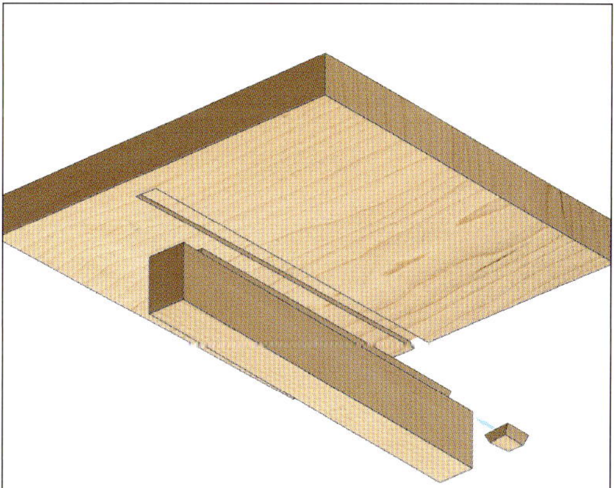

Stopped Dovetail Sliding Batten Joint

To hide the end grain of the sliding batten, one end is stopped, and the entry side is filled with a piece of wood that matches the grain of the tabletop. It's important to allow for shrinkage in the dovetail tenon.

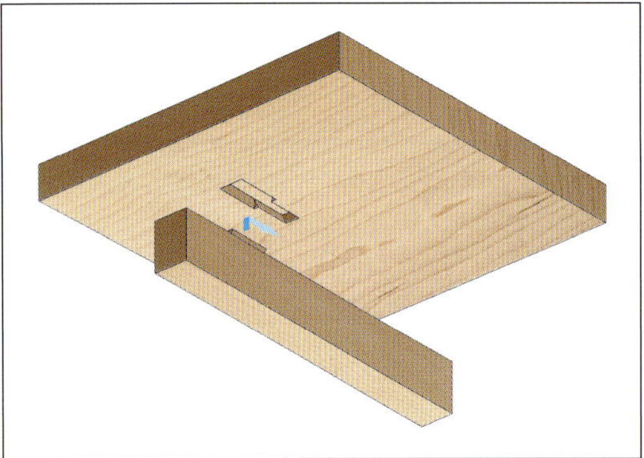

Butterfly Dovetail Joint

Used for joining panels, top boards, and aprons. A square hole and a dovetail groove are made in the female part, and a dovetail tenon made on the apron or other part slides into it.

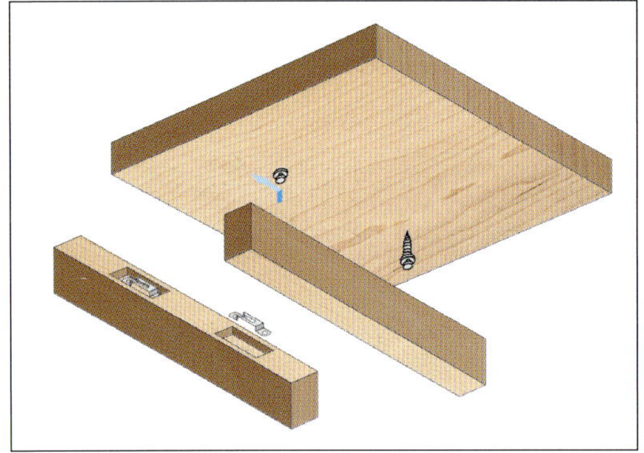

Sliding Batten Joint with Special Fittings

This method uses special fittings to create a sliding batten joint. Machines such as routers or trimmers are often used, making it a versatile method.

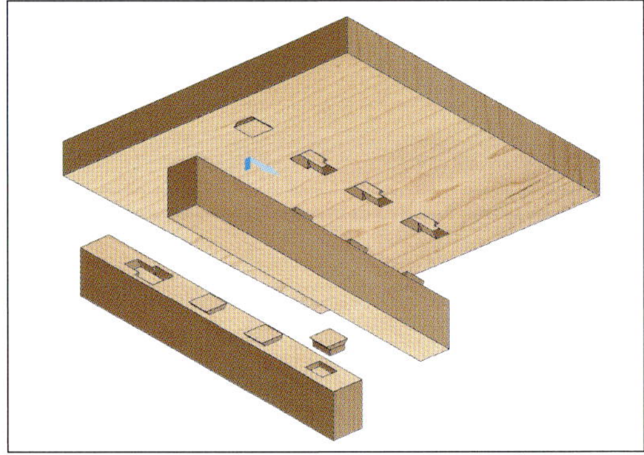

Paired Dovetail Sliding Batten Joint

A dovetail tenon is added to one side of the sliding batten, and only one dovetail tenon is made on the opposite side to be attached to the tabletop.

Most methods to prevent warping or twisting in tables and similar items require significant time when using hand tools alone, and some tools are difficult to obtain. Therefore, fully hand-crafted methods are becoming less common. If you enjoy the process, it can be rewarding to use hand tools, but for functional furniture like tables, using specialized fittings as shown in the photo can be a practical option.

Processing the Stopped Dovetail Sliding Batten Joint

The stopped dovetail sliding batten joint is widely used to prevent warping and twisting in tables and similar items. Previously, a dovetail plane was used for creating the dovetail grooves, but due to time constraints, this explanation models the handwork based on prerouted grooves. The through tenon is cut perpendicular to the end grain on the inside and tapered on the outside. The taper is approximately 1 mm for every 0.39 inches per 30 cm (11.81 in), so for a 450 mm (17.72 in) board, a taper of about 1.5 mm (0.06 in) is applied.

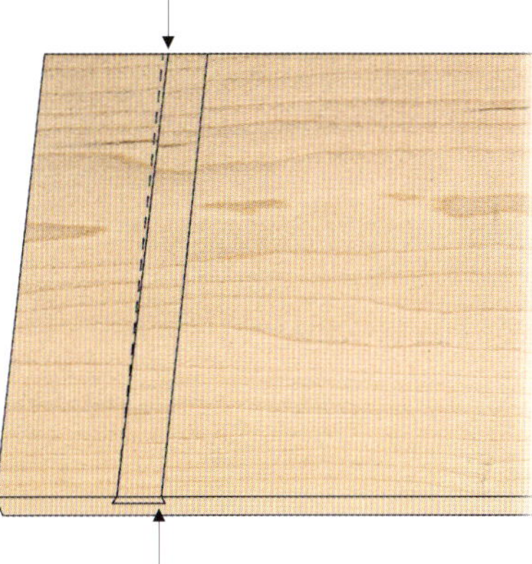

Steps for Stopped Dovetail Sliding Batten Joints

1 Along the marking lines for the groove to be removed, use a straight-edged bar as a guide and make cuts with a rabbet saw.

2 Using a groove plane called a bottom-taking plane, shave the inside of the cuts made with the rabbet saw, and then use a dovetail plane to shave the dovetail groove.

3 Clean the bottom with a paring chisel.

4 Cut the timber used for the batten to the necessary size and mark the insertion direction.

5 Use the dovetail plane to shave the angled part of the dovetail tenon.

6 Perform a dry fit to check for tight or high spots on the tenon.

7 Insert it slightly more forcefully, check the impression in the groove, and adjust the tenon accordingly.

8 Sand the dovetail grooves and dovetail corners with #120 sandpaper and remove any burrs from the corners.

9 If the batten is too tight in the groove, shave the bottom of the tenon slightly to adjust.

10 Use a block of wood and a mallet to tap the batten into the groove.

11 Once the end grain of the board and the batten are flush, place the block of wood end grain against the batten end grain, and tap the batten in until it hits the back of the groove and the sound changes.

12 Once the batten is fully inserted, make a filler piece from the same material as the tabletop.

PRO TIP 17

Groove Processing with a Router

While this book mainly introduces wood joinery using hand tools, for high-risk projects using valuable wood, or when the work would take an enormous amount of time, there's no need to use hand tools. If you have a router or trimmer, using it for long joints like the sliding batten is a viable option. However, if the bit's shank diameter is 6 mm (0.24 in), it can break if the material is hard, so you need to slow down significantly. For more serious work, a 12 mm (0.47 in) shank is recommended.

Routing grooves with a router or trimmer can be done accurately using a straight-edged board or bar as a guide.

Guide the router base along the fixed guide while cutting.

13 Measure the length from the end grain of the tenon on the batten to the end grain of the tabletop. Here, it is 21 mm (0.83 in).

14 To accommodate the expansion and contraction of the tabletop, leave a 3 mm (0.12 in) gap between the tenon and the filler piece. The filler piece is cut to 18 mm (0.71 in), and a mark is made at this position.

15 If the batten is to be removed for storage, do not glue the filler piece or apply just a little glue to the end grain.

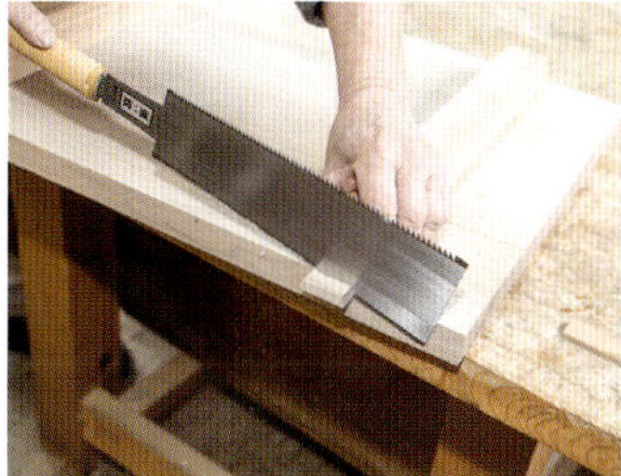

16 Stop at 18 mm (0.71 in) and cut off the excess with a saw.

17 Finish by planing to remove any misalignment.

18 The filler piece is inserted. Use material with a grain pattern close to the tabletop to make the filler piece less noticeable.

Completed stopped dovetail sliding batten joint.

Joining Timber to Timber

Types of Joints

■ Half-Lap Joint

This joint involves cutting half the thickness of each timber piece and joining them together. It's used in doors, furniture, and joinery. Mainly used for T-shaped and cross-shaped joints.

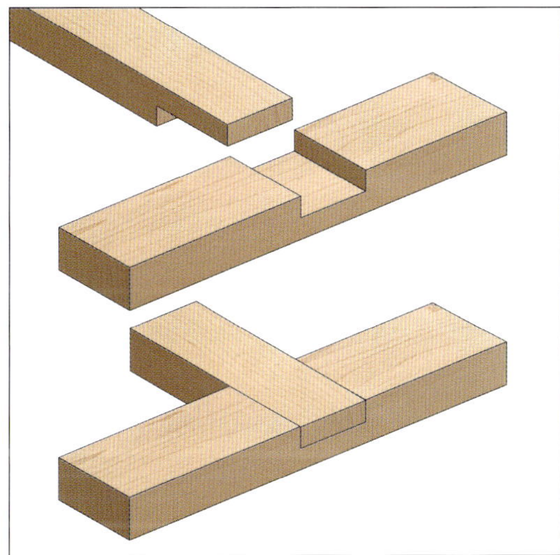

T-Shaped Half-Lap Joint

A method where half the thickness of each material is removed and joined at a 90° angle. Used for attaching middle rails.

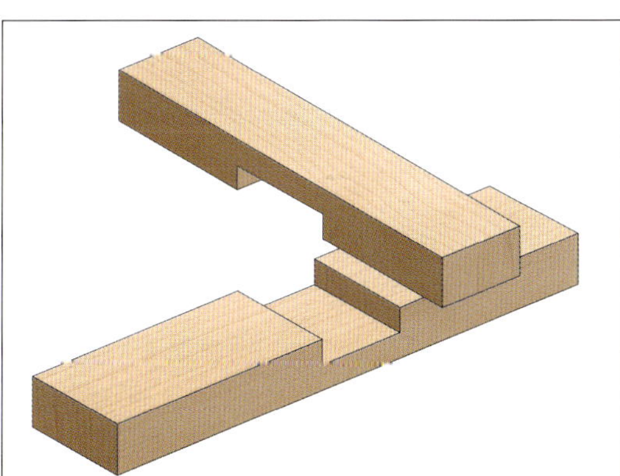

Cross-Shaped Half-Lap Joint

A method where half the thickness of each material is removed and joined to intersect at right angles. Used for latticework, desks, and chair rails.

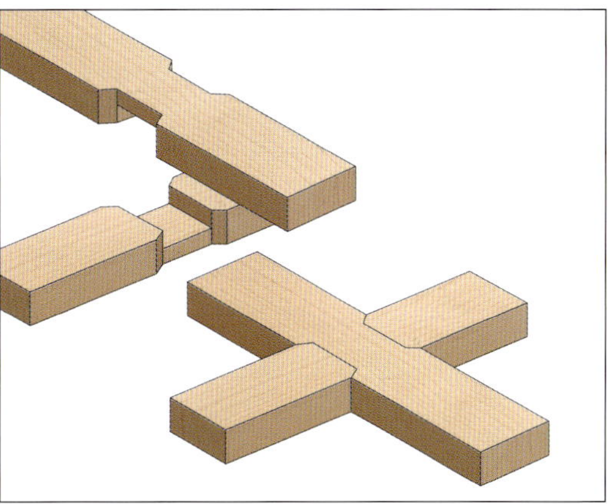

Beveled Cross Half-Lap Joint

A cross half-lap joint with beveled edges on each side, used in high-end furniture.

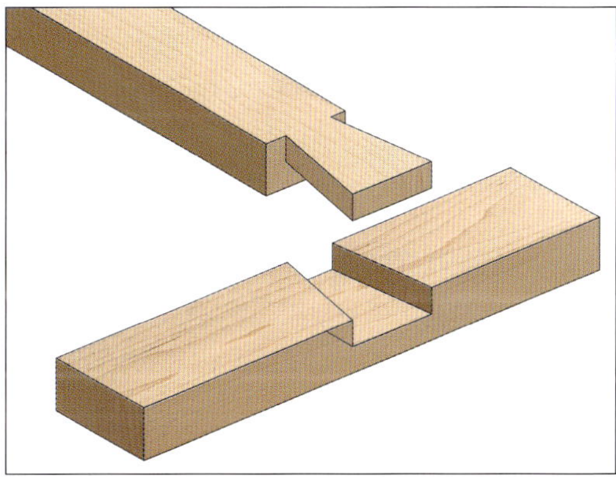

Dovetail Half-Lap Joint

A T-shaped half-lap joint with a dovetail tenon, providing strength against pulling forces.

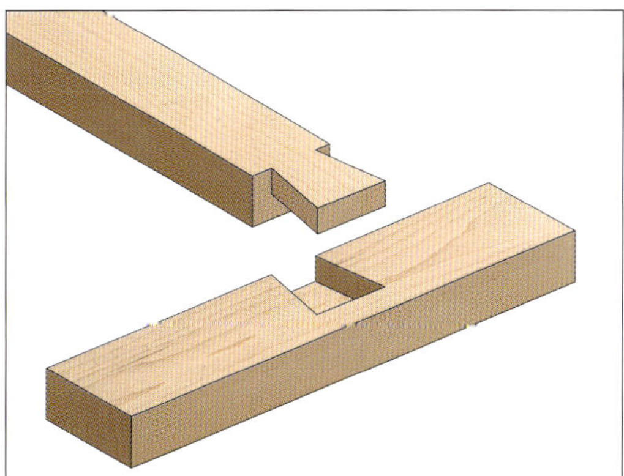

Wrapped Dovetail Half-Lap Joint

A joint that hides the end grain of the dovetail tenon by wrapping it, used for baseboards and aprons.

■ Three-Layer Joint

This joint involves dividing the thickness of the material into three parts, creating male and female parts to be joined. It's used for framed pieces and is also called a framed joint.

T-Shaped Three-Layer Joint
A joint used for joining timber in a T-shape, stronger than a half-lap joint.

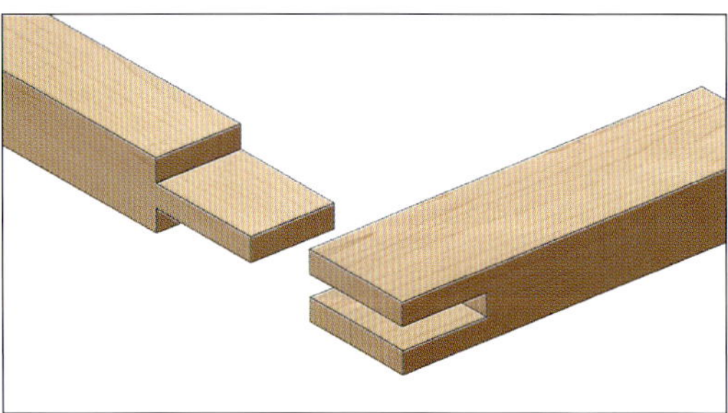

Rectangular Three-Layer Joint
The most basic three-layer joint, dividing the thickness into three parts and joining them at right angles. Used for intermediate level frameworks.

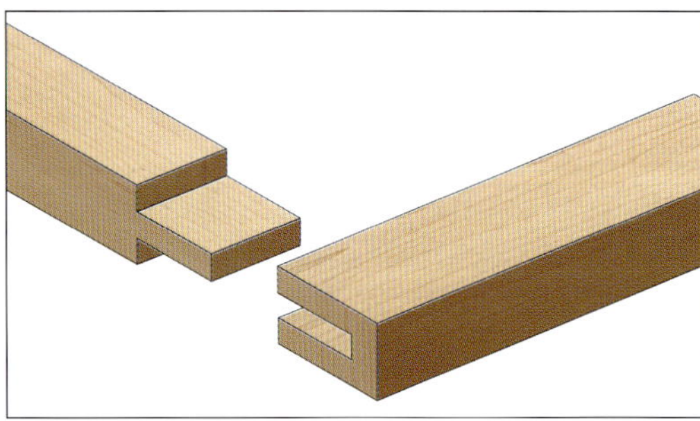

Wrapped Three-Layer Joint
A joint that hides the end grain of the tenon in a rectangular three-layer joint.

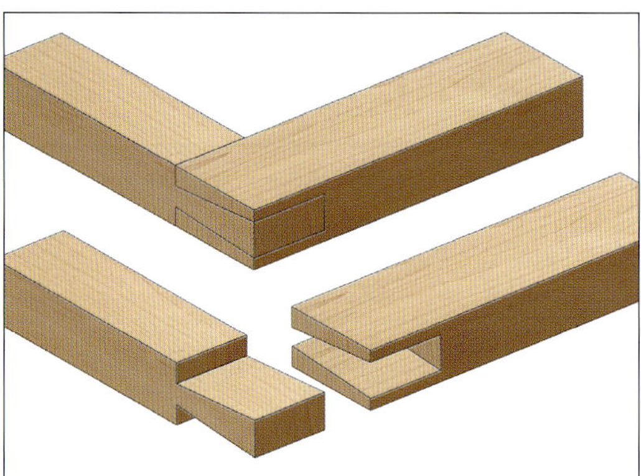

Dovetail Three-Layer Joint
A three-layer joint with a dovetail tenon, used for added strength against pulling forces.

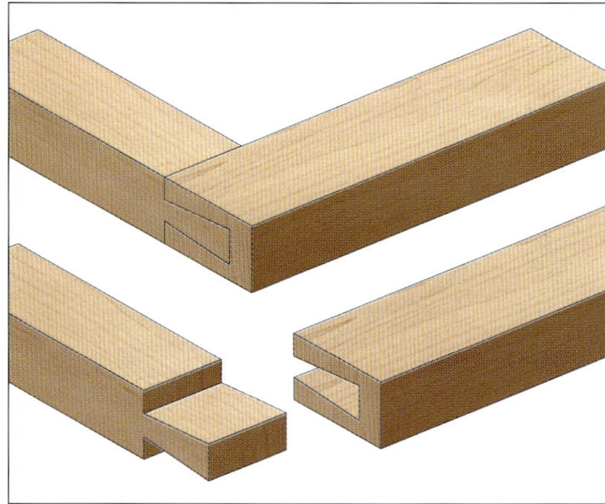

Wrapped Dovetail Three-Layer Joint
A dovetail three-layer joint with the end grain of the tenon wrapped, used for doors and desks requiring both appearance and strength.

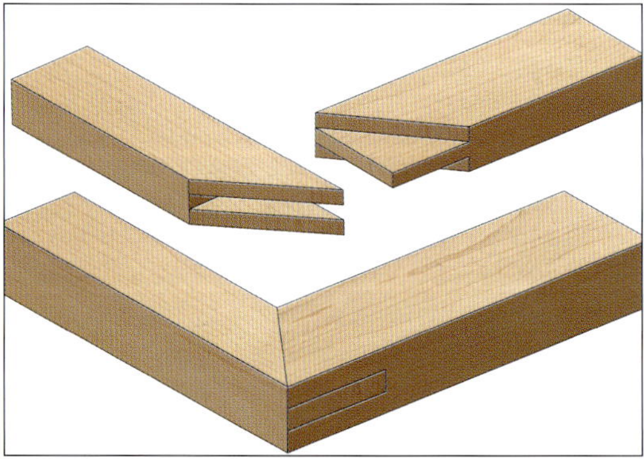

Mitered Three-Layer Joint
A three-layer joint with mitered ends, exposing only one tenon.

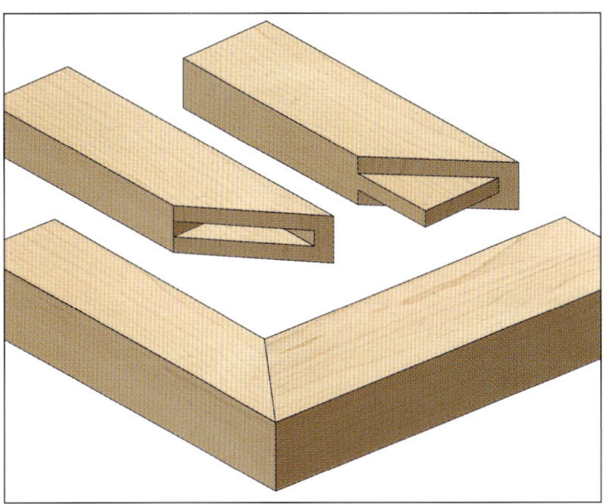

Hidden Mitered Three-Layer Joint
A joint that conceals the tenon inside, used in high-end frameworks.

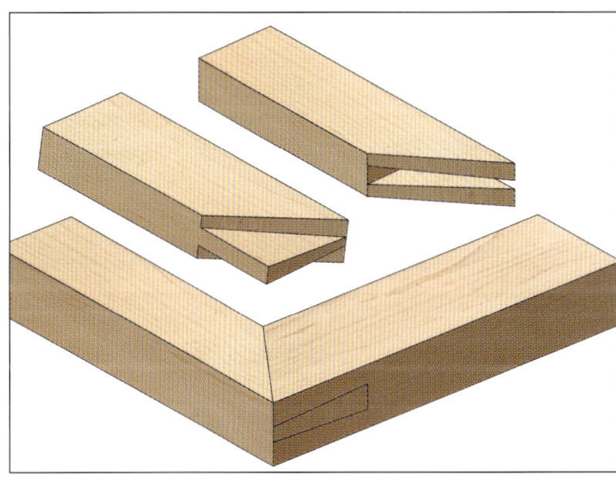

Mitered Dovetail Three-Layer Joint
A mitered three-layer joint with a dovetail tenon, providing additional strength and preventing slippage.

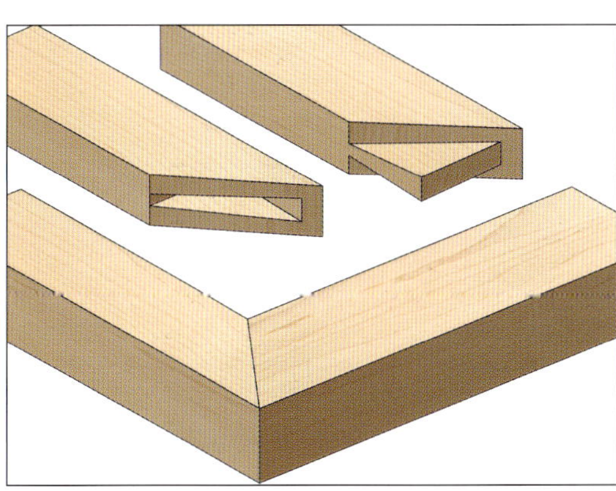

Hidden Mitered Dovetail Three-Layer Joint
A mitered dovetail three-layer joint with a concealed tenon, combining good appearance with strong retention.

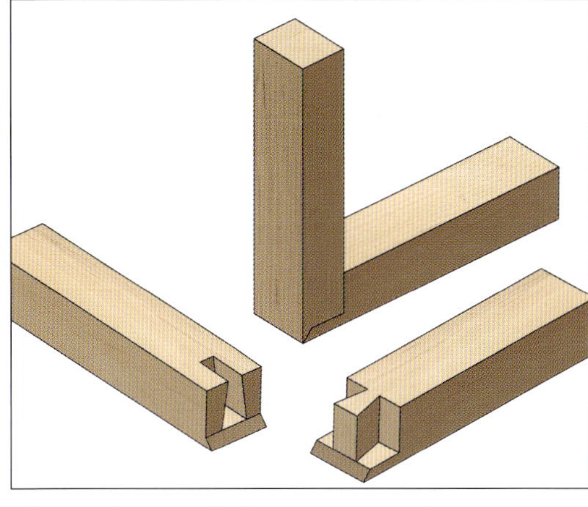

Hidden Dovetail Three-Layer Joint
A joint that conceals the dovetail tenon.

■ Tenon Joint

This joint involves creating a tenon on one piece and a mortise on the other. It's a fundamental woodworking joint used in construction, doors and furniture. Mainly used for T-shaped and L-shaped joints, with through tenons and stopped tenons where the end grain is hidden. The piece with the tenon is the male part, and the piece with the mortise is the female part.

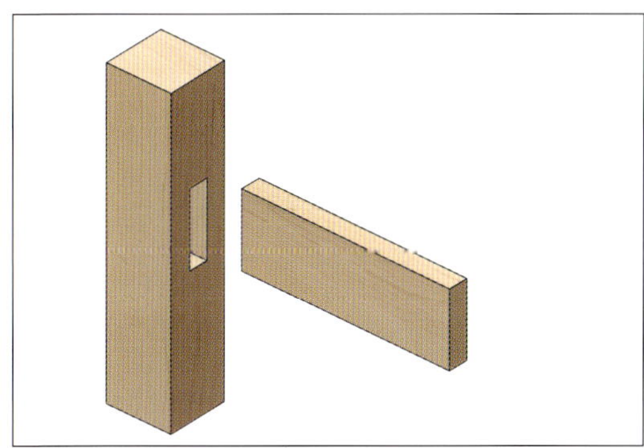

Square Tenon Joint
The simplest tenon joint where a square tenon fits into a mortise. It includes both through tenons and stopped tenons.

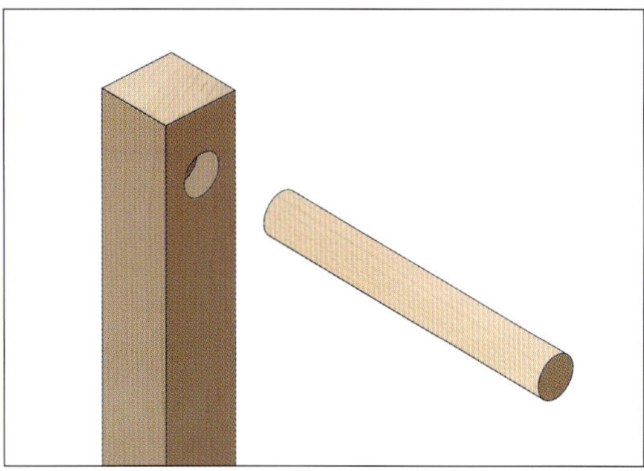

Round Tenon Joint

A joint where the tenon is a round rod, fitting into a round mortise. Both parts can be round rods.

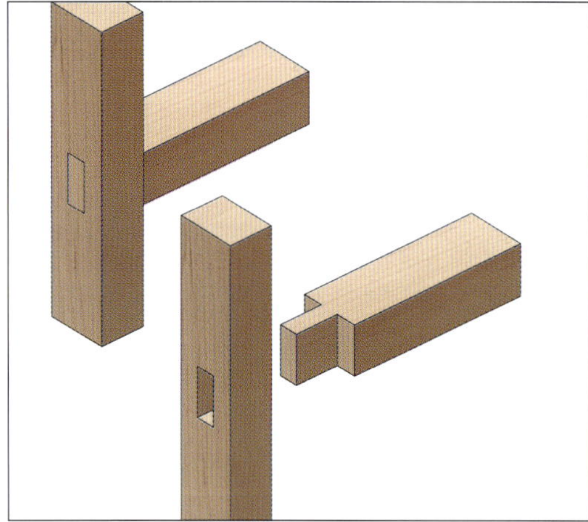

Double Shouldered Tenon Joint

The most common tenon joint used in furniture, joinery, and construction. The tenon thickness is typically one-third of the board thickness.

Triple Shouldered Tenon Joint

A double-shouldered tenon joint with an additional shoulder on one side, used at the ends of frames to prevent shearing at the mortise edge.

Quadruple Shouldered Tenon Joint

A joint with shoulders on all sides of the tenon, ensuring the tenon is completely hidden when assembled, emphasizing appearance.

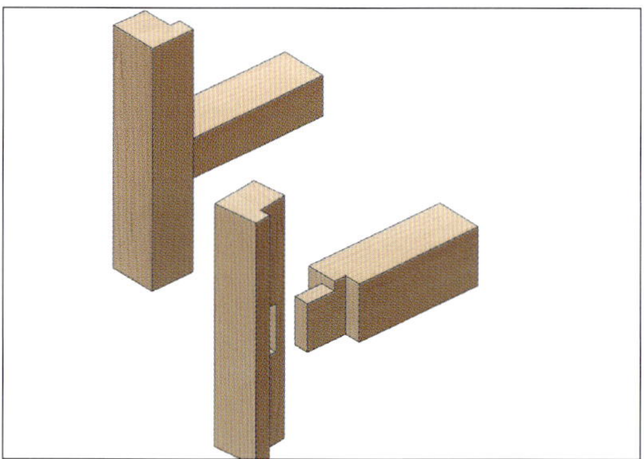

Offset Shouldered Stopped Tenon Joint

A joint with shoulders positioned asymmetrically, creating a stepped cut inside. For through tenons, it's called an offset shouldered through tenon joint.

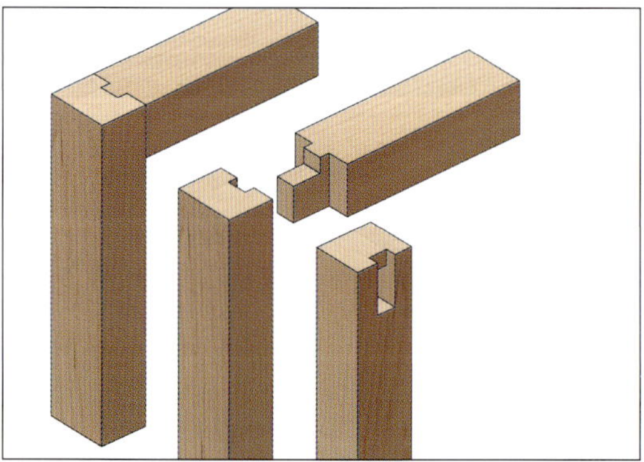

Small Root Tenon Joint (Waist Tenon Joint)

A joint with a small root added to the tenon of the male part in a frame, providing strength against twisting.

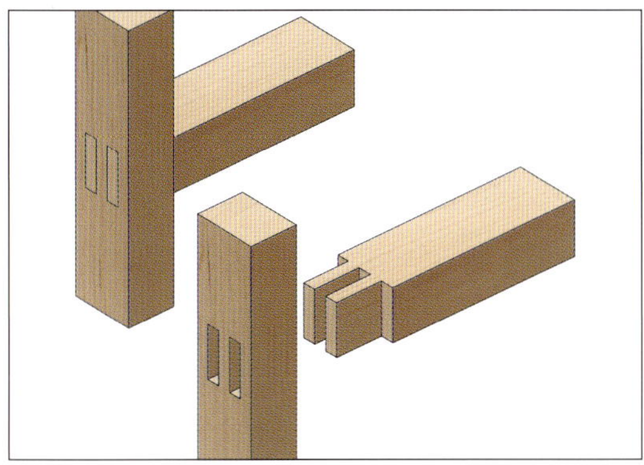

Double Tenon Joint
A joint with two tenons in parallel, used when the female and male parts are thick. Used for joining desk legs to rails, for example.

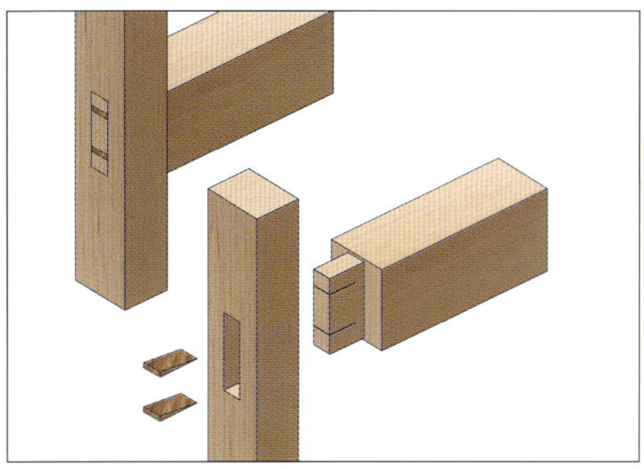

Wedged Through Tenon Joint
A joint where the end grain of a through tenon is split, and a wedge is driven in to secure it.

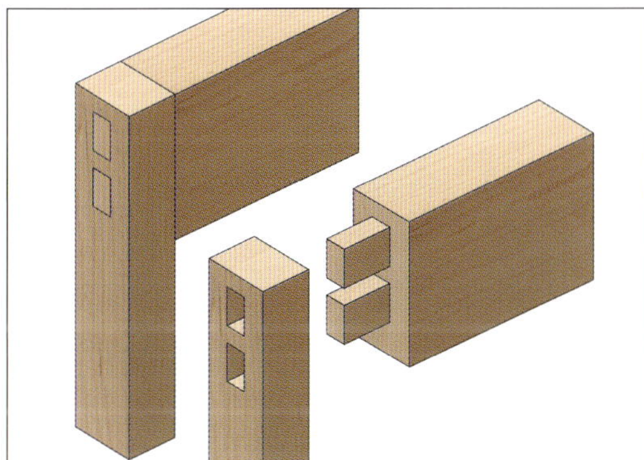

Double-Layer Tenon Joint
A joint with two tenons arranged vertically, used for joining wide materials. The tenon width is smaller than its length for added strength.

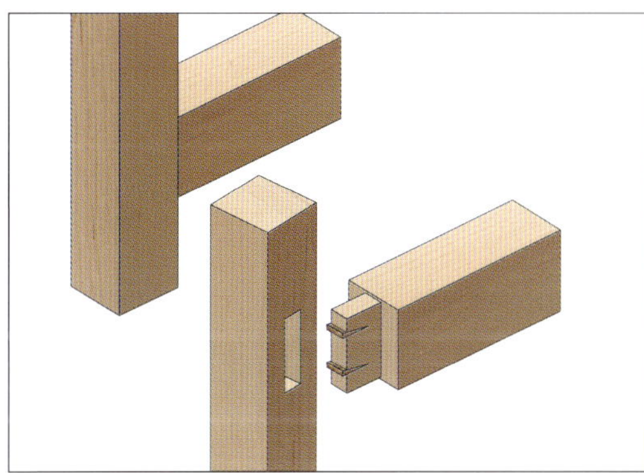

Hell Tenon Joint
A joint where a wedge driven into a stopped mortise spreads the tenon, preventing it from coming loose. Requires precise length to avoid gaps.

Double-Layer Double Tenon Joint
A joint used for thick and wide frames, with two tenons arranged vertically and sometimes with a small root between them.

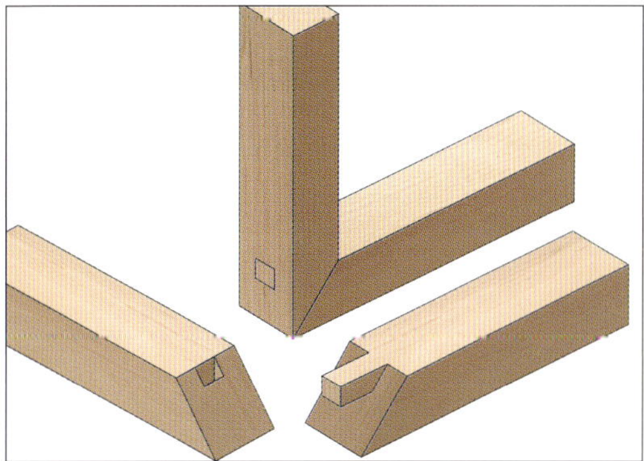

Mitered Through Tenon Joint
A triple shouldered through tenon joint with mitered shoulders. The tenon cross-section is smaller than in a triple shouldered tenon joint, reducing its strength slightly.

Top Mitered Through Tenon Joint

A joint with the front face of a triple shouldered through tenon joint mitered. Combines strength and appearance, used for the top horizontal and vertical parts of a frame.

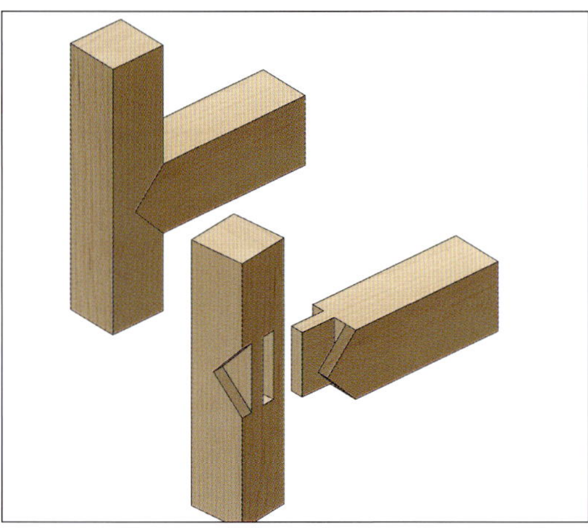

Sword Tenon Joint

Used for joining the front of decorative shelves and tea cabinets in a T-shape, commonly seen in Japanese furniture.

Box Tenon Joint

A complex joint where a box tenon is made inside, appearing as a miter joint from the outside but with a hidden tenon. Classified as both a tenon and a miter joint.

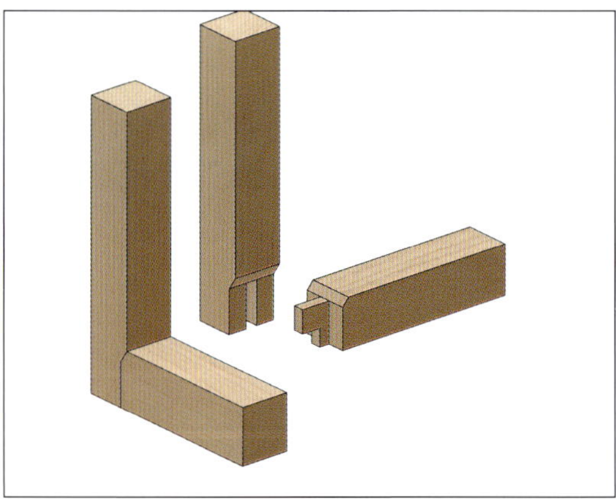

Angled Shouldered Tenon Joint

A joint used in high-end doors and sliding screens, providing high joining strength.

Angled Shouldered Tenon Joint

A high-end joint used when the shoulder is sloped, or the frame width changes.

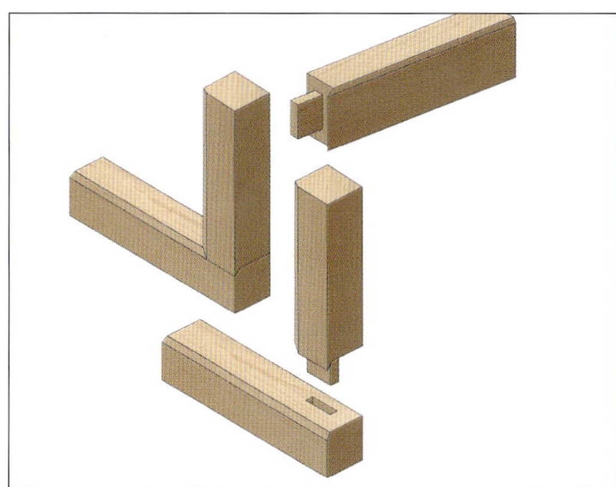

Overlay Tenon Joint (Rider Tenon, Spigot Tenon)

A joint where the tenon fits over a beveled edge inside a frame, matching the bevel.

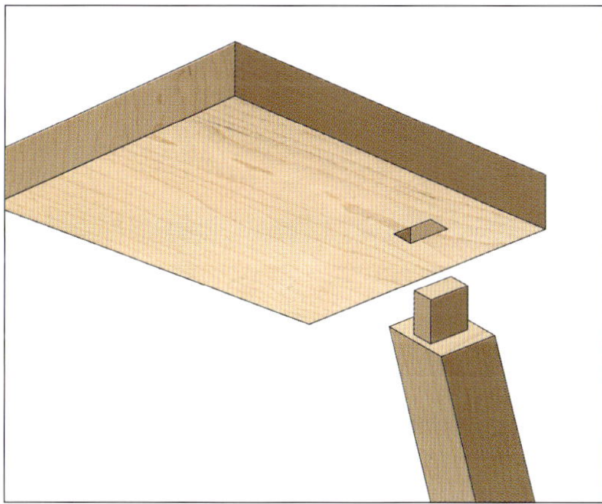

Sloped Tenon Joint

A joint used for stools with angled sides, where either the tenon or the shoulder is sloped. Care is needed to avoid tearing the tenon grain.

■ Miter Joint

A method of joining two pieces at right angles by cutting their ends to 45° angles, so the end grain isn't visible. Often used for joining the side panels of boxes. Since end grain joints fused with glue alone are weak, reinforcement is typically added.

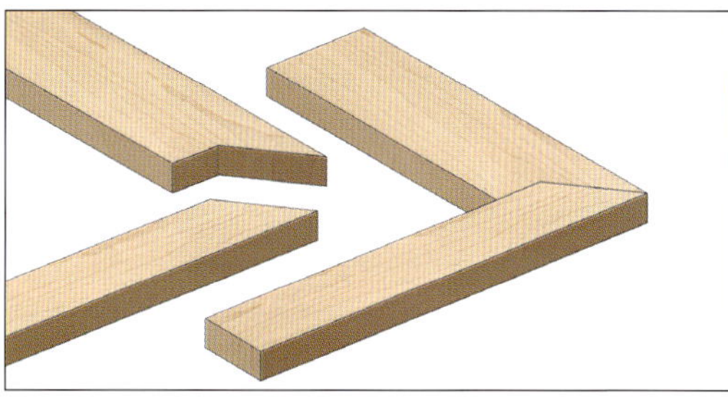

Half Miter Joint

A joint where the narrower piece is mitered and the wider piece is butt jointed. Requires reinforcement due to its weak strength.

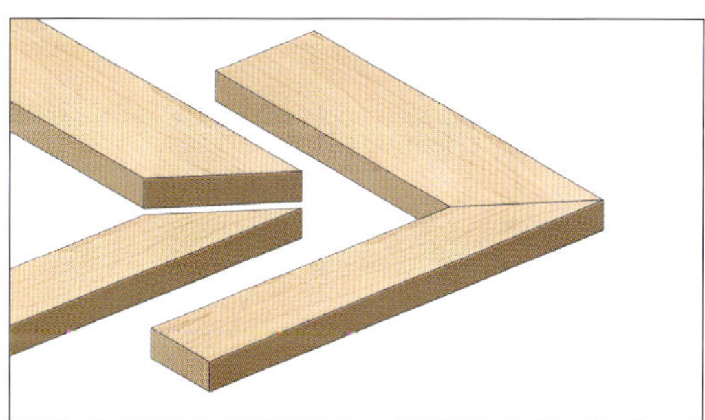

Skew Miter Joint

A miter joint at an angle other than 45°. When joining two pieces of different widths, the angle changes for all the joining surfaces.

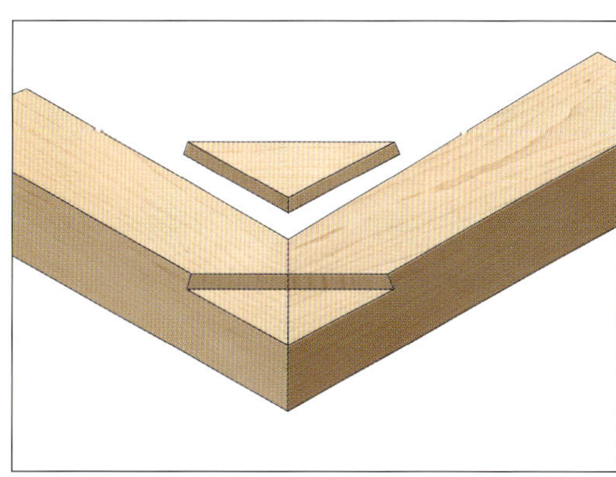

Notched Miter Joint

A simple reinforcement added to a miter joint, with a triangular notch cut into the backside and a thin plate glued in for reinforcement. Used for simple picture frames.

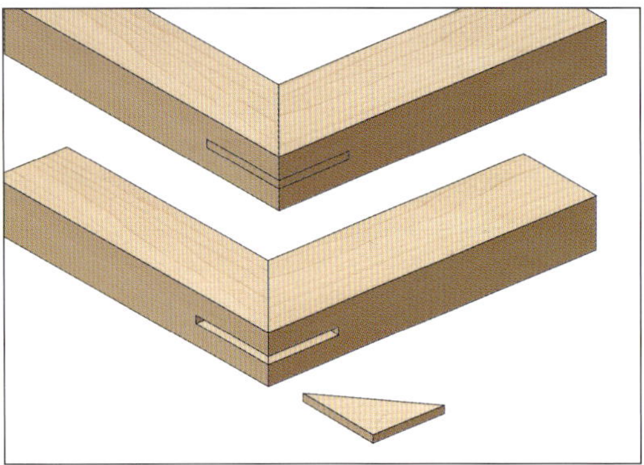

Framed Miter Joint
A method of reinforcing mitered picture frames by inserting a thin plate called a "key" from the outside. Also used for joining boards.

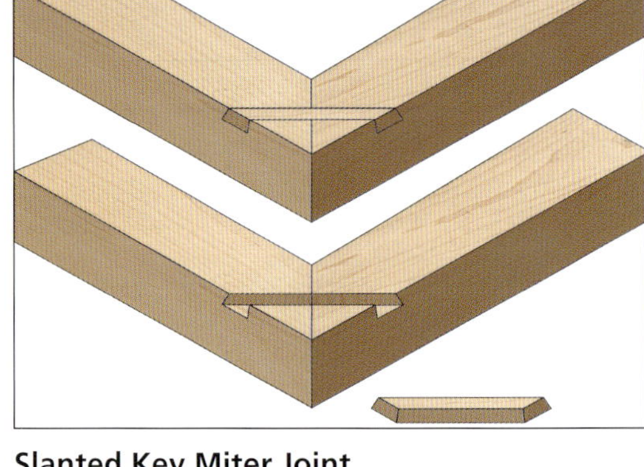

Slanted Key Miter Joint
A reinforced miter joint with a dovetail groove cut into the backside, and a dovetail key inserted. The key is tapered to tighten as it's inserted, increasing strength.

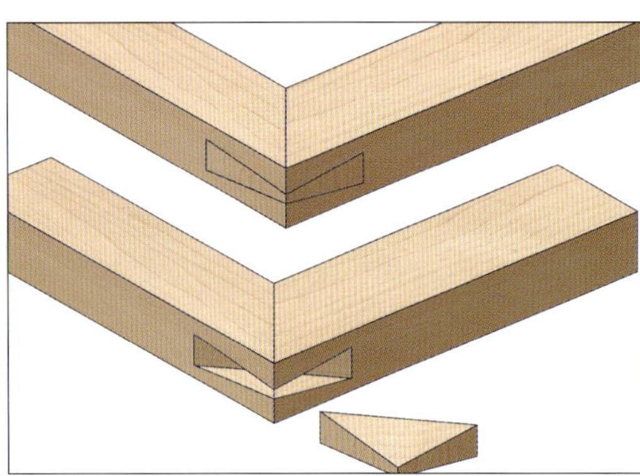

Dovetail Key Framed Miter Joint
A framed miter joint with a dovetail-shaped key and matching notch for added strength.

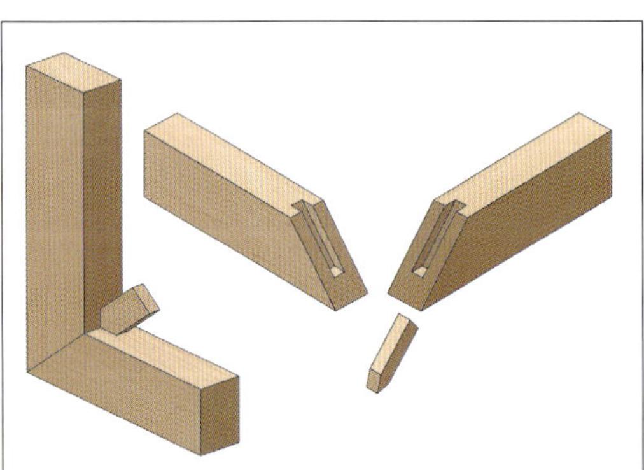

Floating Tenon Miter Joint
A reinforced miter joint where a groove is cut along the joining surface and a thin plate called a floating tenon is inserted.

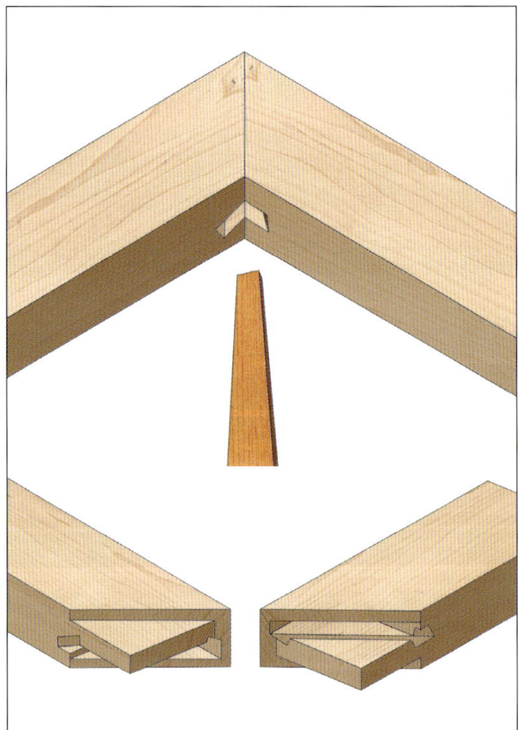

Offset Shouldered Miter Tenon Joint
A strong joint where both parts are mitered and tenoned, with a path for a peg to secure them. Used in frame tables and hearths.

Three-Way Miter Joint

A high-end Japanese furniture joint with mitered connections on three sides. The vertical part has a tenon, and the other two have mortises.

Flowing Three-Way Miter Joint

A variant of the three-way miter joint for parts of different thicknesses and widths, with a single tenon based on the board thickness.

Other Joints

This section covers joints not classified above, including those used for lengthwise joining, frequently used joints and special types.

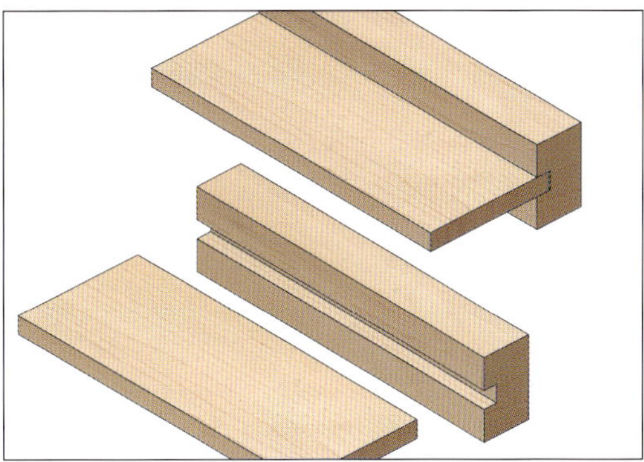

Small Mortise Joint

Used for joining panels within a frame. A groove (small mortise) is cut in the timber, and the panel is inserted, allowing for slight movement to accommodate expansion and contraction if a single board is used.

Four-Sided End Grain Tenon Joint

A joint showing end grain on all sides of a box, used mainly for decorative purposes with limited practical strength.

Box Tenon Joint

A joint where all sides of the female part have shoulders, and the board is sandwiched from top and bottom. Used for joining shelves in decorative shelves.

Processing a Mitered Three-Layer Joint

The mitered three-layer joint, with mitered top and bottom ends, is used for improving the appearance of items like picture frames. Typically, the thickness of the miter should be one-third of the board thickness. To simplify the process, if you have a chisel close to one-third of the board thickness, you can use that width for the tenon thickness, making the work more efficient. The marking of the female part (mortise) involves marking for the miter cut and, after cutting, marking the shoulder line. Another method involves marking from the end grain of the timber initially.

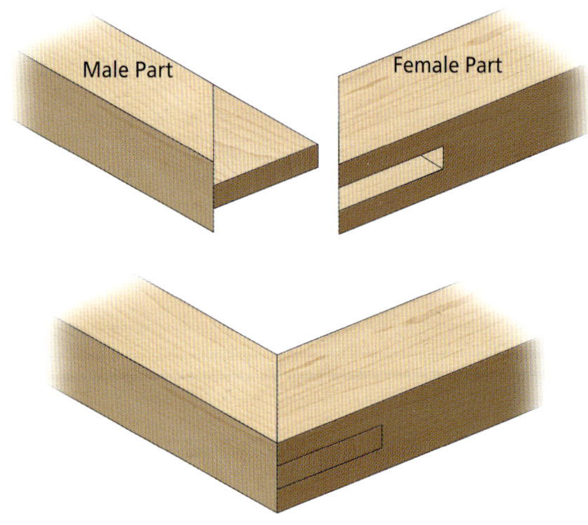

Marking Mitered Three-Layer Joints

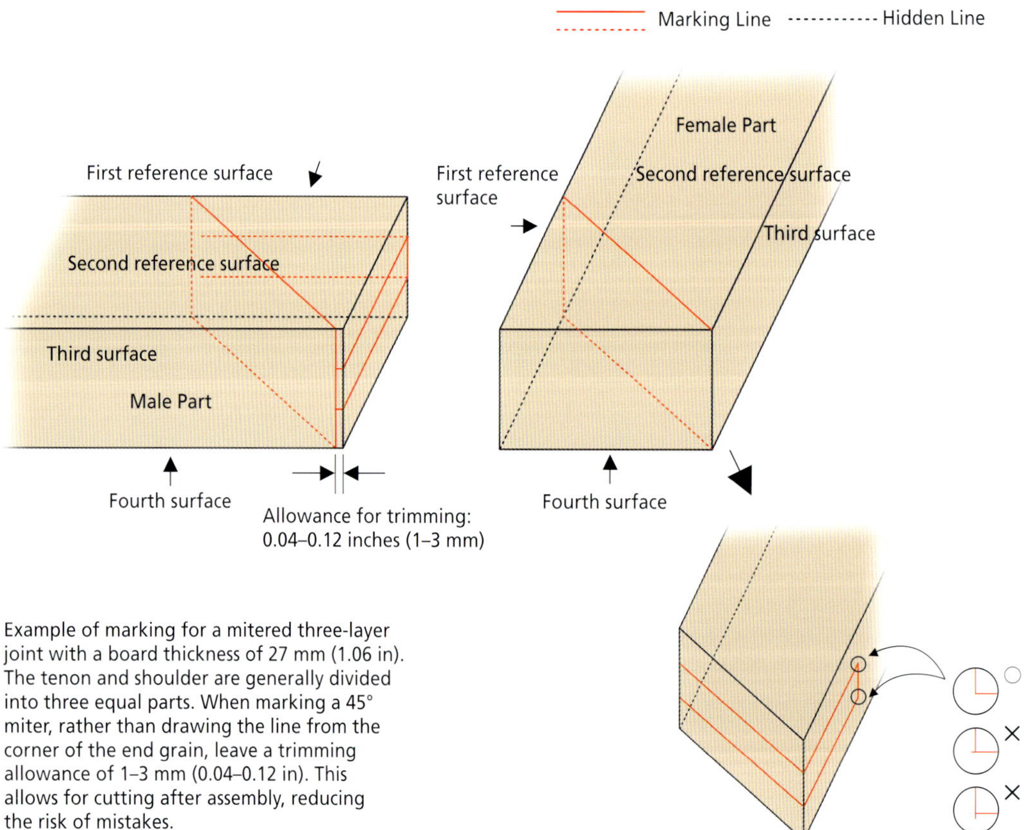

Example of marking for a mitered three-layer joint with a board thickness of 27 mm (1.06 in). The tenon and shoulder are generally divided into three equal parts. When marking a 45° miter, rather than drawing the line from the corner of the end grain, leave a trimming allowance of 1–3 mm (0.04–0.12 in). This allows for cutting after assembly, reducing the risk of mistakes.

Procedure for Making a Mitered Three-Layer Joint

1 Add the width of the female part (mortise) plus an allowance of approximately 1 mm (0.04 in) to the male part (tenon) and use a try square to mark the position.

2 Use a marking knife to draw the miter base line on the primary reference face.

3 Using the line drawn in step 2 as a reference, place the miter gauge and mark the miter line with the marking knife.

4 Draw a reference line with a pencil at the bottom position of the male part's shoulder.

5 Prepare marking gauges set to 9 mm (0.35 in) and 18 mm (0.71 in), and mark the end grain and primary reference face from the secondary reference face of the male part.

6 Place the miter gauge on the female part and draw the miter lines. Use the marking knife for the primary reference face and a pencil for the secondary reference face, which will be cut.

7 Cut the miter on the female part using a crosscut saw. (See page 126, PRO TIP 18).

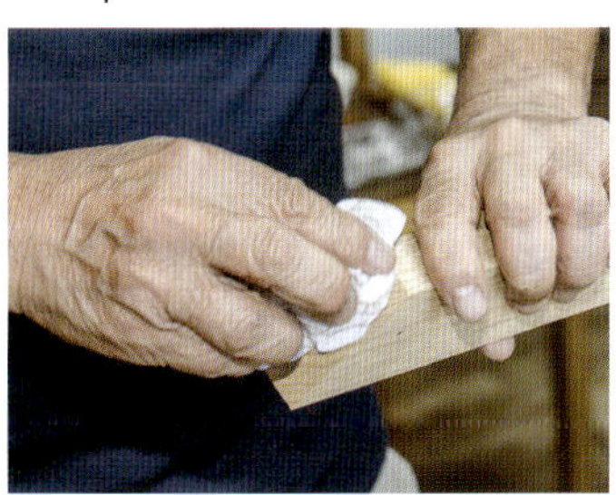

8 Wipe the cut surface of the miter with water to soften the end grain.

9 Use a miter plane trimming platform to finish the miter.

10 Use marking gauges set to 9 mm (0.35 in) and 18 mm (0.71 in) to mark the miter and the third face from the secondary reference face on the female part.

11 Mark the tenon on the female part. The shoulder line was initially marked with a pencil as a reference, so re-mark the parts to be cut with the marking knife.

12 Cut the tenon on the inside of the marking line with a tenon saw, leaving the line visible.

13 Insert a chisel slightly before the inner corner of the miter.

14 From the third face, insert the chisel 2–3 mm (0.08–0.12 in) outside the marking line, keeping the back of the chisel toward the shoulder line.

15 Once you've chiseled deep enough, tilt the chisel forward and chisel in a V-shape.

16 Chisel from the mitered end grain to break up the chiseled section.

17 With the primary reference face facing up, chisel away the remaining parts.

18 Finish the bottom and inner corners of the shoulder.

19 Cut the tenon on the male part with a tenon saw.

20 Cut close to the miter marking line, then cut from the board face as well.

21 Alternately cut from the end grain and the board face to gradually cut away the section.

22 Even if it's not completely cut, if it moves when wiggled, tap it off with a mallet.

23 Clean out any debris in the inner corners of the tenon using the back of a chisel against the end grain to cut the fibers.

24 Finish the inner corners and board face of the tenon with a fine plane.

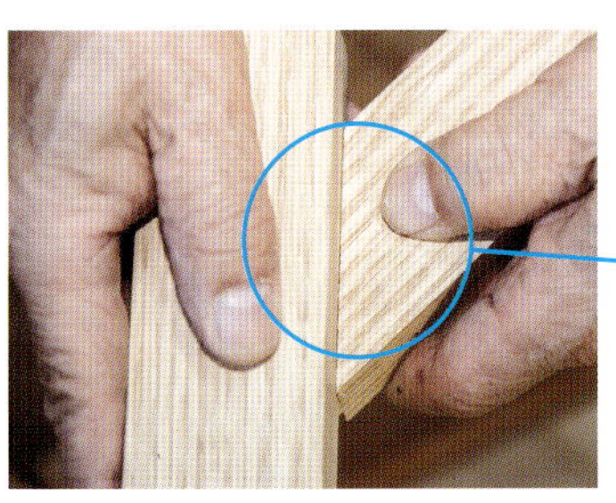

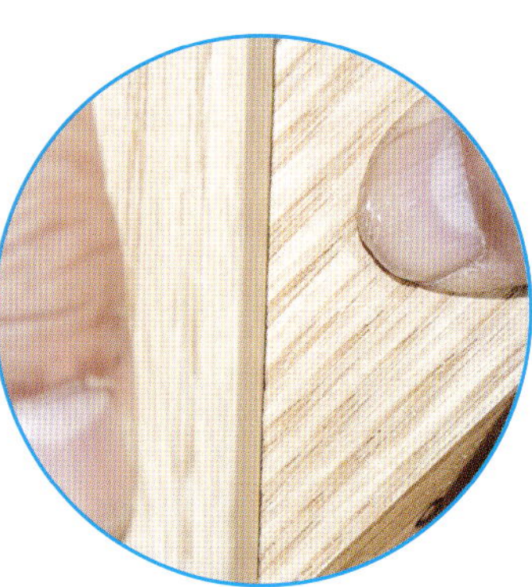

25 Check if the miter fits without gaps by placing it against a square timber or other right-angle guide. If there's still a gap, locate and adjust the inner corners with a chisel.

26 Visually check the gap, and finely adjust the inner corners with a chisel.

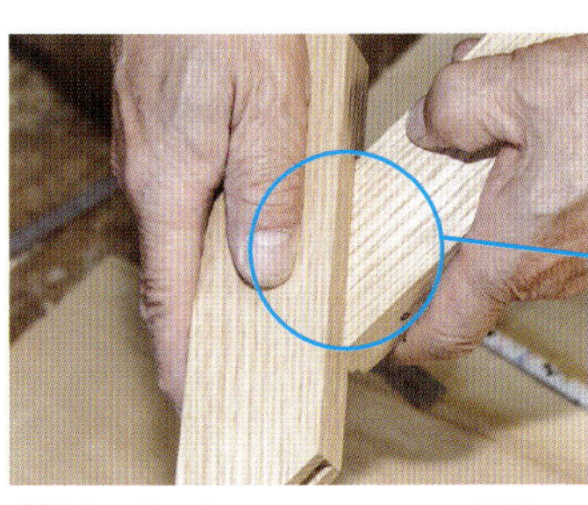

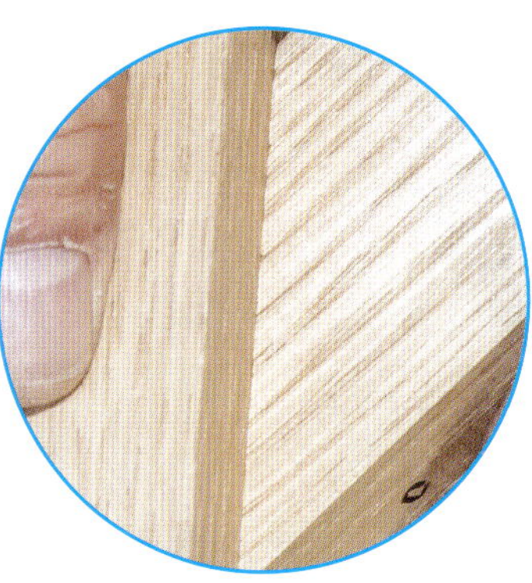

27 Re-check to ensure no visible gaps. If gaps remain, continue fine adjustments as needed.

28 After fine-tuning the miter, dry-fit to check the fit.

29 If there's a visible gap when dry-fitting, determine if it's due to tightness or debris.

30 Clamp with a strong clamp, such as a pony clamp, to see if the gap closes. If it does, proceed to final assembly; if not, adjust the inner corners.

31 Once the male and female parts are finely adjusted, finish the primary reference face with a plane, as it cannot be finished after assembly.

32 With the processing complete, proceed to final assembly.

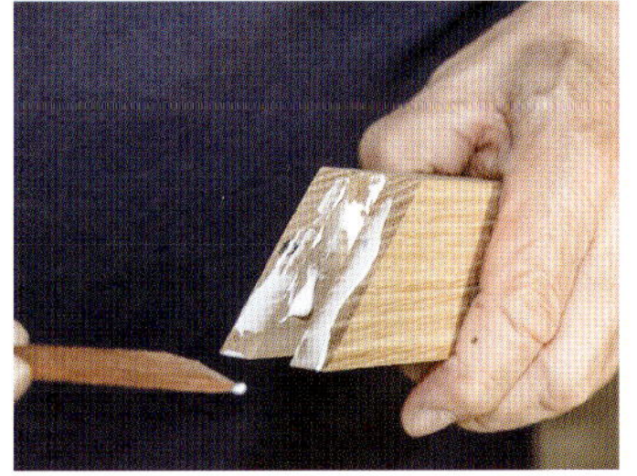

33 Apply glue to the mortise groove, the end grain of the miter, and the shoulder.

34 Place a block of wood and tap in with a mallet, wiping off excess glue with a damp cloth.

35 Clamp tightly until there are no gaps in the miter.

36 Clamp the tenon and mortise of the male and female parts to ensure there are no gaps.

37 Once the miter and tenon are firmly attached, check the right angle with a square.

38 To avoid trimming allowances, clamp the assembly, but for larger frames, use a strap clamp.

39 Once the glue has dried, confirm there are no gaps in the assembly.

40 Plane the trimming allowances and flush the joints for a smooth finish.

Completed mitered three-layer joint

Processing the Keyed Miter Joint

The keyed miter joint enhances the glue surface area by inserting a thin wood spline, or key, into a simple miter joint. While it can be used for joining boards, it's often used for joining timbers where the glue surface area is smaller. For board joints, if strength is the only concern, a flat miter joint with corner blocks for reinforcement is simpler and increases the glue surface area. When creating a keyed miter joint, using a dark-colored wood for the key can provide a decorative contrast with the main wood.

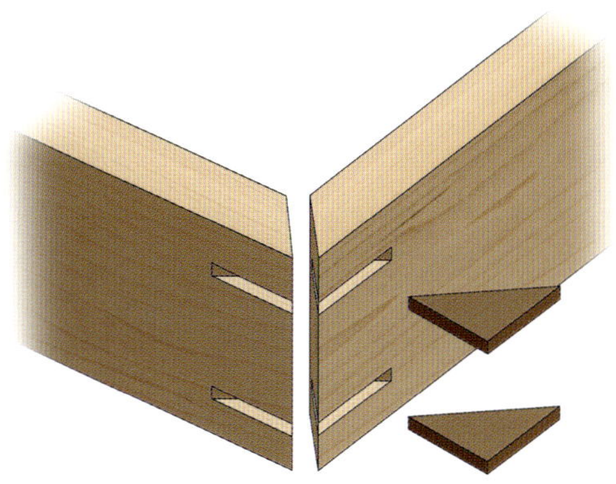

Marking Keyed Miter Joints

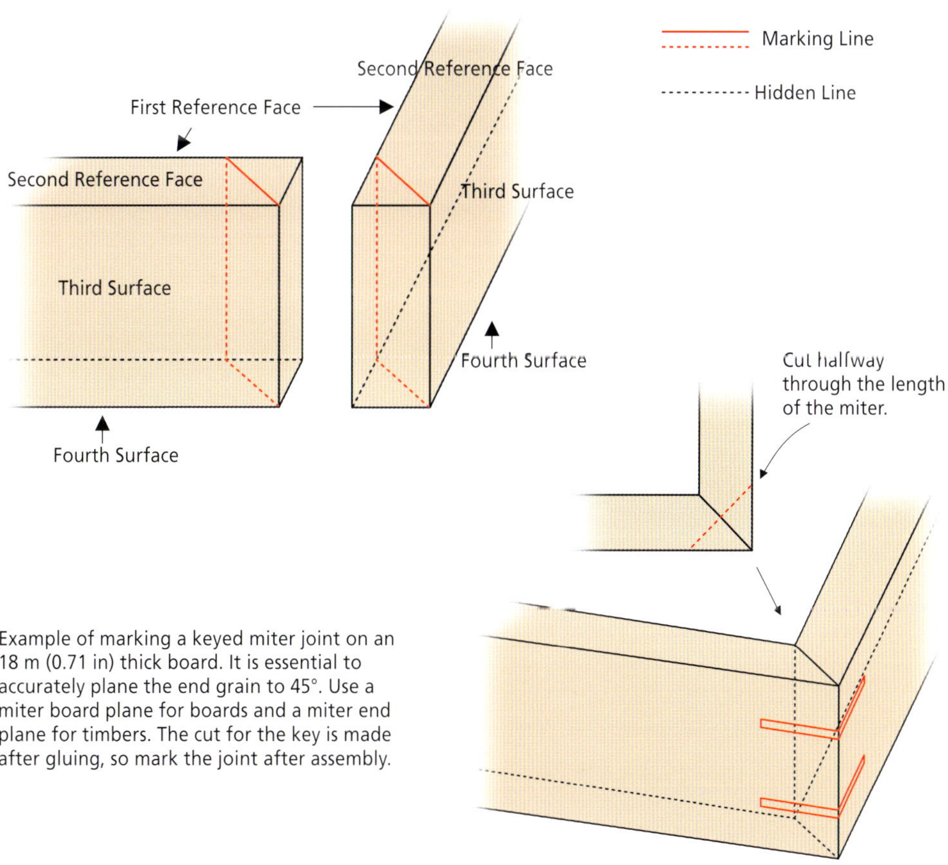

Example of marking a keyed miter joint on an 18 m (0.71 in) thick board. It is essential to accurately plane the end grain to 45°. Use a miter board plane for boards and a miter end plane for timbers. The cut for the key is made after gluing, so mark the joint after assembly.

Procedure for Making a Keyed Miter Joint

1 Since the keyed miter joint has no trimming allowance, determine the cutting position based on the thickness and use a try square to mark on the primary reference face.

2 Use a marking knife and try square to draw the inner miter line on the primary reference face.

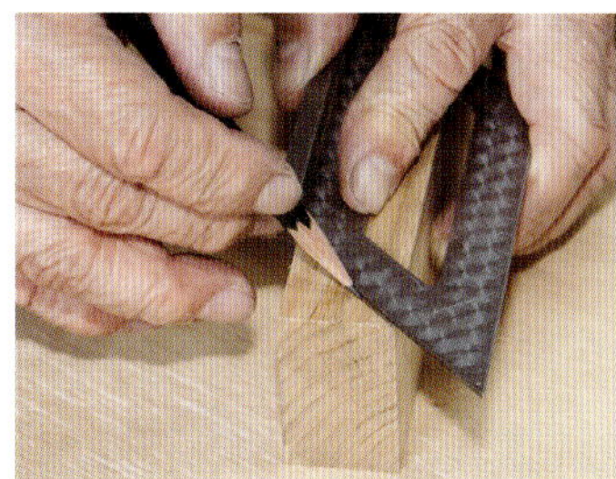

3 Using a miter gauge, extend the line marked in step 2 from the primary reference face to the secondary reference face.

4 Mark the other sides with a pencil for visibility, while the primary reference face is marked with a marking knife.

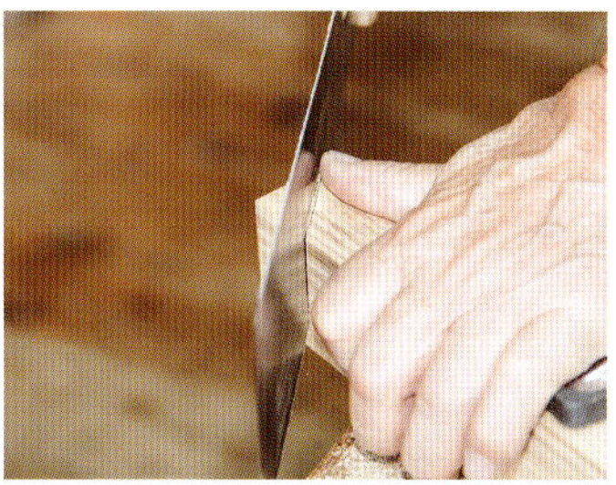

5 Secure the material with clamps and cut along the outside of the marking line with a saw.

6 Wipe the end grain with water to soften it for easier planing.

PRO TIP 18

Marking and Cutting the Miter

When joining timbers with a miter joint in frames, mark and cut the end grain of the joining materials at a 45° angle. For example, if making a square box, all four pieces should be the same length; if even one piece is too short, all pieces will need to be adjusted. Always leave the marking line visible when cutting with a saw, then adjust using a miter end planing board.

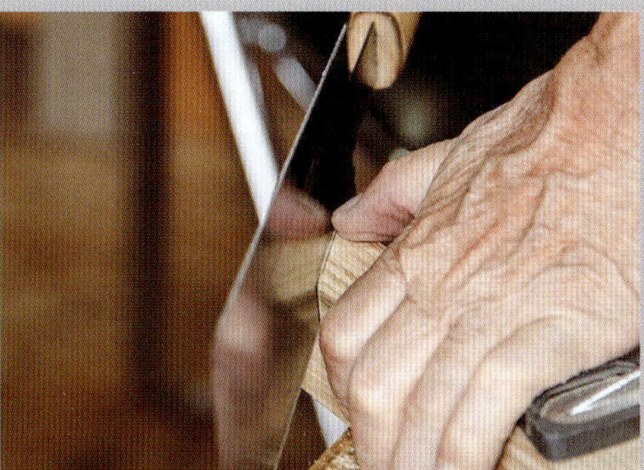

Cut the miter while ensuring the marking line remains visible.

The completed cut miter with the marking line still visible. The finishing is done using a miter end planing board.

7 Use the miter end planing board to finish the miter.

8 Finish the inside (primary reference face) that cannot be finished after assembly using a hand plane.

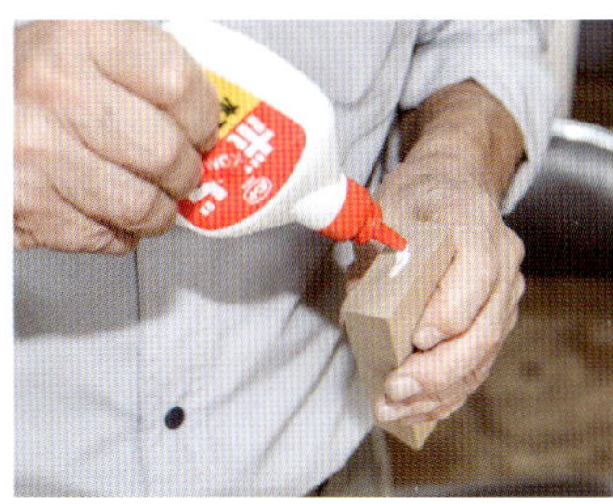

9 Once both pieces are finished, check for gaps in the joint surfaces and apply glue.

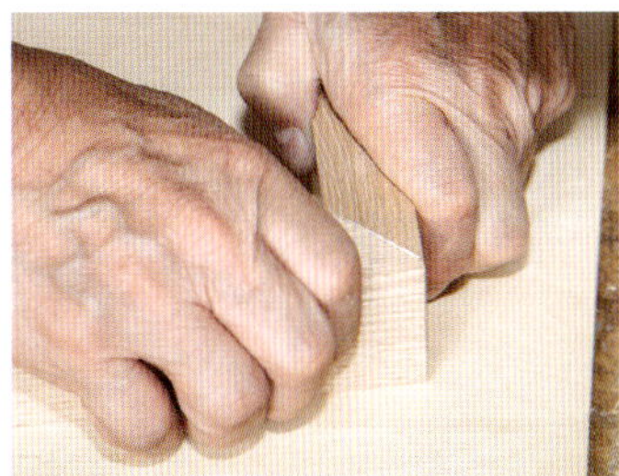

10 Join the mitered ends. For frames, use blocks and a band clamp to secure everything together.

11 Wipe off excess glue with a brush or damp cloth.

12 Once the glue has dried, mark the position for the key. Generally, this is around the middle of the miter length.

PRO TIP 19

Tools for Miter Finishing

Miter joints, where the end grain is planed at a 45° angle to make the end grain invisible when joined, use different tools depending on whether you're working with wide boards or frame timbers. For boards, use a miter board plane with a 45° inclined reference surface, and for timbers, use a miter end planing board with a 45° inclined stop (see pages 46, 47). When planing, the material should protrude 0.1–0.2 mm (0.004–0.008 in) from the reference surface, and the plane should be pressed against the reference surface. End grain offers significant resistance, so wet it before planing.

Miter board plane: Used for finishing thin boards' end grain at a miter.

Miter end planing board: Used for finishing the end grain of timbers at a miter. Plane diagonally to reduce resistance.

13 Use the miter gauge to draw a line on the secondary reference face and match the length from the miter tip.

14 Extend the line drawn on the secondary reference face down to the third face. These lines are drawn with a pencil.

15 Use a marking gauge to draw lines at the cut positions. The balance should be right, so draw the lines from both the top and bottom ends.

16 The marking is complete. Cut along the pencil lines.

17 Secure the material with a vise and make saw cuts just inside the marking gauge lines.

18 Use a narrow chisel to remove the waste and create the groove for the key.

19 Mark a rough outline 3–5 mm (0.12–0.2 in) larger than the miter for the thin wood spline to be used as the key.

20 Use the miter gauge to mark the actual cutting line.

21 Cut along the marking line with a saw.

22 On an anvil, tap the key with a mallet to compress the wood fibers.

23 Insert the key into the groove and compress it lightly by hand.

24 Apply glue inside the groove using a spatula.

25 Insert the key, ensuring there are no gaps where indicated.

26 Clamp the key in place and wipe off any excess glue with a brush.

27 Cut off the protruding part of the key with a saw without set.

28 The key after being cut off with a saw, still slightly protruding from the surface.

29 Finish the joint by planing the protruding key flush with the surface.

30 Plane the top edge to remove any misalignment. Avoid lateral movement of the material, planing at an angle.

Completed keyed miter joint.

Using Marking Tools

Marking out is a crucial step in joint processing. Some even say that once marking out is done correctly, the rest is just processing. This highlights the importance of accurate marking out in joint construction.

The main tools used for marking out are the marking gauge, the scriber and the pencil. While pencils are often thought of as supplementary marking tools to make lines drawn by marking gauges or scribers more visible, there are cases where it's better to draw lines with a pencil.

Marking gauges and scribers make lines by cutting into the wood. When sawing or chiseling, these cut lines guide the blade, ensuring precise cuts. Additionally, when extending lines across adjacent surfaces, a small cut at the corner made by the scriber helps guide the blade, allowing accurate transfer of the line by aligning a try square with the cut. These small cuts do not interfere with the finish, especially if the edges are chamfered during the final finishing.

However, lines drawn with marking gauges or scribers across the grain can remain visible even after finishing and painting. If the line is intended to be cut away entirely, then using the marking gauge or scriber is fine from the start. But for lines that intersect with the wood grain on the visible surface, always draw the grain-parallel lines first with the marking gauge or scriber before drawing cross-grain lines. If cross-grain lines are needed first, use a pencil for preliminary lines, then draw the grain-parallel lines with the marking gauge or scriber before retracing the final cross-grain lines.

For example, the marking out of the shoulder line in dovetail or finger joints involves both the portions to be retained and the waste portions. Use the marking gauge for internal lines and the pencil for external lines, then retrace the lines of the waste portions with the marking gauge after marking out the tenons.

When marking miters, using a pencil initially and leaving the lines visible can make it easier to finish with a miter planing board. This assists in guiding saw cuts and the subsequent planing.

Sawing miters: Pencil marks are more visible and easier to follow when sawing, and residual pencil marks are useful when finishing with a miter planing board.

Marking dovetails: When marking dovetails on the visible surface, use a pencil first, then retrace the lines of the waste portions with the marking gauge.

Processing a Two-Sided Housed Mortise and Tenon Joint

This joint is commonly used in construction as well as in furniture and joinery for frame assembly. The basic principle is to make the tenon thickness ⅓ of the board thickness, though it can be adjusted to match the chisel width used. The tenon length is generally ⅓ of the board width, and the mortise depth should be 3 mm (0.12 in) deeper to allow for glue accumulation. Here, we'll detail the process of mortise cutting.

Female Part

Male Part

Marking a Two-Sided Housed Mortise and Tenon Joint

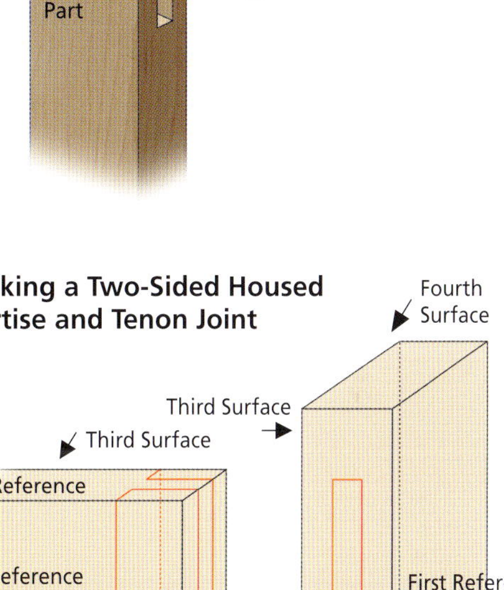

Example of marking a two-sided housed mortise and tenon joint on a board with a thickness of 27 mm (1.06 in). The board width is 50 mm (1.97 in), and the mortise width is copied from the width of the male part. Marking itself is straightforward with few points of caution. As this is a sample joint, there are no fixed rules for the position of the mortise.

Processing a Two-Sided Housed Mortise and Tenon Joint

1 First, mark the mortise on the female part. Determine the position for the hole on the second reference surface, place a square, and use a marking knife to draw the lines.

2 Align one side of the male part with the initial marking line, and on the opposite side, align a square and draw a line with a marking knife.

3 Confirm the thickness of the female part to determine the length of the tenon.

4 Set the tenon length to be ⅔ of the thickness of the female part.

5 Place a square and use a marking knife to draw the shoulder line on the male part. As this is a two-sided housed joint, avoid wrapping the marking around the board.

6 Adjust the marking gauge to ⅓ of the board width or to match the width of the chisel used.

7 Prepare marking gauges set to 9 mm and 18 mm widths, and use these to mark the long edges of the mortise on the female part from the first surface.

8 Use the same marking gauges to mark the tenon on the male part.

9 The marking on both the male and female parts is now complete. Begin processing with the female part.

10 Use a mortise chisel suitable for the mortise width for increased efficiency.

11 Hold the chisel vertically and hammer it into the center of the mortise, with the bevel facing you.

12 Tilt the chisel handle away from you and hammer it toward you, then reverse the angle to create a V-shaped opening.

13 Continue to widen the mortise, placing the chisel's bevel 2 mm (0.08 in) inside the marking line and hammering it vertically.

14 Repeat the above step on the opposite side, creating another V-shaped cut.

15 Use a gouge chisel to clean out the waste from the mortise.

16 Use a wider chisel to refine the wider walls of the mortise.

17 Work vertically along the narrow walls of the mortise, getting closer to the marked line.

18 Mark the desired mortise depth, which should be 3 mm (0.12 in) deeper than the tenon length.

19 Use a bottom-cleaning chisel to remove the waste from the bottom of the mortise.

20 Scrape the bottom clean with the bottom-cleaning chisel, ensuring it is flat.

21 Use a back saw to make diagonal cuts from the ends of the tenon, alternating top and bottom to create a V-notch.

22 Use a shoulder plane to clean and smooth the tenon and shoulders.

23 Chamfer the tenon edges with a chisel for easier fitting.

24 Use a mallet and a block of wood to tap the tenon into the mortise. Check for gaps and adjust the corners if needed.

25 Place a block of wood against the female part and tap next to the male part to remove the tenon.

26 Saw repeatedly from the end grain and the shoulder marking side to separate the unnecessary part of the tenon.

27 If fibers remain attached and the piece does not come off easily, use a mallet to knock it off.

28 If any fibers remain in the corner, it's more accurate to cut them with a chisel than to overcut.

29 Use a corner chisel to remove any remaining waste in the corners.

30 Finish trimming the tenon and shoulder corners with a shoulder plane.

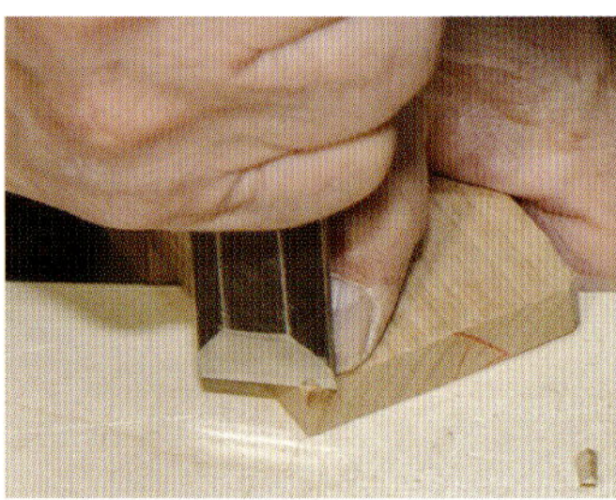

31 Chamfer the corners of the tenon with a chisel.

32 Chamfer the long sides of the tenon with a plane.

33 Place a block of wood and use a mallet to tap the tenon into the mortise. If there are gaps, adjust the shoulder corners.

34 To remove the tenon, place a block of wood against the female part and tap next to the male part with a mallet.

Completed two-sided housed mortise and tenon joint.

Processing of Four-Way Housed Tenon Joint

Since the shoulders of the tenon are on all four sides of the male part, the tenon width is slightly narrower; but this method is used when the appearance is prioritized. The tenon thickness is generally ⅓ of the board thickness, similar to the two-way housed tenon joint. The four-way housed tenon joint is also typically a stopped tenon, so the tenon hole isn't visible. The method of carving the tenon hole is basically the same as for the two-way housed tenon, so details are omitted. In a two-way housed tenon, the corners of the tenon and shoulder may be slightly visible at the joint, but in a four-way housed tenon, if properly fitted, the tenon isn't visible at all.

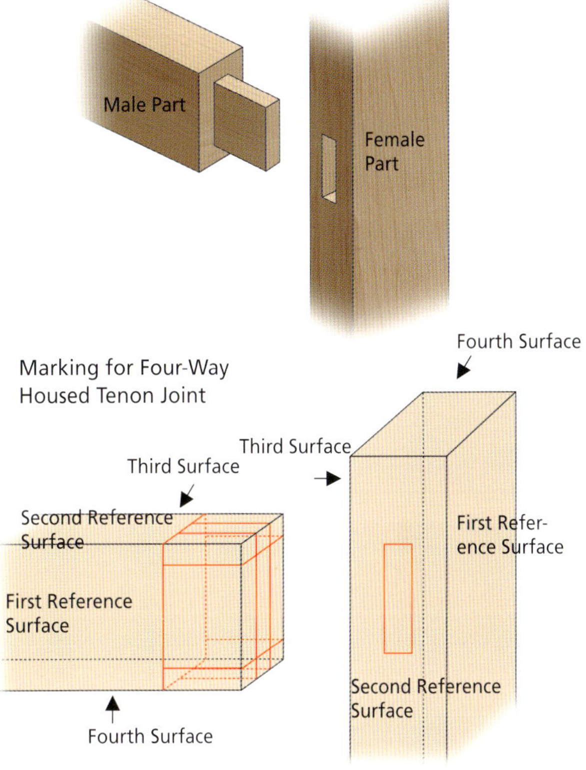

Example of marking for a four-way housed tenon joint with a board thickness of 27 mm (1.06 in). The board width is 50 mm (1.97 in), and the width of the tenon hole is marked from the male part's width. The tenon hole is drilled about 3 mm (0.12 in) deeper for glue accumulation.

Marking Four-Way Housed Tenon Joints

1 Determine where the male part attaches to the second face of the female part. Use a pencil mark at the hole will be on the inside.

2 Measure 6 mm (0.24 in) inside from the pencil line using a ruler, then use a square and a marking gauge to make a mark.

3 Prepare marking gauges fixed to 9 mm (0.35 in) and 18 mm (0.71 in) and mark the long edges of the hole from the first face of the female part.

4 Once the vertical lines of the tenon hole are drawn, draw the horizontal lines at the positions marked in step 2.

5 Carve out the tenon hole. Since it is a stopped tenon, the procedure is the same as for the two-way housed tenon.

6 Once you have reached the required depth, including the 3 mm (0.12 in) for glue accumulation, use a bottom-cleaning chisel to clear the debris.

7 Finish the opening of the tenon hole.

8 Using the gauge from step 3, draw lines on the end grain and second and fourth faces of the male par, starting 9 mm and 18 mm from the first reference face.

9 Mark the housing lines at 30 mm from the end grain. From the second face, mark 6 mm and 44 mm lines on the first and third faces and the end grain.

10 Make vertical cuts from the end grain to the housing lines using a crosscut saw.

11 Use a backsaw to remove the waste from the housing lines. Ensure all four faces are flush; using a jig improves accuracy.

12 Carefully separate the waste, cutting a little from the end grain and the board face each time.

13 After removing the waste, use a chisel to clean out any fibers left in the corners.

14 Clean out the corners of the tenon and housing carefully to avoid gaps when assembled.

PRO TIP 21

Using Multiple Marking Gauges

Marking gauges are handy for marking multiple components with the same width, such as tenons and tenon holes. It's best to avoid changing the width once it's set until all markings are completed. Having multiple marking gauges set to different widths can be very convenient.

Fix the blade width of the marking gauge with a ruler.

Once fixed, don't change the width of the marking gauge until all markings are complete.

15 Use a square stock with a straight edge to check the male part's housing face and ensure there are no gaps.

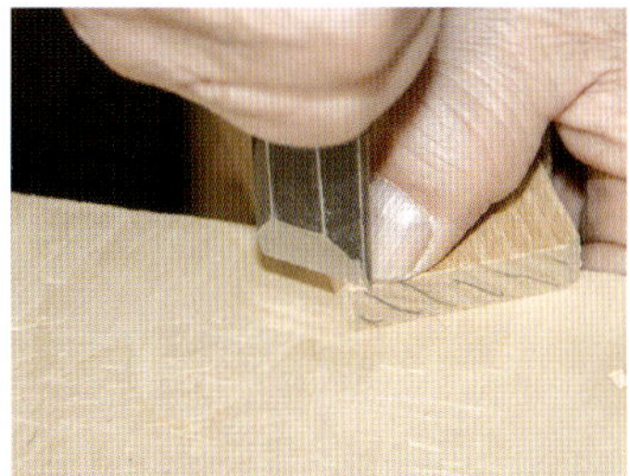

16 Bevel the edges of the tenon with a chisel and a plane.

17 Test fit to ensure there are no gaps in the housing. If gaps are found, make further adjustments.

18 Once the male and female parts are properly fitted, move on to final assembly.

19 Apply glue to the tenon hole of the female part. It is sufficient to apply glue only at the entrance, as the male part will push the glue in.

20 Use a mallet to tap the tenon into place with a block of wood. Wipe off any excess glue with a wet cloth.

Completed four-way housed tenon joint.

Double Tenon Joint

This joining method is used when the male part is wide and the female part is thick. It provides strength and resistance to twisting. The process of creating two side-by-side tenons is similar to that of a two-way housed tenon. Here, only the marking diagram and a photo of the completed joint are presented.

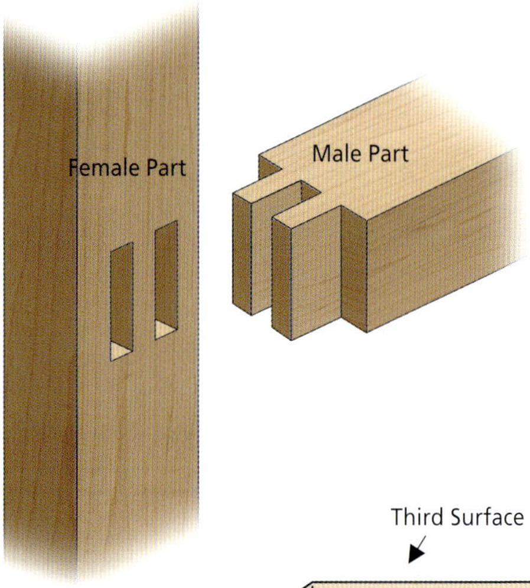

Female Part
Male Part

Marking Double Tenon Joints

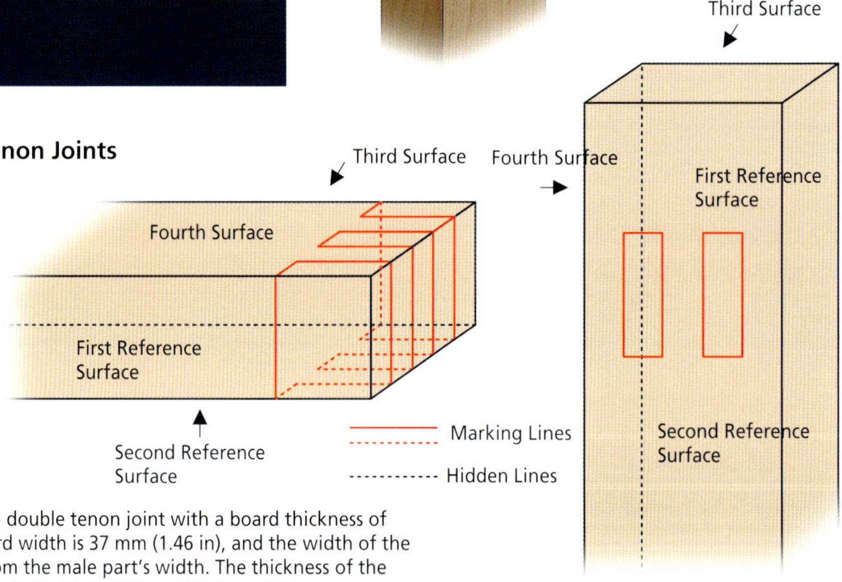

Third Surface
Fourth Surface
First Reference Surface
Second Reference Surface
Marking Lines
Hidden Lines
Third Surface
Fourth Surface
First Reference Surface
Second Reference Surface

Example of marking for a double tenon joint with a board thickness of 50 mm (1.97 in). The board width is 37 mm (1.46 in), and the width of the tenon holes is marked from the male part's width. The thickness of the tenons and tenon holes is divided into fifths of the board thickness.

Double Tenon Joint

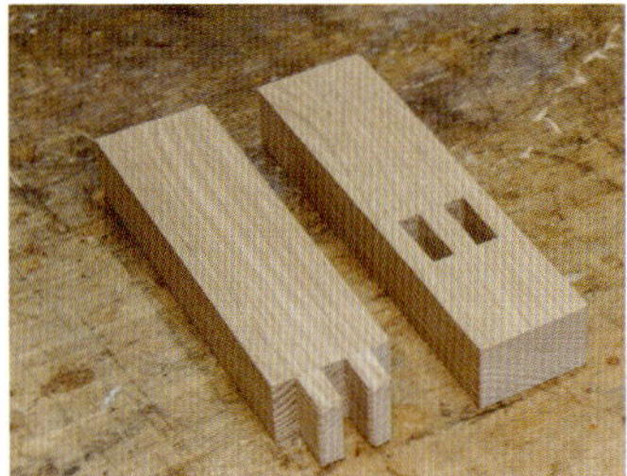

Before and after assembly of a double tenon joint. The process is not significantly different from a two-way housed tenon joint.

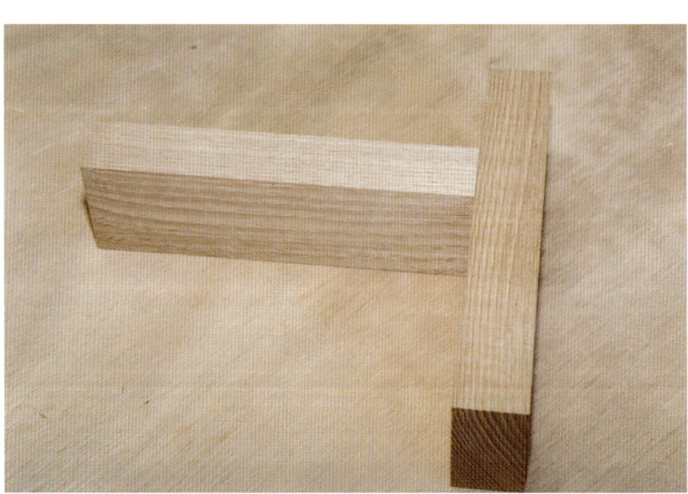

PRO TIP 22

Cutting Holes Using a Chisel

When creating mortises with a mukomachi chisel, there are various methods, but the basic principle is to leave a finishing allowance of about 2 mm (0.08 in) from the marked line to avoid cutting beyond it, thus reducing resistance when chiseling along the line. There are two main methods: chiseling along the marked line with the back of the chisel facing the marked line or starting from the center of the mortise, deepening it into a V-shape before chiseling along the line. Either method works, but when chiseling from the marked line, the chisel may tend to enter at an angle due to the pressure on the bevel, so leaving a slightly larger finishing allowance can prevent mistakes. The illustrations show the process using only the mukomachi chisel, but using a mortise chisel or a bottom-cleaning chisel to clear out debris will improve efficiency. When using an electric drill for pilot holes, it's advisable to leave an even larger finishing allowance to reduce mistakes.

Processing a Tenon with a Haunch

This method involves adding a haunch to the tenon, making it resistant to twisting, and is often used where the joints of a table leg and apron are concealed. When processing, there is a risk of the female part's haunch chipping off from the end grain. For hardwoods, a thickness of about 15 mm (0.6 in) is used, and for softwoods such as conifers, about 20 mm (0.8 in) is taken. If the male part's width is narrow, resulting in a narrow tenon, a shoulder is added to the female part to be trimmed off after assembly.

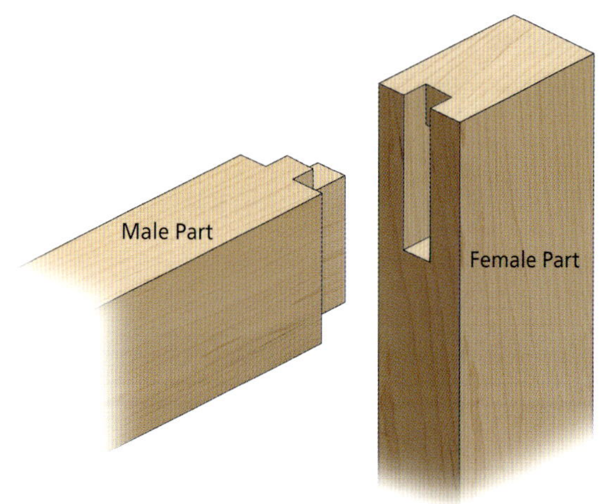

Marking a Tenon with a Haunch

The haunch on the female part is taken from the end grain, about 15 mm (0.6 in) for hardwoods and about 20 mm (0.8 in) for softwoods.

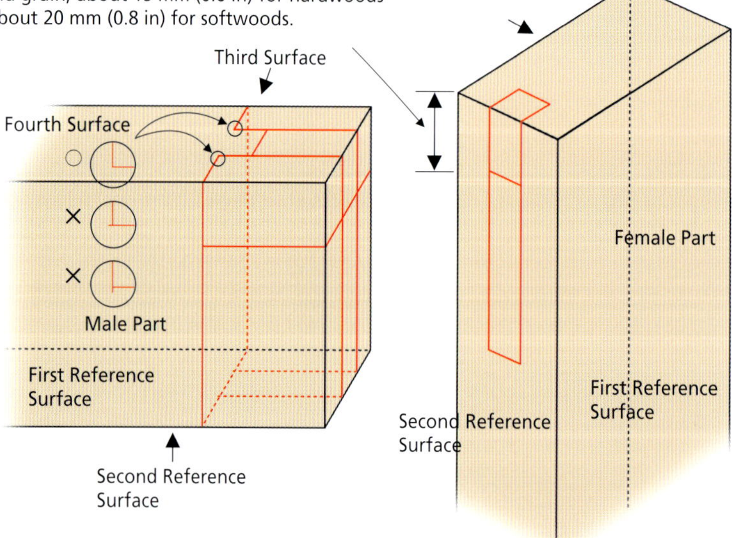

When the male part's width is narrow, resulting in a narrow tenon, the tenon width is widened, a shoulder is added to the haunch, and the shoulder is trimmed off after assembly. The shoulder allowance is about 5 mm (0.2 in).

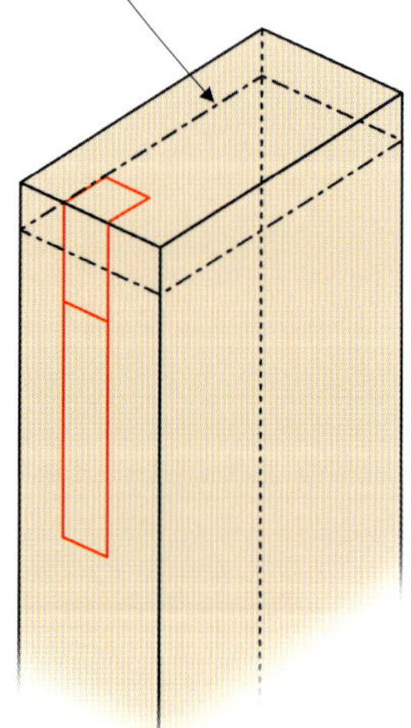

Example of marking a tenon with a haunch on a piece of timber with a thickness of 27 mm (1.06 in) and a width of 50 mm (1.97 in). The tenon thickness is one-third of the timber thickness, with the tenon width being 35 mm (1.38 in) and length 30 mm (1.18 in), while the haunch length is 9 mm (0.35 in). The depth of the mortise in the female part, including the glue pocket, is 33 mm (1.3 in).

Tenon with Haunch Joint Process

1 Transfer the width of the male part to the female, scribe the tenon mortise on the second surface of the female part, then draw a line 35 mm to the end grain.

2 From the first reference surface, mark the shoulders 30 mm (1.2 in) from the end grain of the male part with a marking gauge.

3 Continue marking the shoulders with the marking gauge, and draw lines with a pencil only on the third surface, which will retain the haunch.

4 On the second reference surface of the female part, mark lines 9 mm (0.35 in) from the first reference surface using a marking gauge, extending these marks to the bottom of the haunch on the end grain.

5 Scribe the same lines on the male part's second reference surface, end grain, and fourth surface using the same marking gauge. Then, use a marking gauge set to 18 mm (0.7 in) and mark similarly from the first reference surface.

6 Mark a line 9 mm (0.35 in) toward the end grain from the shoulders drawn on the male part for the haunch.

7 Retrace the pencil lines on the fourth surface of the male part, which were drawn in step 3, using the marking gauge for the cut parts.

8 Chisel out the mortise on the female part using a mukomachi chisel, following the same steps as for a two-way housed tenon.

9 As it is a stopped tenon, use a bottom-cleaning chisel to clear out the bottom.

10 Saw the waste from the haunch, leaving the line slightly intact, using a tenon saw.

11 Chisel out from the end grain to the bottom of the haunch.

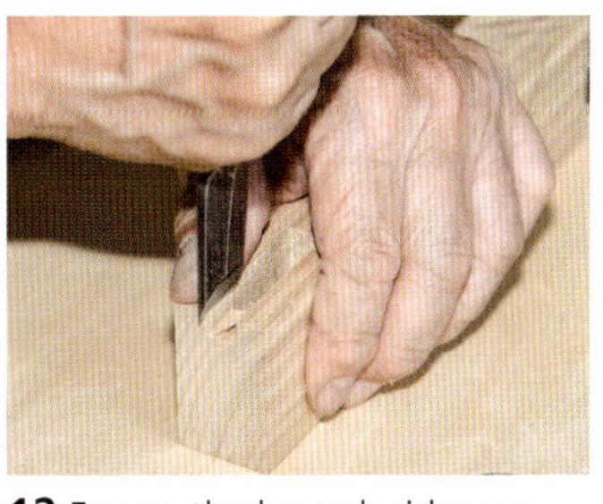

12 Ensure the haunch sides are flush with the mortise sides.

13 Cut the male part's tenon from the end grain using a rip saw.

14 Cut the bottom of the shoulders and haunch with a shoulder saw.

15 Finish the corners and inner sides of the tenon with a shoulder plane.

16 Remove any remaining debris from the corners with a chisel.

17 Dry fit the joint to check for tight spots.

18 Smooth any tight areas or debris in the corners of the tenon with a chisel.

19 Bevel the edges of the tenon. Since it will be hidden, the size of the bevel can be approximate.

20 Also, bevel the long sides of the tenon with a plane.

21 The male and female pieces are now prepared for final assembly.

PRO TIP 23

Using a Marking Knife for Accuracy

For accurate marking, small incisions made by the marking knife are useful. Even an incision less than 1 mm (0.04 in) deep can help the blade of the marking knife slide into the cut, ensuring precise marking.

Slide the knife blade toward the incision at the corner to align the marking.

When the blade reaches the incision, it stops precisely.

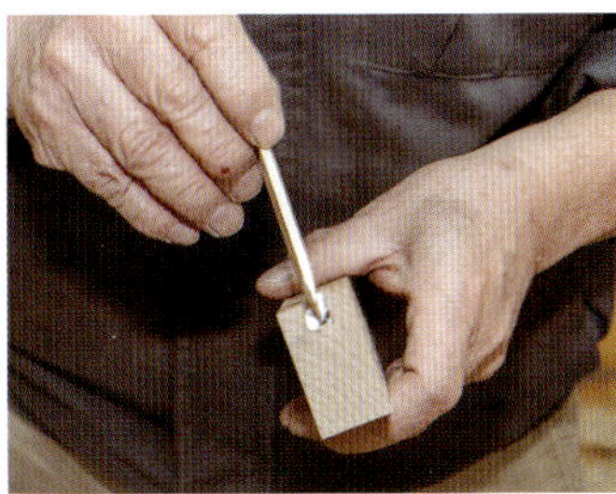

22 Apply glue evenly inside the mortise of the female piece.

23 Place a block of wood over the joint and hammer it in with a mallet.

24 Wipe off any excess glue.

25 Clamp the joint securely.

26 Check the squareness with a try square and let it dry.

27 Wipe the end grain of the female part with water and plane down any discrepancies.

Completed tenon with haunch joint.

Wedge Tenon Joint Process

This joint enhances the two-way through tenon joint by inserting wedges to make the tenon more secure. The slots for the wedges should be cut to a depth of ½ to ⅔ the length of the tenon, with the cut starting 5 mm (0.2 in) from the end and angled approximately 8° inward. If the cut is too close to the end, the tenon may crush when the wedge is inserted, so ensure a minimum of 5 mm (0.2 in) from the end. The mortise should be cut about 1 mm (0.04 in) narrower to allow for the wedge.

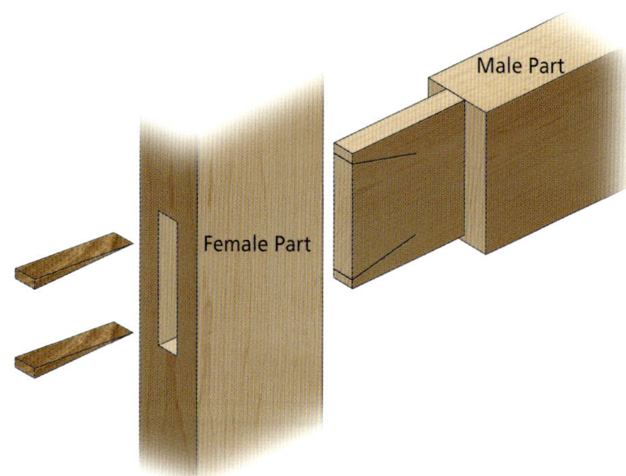

Wedge Tenon Joint Marking

Third Surface

Second Reference Surface

Third Surface

Fourth Surface

Female Part

Second Reference Surface

Male Part

First Reference Surface

Fourth Surface

First Reference Surface

The tenon of the male part is marked 3 mm (0.12 in) longer to allow for trimming later.

Interior of the mortise. Make the middle 0.5 mm (0.02 in) narrower than the marked lines so that when the male tenon is inserted, it compresses the wood.

The slots for the wedges should start about 5 mm (0.2 in) from the end.

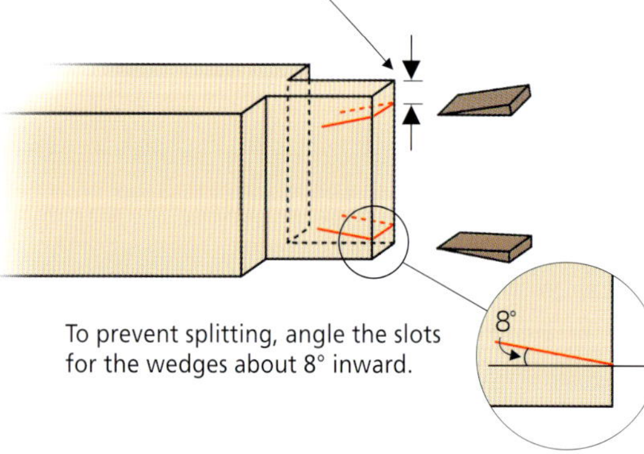

To prevent splitting, angle the slots for the wedges about 8° inward.

Marking Lines ------------ Hidden Lines

Example of marking a wedge tenon joint on 27 mm (1.06-in) thick and 50 mm (1.97-in) wide timber. Mark the mortise on the female part about 1 mm (0.04 in) narrower to allow for the wedge. The inside of the mortise should be slightly narrower in the middle so that when the male tenon is inserted, it compresses the wood. The end of the tenon will protrude slightly from the fourth surface of the female part, allowing for a small gap to insert the wedges.

Wedge Tenon Joint Process

1 Use a marking knife to mark the thickness direction on the second reference surface of the female piece.

2 Add small marks on the corners and extend the marks to the fourth surface.

3 Align the width of the male piece with the initial line and draw another line 1 mm (0.04 in) narrower.

4 Mark the shoulder of the tenon on the male piece 3 mm (0.12 in) beyond the mortise, aligning the female piece and offsetting the line from the end of the male piece by 3 mm (0.12 in).

5 Use a square and marking knife to draw the shoulder line, extending it from the first to the fourth surface.

6 Draw lines 9 mm (0.35 in) and 18 mm (0.71 in) from the first reference surface for both the tenon and mortise.

7 Use a 3-bun mortising chisel to cut the mortise in the female piece.

8 Use a rip saw to cut the tenon on the male piece.

9 Use a shoulder saw to cut along the marked lines for the shoulders.

10. Once the waste has been removed, use a chisel to clean the corners of the shoulders.

11 Test fit the tenon into the mortise and use a rabbet plane to adjust the thickness of the tenon as needed.

12 With the male and female pieces prepared, proceed to mark and prepare the wedges.

13 Mark the slots for the wedges, aiming for about 8° inward and halfway up the tenon length. A custom jig can be useful for this.

14 Mark the wedge slots at an inward angle to prevent splitting.

15 Use a coarse saw to cut the slots for the wedges.

16 Prepare the wedges using thin walnut strips, planing them to the required thickness.

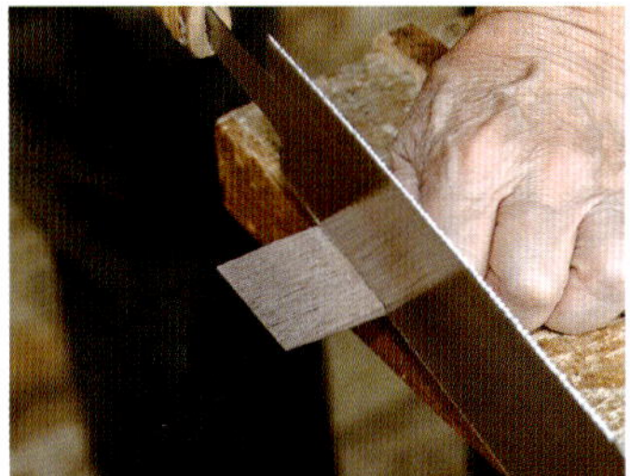

17 Cut the wedges 1 to 2 cm (0.39 to 0.79 in) longer than the slot depth.

18 Use a marking gauge to mark the thickness of the tenon, and then split the wedges slightly wider by 1 to 2 mm (0.04 to 0.08 in).

19 Check the fit of the wedges, ensuring they are slightly wider than the tenon.

20 Use a plane to gradually adjust the width of the wedges for a precise fit.

21 Bevel the corners of the tenon with a chisel.

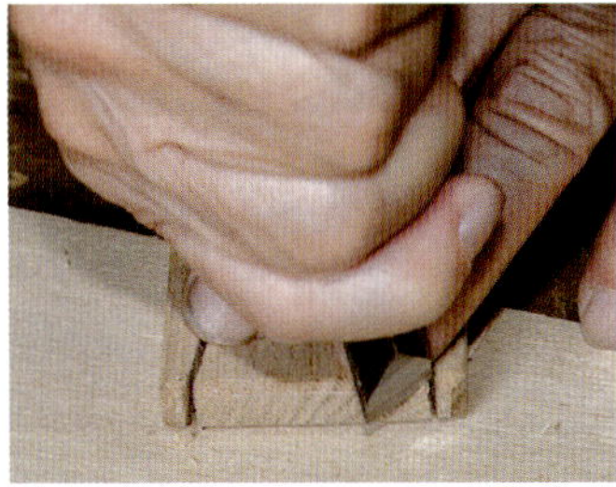

22 Bevel the slots for the wedges to make insertion easier.

23 Use a mallet to assemble the joint for a trial fit.

24 Check the fit, ensuring the tenon is compressed and there are slight gaps along the short edges.

25 If the wedge slots are too tight, widen them with a chisel.

26 Once the fit is confirmed, disassemble the joint and apply glue to the first reference surface of the female piece.

27 Reassemble the joint as before, apply glue to the wedge tips, and insert the wedges.

28 Wipe off excess glue with a damp cloth or brush and let it dry.

29 Trim the protruding tenon and excess wedge with a flush-cut saw.

30 Finish the joint with a smoothing plane.

Completed wedge tenon joint.

Upper End Mitered Through Tenon Joint Process

This method involves mitering the exposed side of a three-sided housed tenon joint and using a through tenon. The tenon thickness is typically one-third of the board thickness. The housed section between the mitered part and the tenon is determined by the chisel width, with the miter thickness being at least 5 mm (0.2 in) for strength. The tip of the male piece is placed about 6 mm (0.24 in) back from the end grain, and the tenon is extended, allowing for the excess to be cut off after assembly.

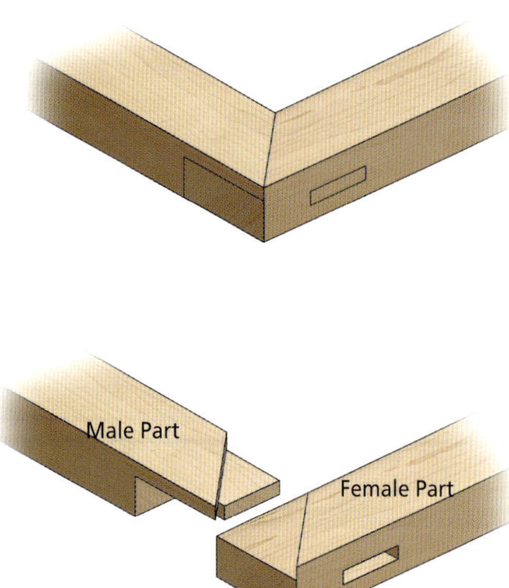

Upper End Mitered Through Tenon Joint Marking

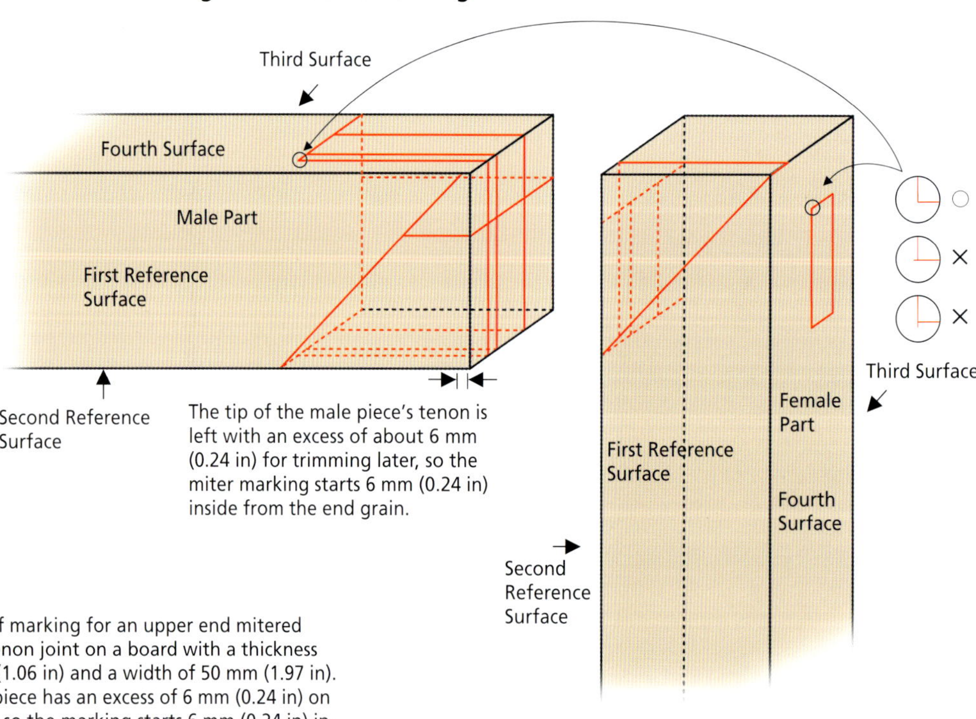

Example of marking for an upper end mitered through tenon joint on a board with a thickness of 27 mm (1.06 in) and a width of 50 mm (1.97 in). The male piece has an excess of 6 mm (0.24 in) on the tenon, so the marking starts 6 mm (0.24 in) inside from the end grain. Generally, the board is divided into thirds, distributing the miter and housed sections. Here, the housed section is set to 4 mm (0.16 in) to match a 3 mm (0.12 in) chisel, with the miter thickness set to 6 mm (0.24 in) for strength. Thus, the tenon thickness is 9 mm (0.35 in), and the housed section on the third side is 8 mm (0.31 in).

Upper End Mitered Through Tenon Joint Process

1 Place the female piece on the second face of the male piece, and add 6 mm (0.24 in). Use a square to draw a marking gauge line for the housed joint.

2 Extend the marking gauge line drawn on the second reference face to the third face.

3 For the fourth face, leave the mitered section and mark with a pencil to serve as a guide for vertical marking.

4 Align the miter gauge with the line drawn on the second reference face, and mark the miter on the first and third faces.

5 Mark the miter on the female piece as well. Take 1 mm (0.04 in) for the margin from the corner of the end grain, align the gauge, and mark with a marking knife.

6 From the bottom line of the miter marked on the second face of the female piece, mark the width of the hole 30 mm (1.18 in) toward the end grain. Use a square to mark.

7 Prepare gauges fixed at 6 mm (0.24 in), 10 mm (0.39 in), and 19 mm (0.75 in). Mark the male piece on the first and second faces, end grain, and fourth face.

8 Mark 6 mm on the end grain and second reference face of the female piece. Then use the 10 mm and 19 mm gauges to mark the tenon hole on the second and fourth faces.

9 From the second face of the male piece, use the 30 mm (1.18 in) gauge to extend the tenon tip marking to the first face, end grain, and third face.

10 Use a rip saw to cut the tenon hole in the female piece. Since it's a through tenon, carve halfway through, then carve from the opposite side.

11 Finish the sides of the through tenon hole with a chisel.

12 On the male piece, use a rip saw to cut up to the marking for the bottom of the miter and just before the tenon marking for the housed joint bottom.

13 Fix the third face upward and cut the upper end of the tenon. Be careful not to cut the bottom face as it is the miter.

14 The first reference face of the cut miter (upper end of the miter) stops just before the miter marking.

15 Similarly, make vertical cuts on the miter of the female piece and use a gauge to cut the first reference face with a tenon saw.

16 Alternate between vertical and horizontal cuts to avoid over-cutting, gradually separating the excess parts.

17 The miter of the female piece after separation. If the part becomes loose, it can be tapped off with a hammer to avoid over-cutting.

18 Use a rabbet plane to finish the corners of the miter.

PRO TIP 24

Using Fingertips as a Guide for Saw Cuts

When sawing wood, guide the saw blade with your fingertips to avoid deviation. There's no fixed rule; you can use either the index finger or thumb as a guide. While this method is generally safe, there's a risk of scratching your nails if the saw teeth catch, so proceed carefully and at your own risk.

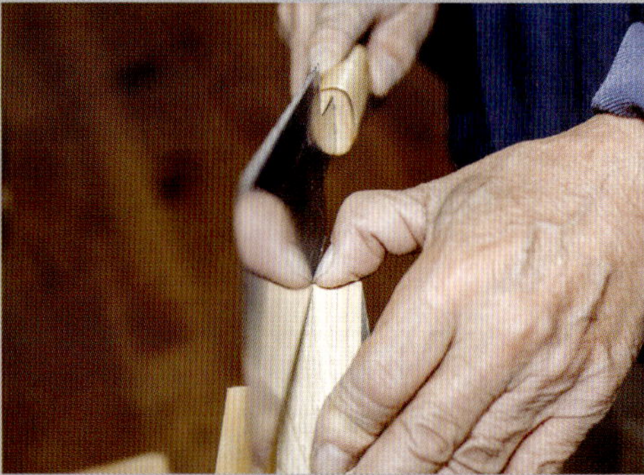

Example of using the thumb as a guide. Raise the nail and align it with the marking line, matching the saw blade's tip.

Example of using the index finger as a guide. Like the thumb, raise the nail and align it with the saw blade tip. Always saw slowly and carefully.

19 Use a rabbet plane to remove any remaining debris from the corners.

20 Place a square bar with right angles on the mitered corner to ensure no gaps.

21 Chisel out the space between the tenon and miter on the male piece using a 3 mm (0.12 in) chisel.

22 Use a tenon saw to cut the housed section of the male piece.

23 After separating, use a rabbet plane to finish the corners of the tenon and a chisel for final touches.

24 Place a square bar with right angles on the tenon and housed section to ensure no gaps.

25 Chisel away the remaining unwanted part at the top end of the tenon on the fourth face of the male piece.

26 Use a skew chisel to carve the top end of the tenon straight to the housed section.

27 Finish the housed section and remove any remaining debris from the corners with a chisel.

28 Cut the miter on the male piece. The miter tip is prone to chipping, so cutting it last minimizes the risk of failure.

29 Finish the exposed sides of the tenon with a chisel. Since there's only a 4 mm (0.16 in) gap, use a thin chisel.

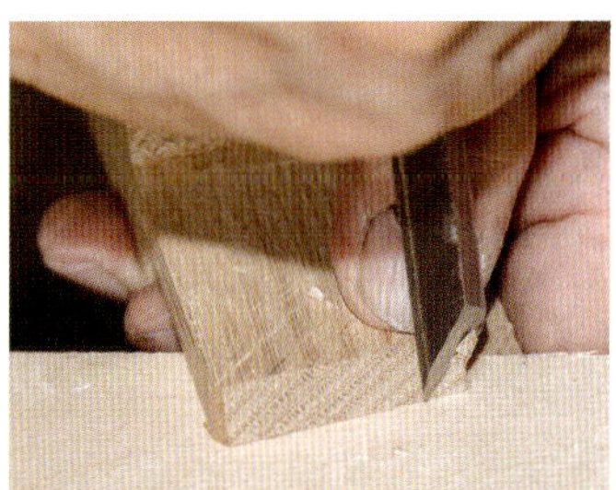

30 Bevel the short edges of the tenon with a chisel.

31 Carefully bevel the long edges of the tenon as well, avoiding the miter tip.

32 Test fit by hand before hammering to check for any contact points.

33 There's a narrow gap between the miter and tenon. Adjust the housed section bottom if any debris remains.

34 Use a 3 mm (0.12 in) chisel to clear debris from the housed section bottom, ensuring no gaps between the miter and housed section.

35 Once you've confirmed there are no strong contact points, use a hammer with a block to test fit.

36 Use a smoothing plane to finish the second reference faces of both male and female pieces before final assembly.

37 With the final fitting confirmed, apply glue and allow it to dry.

38 Apply glue to the miter, housed section, and tenon hole of the female piece.

39 Hammer in the male piece using a block, ensuring the excess tenon does not hit the work surface. Place a board underneath to avoid this.

40 Use clamps to tighten and eliminate gaps. Wipe off any excess glue with a damp cloth.

41 Tighten with clamps. Check for any indentations caused by wood debris and address them carefully.

42 Use a damp cloth and iron to remove indentations by swelling the wood.

43 Use a smoothing plane to remove any indentations and unevenness.

44 Use a saw without set teeth to trim the tenon's excess.

45 To smooth out unevenness, dampen the end grain to soften the wood.

46 Use a smoothing plane to smooth out the unevenness.

47 Smooth out any unevenness on the first reference face and third face. Use the plane at an angle to avoid dragging the wood along the joint.

Completed upper end mitered through tenon joint.

Processing the Dovetail Housed Tenon Joint with Wedge Pins

This joint, used in structures like sunken hearths and table frames, is known as the dovetail housed tenon joint with wedge pins (referred to as wedge pin joint hereafter). The two parts to be joined are made identically, and while the structure may appear complex, the critical aspect is the appearance of the mitered joint. The internal dovetail mortises are secured with wedge pins, ensuring the joint rarely comes apart.

This joint is also called the wedge pin joint because of the wedge pins used for fixing. However, since other joining methods also use wedge pins, it can be considered a general term for joinery involving wedge pins. Typically, the tenon end is left square and the mortise is cut to fit, but for efficiency, the tenon end is cut at an angle, allowing for shallower mortises. As the shapes of the combining parts are identical, there's no distinction between the male and female pieces. Therefore, the process is explained for one side, with the understanding that two identical pieces are to be made.

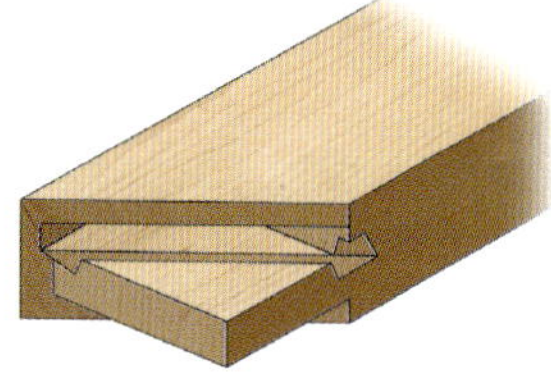

Steps for Wedge Pin Joints

1 Use a square to transfer the width of the part onto the working piece.

2 Draw the marking line ① on the first reference face using a marking knife.

3 Align the miter gauge with line ① and use a marking knife to mark lines on the second reference face and the fourth face.

4 From marking line ①, mark line ③ at a position 15 mm (0.59 in) toward the tip of the miter.

5 From marking line ①, mark a point 18 mm (0.71 in) in the opposite direction. It's the reference for the bottom of the tenon mortise.

6 Use a miter gauge and square to extend marking line ③ around, and draw lines ④ and ⑤ on the first and second reference faces.

Marking for Wedge Pin Joint

Marking Lines ---------- Hidden Lines

Marking Diagram 1

Second Reference Face
Third Face
15 mm (0.59 in)
18mm
Fourth Face
First Reference Face

Marking Diagram 2

Second Reference Face
Third Face
Fourth Face
First Reference Face

This example shows marking a wedge pin joint on a square timber piece with a board thickness of 36 mm (1.42 in) and a board width of 70 mm (2.76 in).

Diagram 1: The tenon end is cut at an angle to make the mortise shallower without compromising strength. This position is marked 15 mm (0.59 in) from the miter marking ②. The spacing of 18 mm (0.71 in) between lines ② and ④ represents the depth of the mortise, allowing a clearance of 3 mm (0.12 in) for the tenon's 15 mm (0.59 in). Precision is not crucial. Lines ④ and ⑤ are reference lines and are drawn with a pencil.

Diagram 2: The tenon, mortise, and housed sections are divided into four equal parts for marking. Here, with a board thickness of 36 mm (1.42 in), lines are marked at 9 mm (0.35 in), 18 mm (0.71 in), and 27 mm (1.06 in) from the second reference face.

Diagram 3: Cut the tenon 20 mm (0.79 in) from the tip of the miter to create the housed section (marking line ⑨). Line ⑩ is the mortise line. Draw a right-angle line (marking line ⑪) from the bottom of line ⑨ (the corner of the tenon and housed section) to line ⑩. Mortise up to this line.

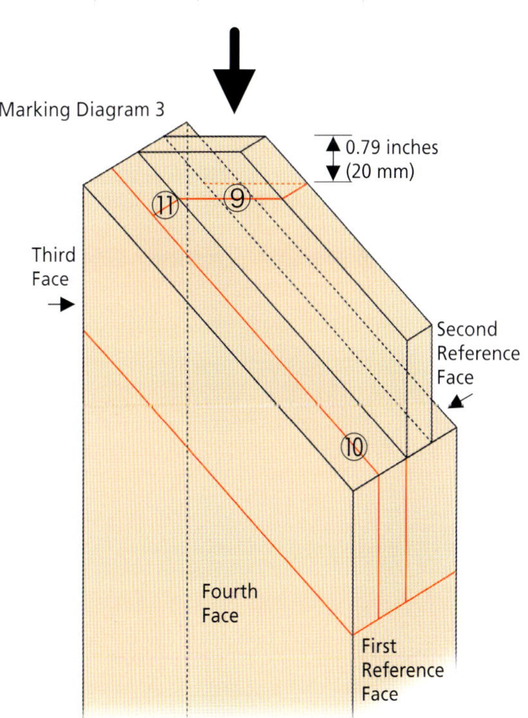

7 Cut along marking line ③ with a saw. This cut will be hidden inside the mortise, so precision is not critical.

8 Draw a line on the cut face and the first reference face, 18 mm (0.71 in) wide, using a marking gauge set at this width from the second reference face (marking line ⑥).

9 Use a marking gauge set at 9 mm (0.35 in) to draw a line from the first reference face to marking line ① (marking line ⑦).

10 Set the marking gauge to 27 mm (1.06 in) and draw a line from the second reference face to marking line ⑤ on the first reference face (marking line ⑧).

11 After completing the marking as shown in Diagram 2, lines ⑥ and ⑧ should reach marking line ⑤ , while line ⑦ stops at marking line ① .

12 Indicate the parts to be cut and retained. The actual cuts are made along lines ⑥ and ⑦ ; line ⑧ will be used for the mortise later.

13 Cut along marking line ① with a rip saw. Don't extend the cut to the tip of the miter on the wood end.

14 Cut precisely along marking line ⑦ if possible.

15 Cut along marking line ⑥ , stopping at marking line ① , then cut along the board face.

16 Insert a crosscut saw into the cut made along marking line ⑦ and cut off the unnecessary parts from the board face.

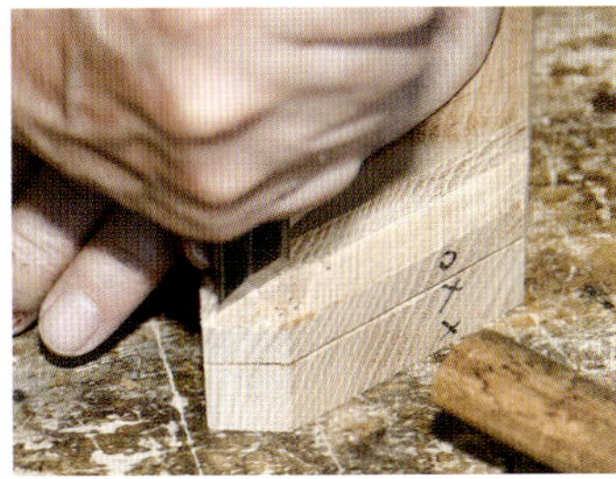

17 Remove any remaining parts in the corner with a chisel.

18 Finish the area with a shoulder plane.

PRO TIP 25

Verifying Marking Gauge Width for Halving

When dividing the thickness of the board into four equal parts for marking the tenon and mortise, begin by accurately halving the board thickness with a marking gauge. For example, with a 36 mm (1.42 in) thick board, set the marking gauge at 18 mm (0.71 in) and draw lines from both the reference face and the opposite face to verify the correct width. Since the line follows the grain, it won't be very noticeable. For joints tightened with a wedge pin, the tenon thickness doesn't require extreme precision; ensuring the center marking is accurate is sufficient. If you have two marking gauges, you can complete the marking by drawing lines from both sides at 9 mm (0.35 in) without significant impact on the process.

Use a marking gauge set to half the board thickness to draw a line from the reference face. Draw a line from the opposite face at the same position.

If the lines match, the marking gauge is set accurately at half the board thickness.

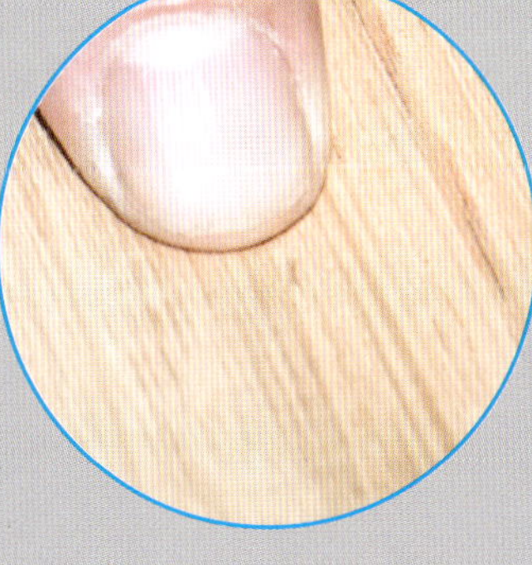

If the lines match, the marking gauge is set accurately at half the board thickness.

19 If the lines match, the marking gauge is set accurately at half the board thickness.

20 After cutting away the unnecessary parts to leave only the tenon, proceed with marking as shown in Diagram 3.

21 From the remaining line ⑧ on the first reference face, draw marking line ⑩ . Use a mortise marking gauge to ensure the tenon fits.

PRO TIP 26

Using a Drill for Mortising in the Wedge Pin Joint

Since the wedge pin joint relies on wedge pins to secure the parts, the precision required for the tenon and mortise is not very high. While achieving a snug fit without gaps is satisfying, a slightly loose assembly is fine as the wedge pin will tighten it. For efficiency, you can use a power drill for mortising. The extent to which you rely on the drill is up to personal preference.

1 Use a 6 mm (0.24 in) bit for a 9 mm (0.35 in) mortise to avoid tightness.

2 Check the alignment and depth of the mortise using marking lines ④ and ⑤ , then start removing the unnecessary parts.

3 Gradually adjust the drilling position to break up the interior rather than drilling through.

4 The interior of the mortise is roughly hollowed out. Chisel the bit marks off the sides and bottom of the mortise.

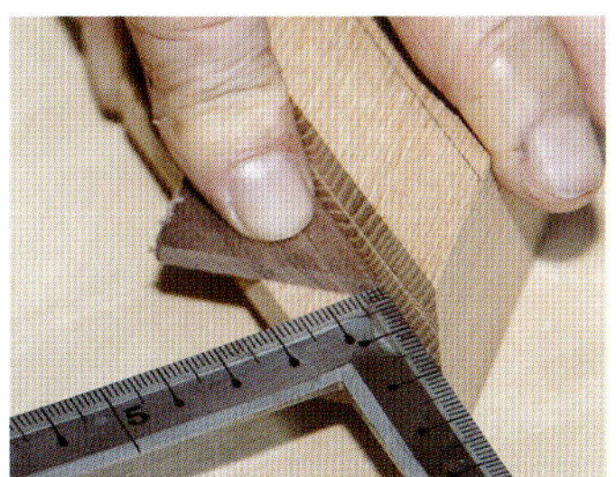

22 Mark a 45° line from the tenon tip. Use a thin board processed to 45° as a gauge since the miter gauge base gets in the way.

23 Marking line ⑨ measured in photo 19. This will also be cut off with a saw. Precision is not highly necessary, so it is marked with a pencil.

24 Cut along line ⑨ with a tenon saw. Be careful not to cut the shoulder face.

Using a bit close to the tenon thickness shortens the chiseling time but may leave bit marks, whereas using a smaller bit requires more handwork but results in a cleaner finish. Be cautious of bit marks on the adjacent tenon during drilling. You may choose to avoid this area, or if planning to use a drill from the start, cut outside the marking lines and finish at this stage.

5 Use a wide chisel, placing the back of the blade against the side of the mortise, to remove remaining material.

6 Clean the bottom of the mortise from the first reference face side.

7 Check the depth of the mortise with calipers or a stop gauge.

8 Remove debris with a chisel. This will be detailed in the steps on page 158, photo 28.

25 Touch the shoulder face cut off in the previous page, photo 21, to confirm its accuracy. This face will be the miter shoulder face, so precise processing is required.

26 If there is a step, use a chisel to remove it to ensure there are no gaps when assembled.

27 Chisel the mortise between the tenon and marking line ⑩ up to marking line ⑪ using a mortise chisel. Start by holding the back of the chisel towards you and making perpendicular cuts to the shoulder face.

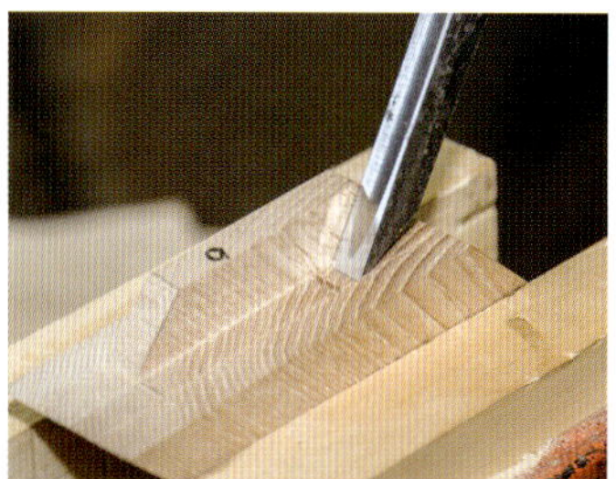

28 Then tilt the head of the chisel away, creating a V-shaped groove with the chisel blade.

29 Place the first reference face up on the bench and chisel vertically using marking line ④ as a guide.

30 Continue chiseling parallel to marking line ④ from the reference face.

31 Chisel parallel to marking line ⑪ from the shoulder face side.

32 Finish the bottom from the first reference face side, ensuring the tenon of the connecting piece does not hit.

33 Finish processing the tenon and mortise of the two pieces. Test fit to ensure there are no gaps at the miter joint. Pay particular attention to the part marked by line ⑨ , as steps can easily form here after sawing.

Sawing lines for the shark fin wedge with a shoulder saw

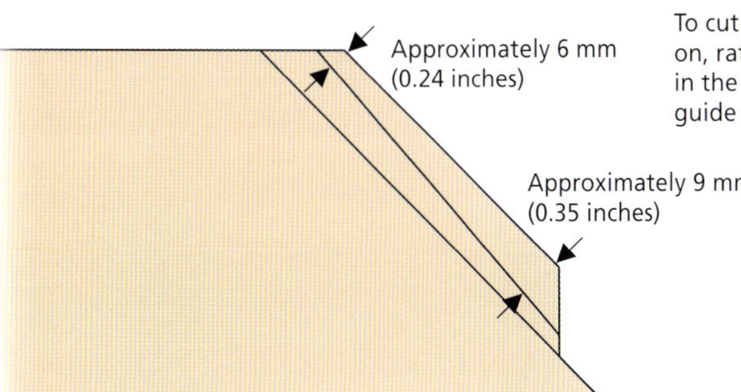

To cut a groove for the shark fin wedge in the tenon, rather than relying on marking lines as shown in the diagram, it is more accurate to use a jig and guide the shoulder saw blade along the jig's edge.

Prepare a jig with a tightening taper of 5° and a wedge angle of 10°. The exact angles are not critical, but it is important that the wedge fits securely. This jig can also be used to set the taper for the wedge.

85°

100°

34 Draw a saw line on the tenon for the shark fin wedge.

35 Using the jig, measure the width from the tenon tip, which should be approximately 6 mm (0.24 inches) on the inside and approximately 9 mm (0.35 inches) on the outside.

36 Sawing is more accurate using the jig due to the tightening taper and wedge angle.

37 Place the jig against the tenon's shoulder and mark the width for the cut. Once marked, fix the jig to the same position on the other component.

Balancing the Groove for the Shark Fin Wedge

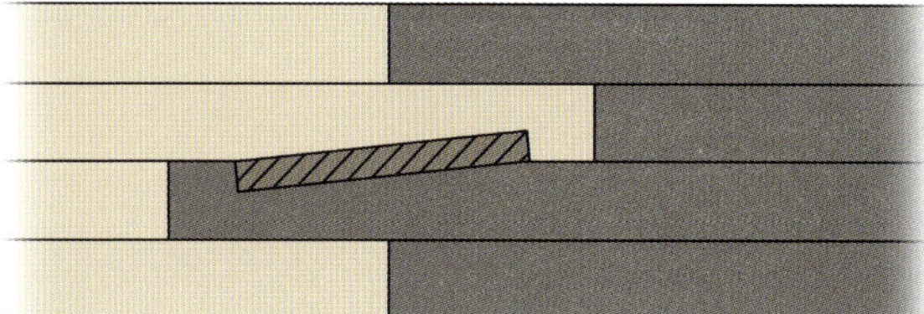

When fitting the two pieces together, the grooves cut to a depth of 3 mm (0.12 inches) should align so that the shark fin wedge (the shaded area) fits into them. Use a chisel to carve diagonally from the saw cuts as shown in the diagram. Since there are no marking lines, you need to rely on visual judgment, but be careful not to damage the saw-cut line as this is the tightening point.

38 With the shoulder saw blade against the jig, cut a groove to a depth of approximately 3 mm (0.12 inches).

39 Initially, use a wide chisel to carve diagonally from the saw-cut line.

40 Inside the mortise, use a thin chisel or shoulder chisel as a high-backed chisel will not fit.

41 Clean out the bottom of the saw-cut line to ensure no debris remains.

42 You should now have an inclined groove, though some debris may still be visible. From here, adjust as you fit the parts together.

43 Combine the two parts and check the narrow groove visible inside, where the shark fin wedge will be inserted.

44 Make the shark fin wedge. It is recommended to use bamboo or hardwood; here, cherry wood is used.

45 Measure the width of the groove for the wedge on both the inner and outer sides.

46 Transfer the taper of the jig, used for the saw cut in the tenon, to the shark fin wedge.

47 With the plane's bottom facing up, shave the width of the shark fin wedge. Avoid using a marking gauge for splitting as it might break, instead, use a plane or saw.

48 The shark fin wedge is complete. The length will be cut after assembly, so leave it as is.

49 Insert the shark fin wedge and check to ensure the parts are tightened together.

50 Check that the joints fit seamlessly.

51 Use a hand plane to smooth out any unevenness. Hold the plane at an angle to avoid grazing the end of the other piece's miter.

52 Draw the hand plane diagonally and feel the joint with your fingers to eliminate any unevenness.

Completed differential mortise and tenon joint with shark fin wedge.

Makoto Igarashi's Wood Crafts

We have introduced the procedures for making joints used in furniture and joinery by dividing them into joining boards, joining boards to timbers, and joining timbers. Many of these joints can be processed entirely with machines, and we have also introduced processes that professional woodworkers, considering work efficiency, might not perform with hand tools alone.

So, how are hand tools utilized in the workshop? We visited the workshop of woodworking artist Makoto Igarashi, who is busy preparing for an exhibition, to talk about the hand tools and parts that can be processed by machines. We also discussed the tools used in his work and his approach to creating art.

Working as a Woodworking Artist

We have introduced the procedures for making joints used in furniture and joinery by dividing them into joining boards, joining boards to timbers, and joining timbers. Many of these joints can be processed entirely with machines, and we have also introduced processes that professional woodworkers, considering work efficiency, might not perform with hand tools alone.

So, how are hand tools utilized in the workshop? We visited the workshop of woodworking artist Makoto Igarashi, who is busy preparing for an exhibition, to talk about the hand tools and parts that can be processed by machines. We also discussed the tools used in his work and his approach to creating art.

Working as a Woodworking Artist

There are various fields in the job of making things with wood. Even within the realms of furniture making and joinery, there are artisans known as traditional craftsmen who have mastered local techniques and support the local industry. Others work with furniture and joinery on a different level, creating fine art pieces. Additionally, items like lacquerware, made from wooden pieces crafted by artisans called wood turners, are also part of the woodworking profession.

Makoto Igarashi considers himself a "woodworking artist" rather than a furniture maker or joiner because he does not want to be confined to creating decorative pieces and has a clear direction

The side and bottom panels are joined with stopped hidden dovetail joints, and the board supporting the flower insert is joined with a butterfly dovetail joint.

toward creating artistic expressions with wood. During our visit to his workshop, we observed his work on a flower vase, including finishing a stopped hidden dovetail joint for the side and bottom panels and joining the board supporting the flower insert with a butterfly dovetail joint. We discussed the use of hand tools and power tools for these processes.

Since the board thickness is less than 0.24 inches (6 mm), a carving knife is easier to use. The box-like structure below is the workbench, which can be adjusted for height and orientation based on the task.

About the Workbench and Tools

Igarashi's workshop is a renovated room in his house. He usually works seated at a high workbench used by joiners. While traditional Edo-style joiners' benches are typically 33 cm (13 inches) wide, he uses a bench about 24 cm (9.4 inches) wide because he doesn't make large items. This width allows him to plane the bench surface using a jointer in his workshop. He adapts traditional forms to his style for ease of work.

When we visited, he was adjusting the tenons of a stopped hidden dovetail joint for the side and bottom panels of the flower vase using a carving knife. For exhibitions, many of his pieces are made from boards less than 6 mm (0.24 inches) thick, and for softwoods, a carving knife is easier to use for adjusting the joints, especially for the inner corners of the male tenons, which require a thin, sharp blade.

Use chisels to trim the tenons at both ends. Since the joint surfaces are not perpendicular to the end grain, a triangular jig made of plywood is used to adjust the angle.

Efficient Handwork

After adjusting the side and bottom panels, he moved on to processing the board supporting the flower insert, made from black persimmon. In custom work, the use of wood grain is crucial, especially

A miter plane that can be used for both right-handed and left-handed operations is used.

for materials like black persimmon, which have distinctive grain patterns. He selects the portion to use from the board, cuts it with a saw, and preps the wood. For professional woodworkers, using a jointer and planer is standard, but for valuable woods, this may differ.

Running long materials through a planer is possible, but it involves planing unused portions. While it's feasible to cut the needed part and use other materials as holders in the planer, adjusting the machine and creating holders can be time-consuming for a single piece. Hand planing the necessary material from the rough piece is often quicker.

After planing the cut material, he marks and processes the butterfly dovetail joint.

When using valuable wood like black persimmon, the board is sometimes cut before planing to minimize waste.

A chisel with a highly precise back is suitable for this type of work.

In custom work, hand tools are often faster. The board is planed to the planned thickness using a rough plane.

Mark the position of the relief hole. Drill a round hole in the center of the tenon mortise with a router to make it easier to chisel the sides of the tenon.

For this type of work, using power tools like a router improves efficiency. The base plate of the router is custom-made from acrylic to facilitate precise work.

Partial Use of Power Tools

For the butterfly dovetail joint supporting the flower insert, the black persimmon is the male part, and the side panels are the female parts. As shown in the dry fit on page 165, the side panels are inclined at different angles, making it challenging to mark from the reference surface. He processes one female part first, marks the tenon position on the male part, and transfers the tenon position from the male part to the other female part. The initial relief hole in the female part is made with a router, then squared with a carving knife. The dovetail tenon has a taper of about 1 mm (0.04 inches), and he uses tape to adjust the thickness when marking the dovetail groove.

After processing the male dovetail tenon and the female butterfly dovetail groove, he performed a dry fit, concluding the day's work. The finished flower vase on page 170 has its inner side and bottom panels lacquered with roiro (a type of lacquer), the board supporting the insert is coated with raw lacquer, and the surface is finished with prepolymer.

Although the detailed joints are not visible in the finished work, observing the workshop reveals the intricate processes involved.

Machine and Handwork in Making a Heptagonal Sake Cup

Preparing for an exhibition, we observed the making of a heptagonal sake cup.

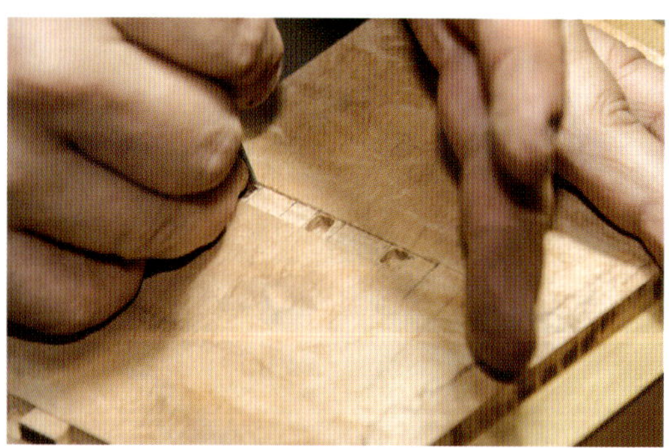

After drilling with the router, the hole is precisely squared using a carving knife. The thin board makes the carving knife easier to use.

Since the dovetail groove is narrowed by about 0.04 inches (1 mm) in the thickness direction, tape is used on a thin board to adjust the thickness for the marking gauge.

After processing, adjust the fit with the male part by combining them several times.

Use a block of wood and a mallet to tap the male part from the side until it is fully inserted. The depth can be confirmed by the sound and feel of the mallet.

Assembling a piece with mitered joints, we noted an unexpected use of machines and hand tools. Typically, you would plane a sizable piece to the required thickness with a jointer and planer, cut the components, and use a bevel jig to trim the edges. However, Igarashi's cups, though of consistent size, are made from various wood species, and he found handwork more efficient than adjusting machines for each species.

Additionally, making the small mortise for the cup's bottom panel often results in breakage when processed close to the end grain with traditional hand tools. He found it more reliable to use a router table for gradual cuts after cutting the components.

Conclusion

Observing a woodworking artist's daily work, it's evident that the choice of tools—hand tools or machines—depends on the required precision and efficiency. There is no need to use hand tools for tasks machines can handle, but for tasks only achievable by hand, time should not be spared. This approach provides valuable insights for anyone creating things, whether professional or amateur.

Made from at least five different wood species, adjusting machinery for such varied materials is difficult.

Approximately 0.12 inches (3 mm) thick, with small mortises made about 0.12 inches (2 mm) from the end grain. Using a router table reduces the chance of errors.

While the tool is available, it may not be used if unsuitable for the task.

Chestnut Wood Flower Vase
The vase uses spalted chestnut on the exterior, with the interior finished using roiro lacquer and raw lacquer.

Chestnut Wood Cabinet

The cabinet uses parts of the chestnut wood known as "kane-suji," which are avoided due to their hardness that can chip plane blades, as well as the reddish parts rarely used in chestnut wood, to create a unique visual effect for the entire piece.

Kamiyosugi Carved Box

The lid is made from ancient cedar (kamiyosugi) and the body from Yoshino cedar. The side panels of the body feature marquetry with the grain turned 90°, creating a visual effect that widens the grain from inside to outside.

Five-Pointed Box "Hoya"

The pentagonal box is made from Kenpo pear wood, joined using a large floating tenon miter joint. The petal-like support is made from iroko wood.

Workshop Konjyakudo
Makoto Igarashi

After graduating from Kyoto Traditional Craft School (now Kyoto Traditional Craft University) in 2000, Igarashi started working under the name "Workshop Konjyakudo." He made his first entry in the 59th Japan Traditional Crafts Exhibition in 2012. Currently, as a full member of the Japan Kogei Association, he actively participates in craft exhibitions and various activities. He follows the advice from his teacher at the Kyoto school: "Even if you don't have work, keep your hands moving, and eventually, something will come of it," taking on tasks such as repairing antiques and handling challenging woodworking orders.
https://www.facebook.com/konnzyakudou

Index

Books to Span the East and West

Tuttle Publishing was founded in 1832 in the small New England town of Rutland, Vermont [USA]. Our core values remain as strong today as they were then—to publish best-in-class books which bring people together one page at a time. In 1948, we established a publishing outpost in Japan—and Tuttle is now a leader in publishing English-language books about the arts, languages and cultures of Asia. The world has become a much smaller place today and Asia's economic and cultural influence has grown. Yet the need for meaningful dialogue and information about this diverse region has never been greater. Over the past seven decades, Tuttle has published thousands of books on subjects ranging from martial arts and paper crafts to language learning and literature—and our talented authors, illustrators, designers and photographers have won many prestigious awards. We welcome you to explore the wealth of information available on Asia at **www.tuttlepublishing.com.**

Published by Tuttle Publishing, an imprint of Periplus Editions (HK) Ltd.

www.tuttlepublishing.com

ISBN: 978-4-8053-1913-0

Staff (original Japanese edition)
Project Planning/Editing: Senyosha Inc.
Editing: Yutaka Takashima
Photography/Design: Yutaka Yamaguchi
Book Design: Masahiro Tanimoto

Distributed by:
North America, Latin America & Europe
Tuttle Publishing
364 Innovation Drive
North Clarendon
VT 05759-9436 U.S.A.
Tel: (802) 773-8930
Fax: (802) 773-6993
info@tuttlepublishing.com
www.tuttlepublishing.com

Japan
Tuttle Publishing
Yaekari Building 3rd Floor
5-4-12 Osaki Shinagawa-ku
Tokyo 141 0032
Tel: (81) 3 5437-0171
Fax: (81) 3 5437-0755
sales@tuttle.co.jp
www.tuttle.co.jp

Asia Pacific
Berkeley Books Pte. Ltd.
3 Kallang Sector, #04-01
Singapore 349278
Tel: (65) 6741-2178
Fax: (65) 6741-2179
inquiries@periplus.com.sg
www.tuttlepublishing.com

Printed in China 2412EP
28 27 26 25 24 10 9 8 7 6 5 4 3 2 1